THE UNIVERSAL EYE

World Television in the Seventies

BY THE SAME AUTHOR

The World of Gold
The Smugglers
The Adventurers

THE UNIVERSAL EYE

World Television in the Seventies

TIMOTHY GREEN

THE BODLEY HEAD
LONDON SYDNEY
TORONTO

ISBN 0 370 01356 5
Printed and bound in Great Britain for
The Bodley Head Ltd
9 Bow Street, London WC2E 7AL
by Richard Clay (The Chaucer Press), Ltd.
Bungay, Suffolk
Set in Linotype Plantin
First published 1972

CONTENTS

CONTENTS

PREFACE

THE idea for this book came from a conversation I had in Geneva in 1968 with Neville Clarke, then director of the European Broadcasting Union's news exchange. Without his initial prompting and then continuing help it would never have been written. My special thanks, therefore, go to him.

Over the two years that I have been working on the book several hundred broadcasters in forty countries on five continents have taken time out to talk to me about their own television scene. I have appreciated their courtesy and hospitality immensely. In particular, I am most grateful for the assistance and encouragement of Sir Hugh Greene; Michael Type, assistant to the secretary-general of the European Broadcasting Union; Sir Charles Moses, secretary-general of the Asian Broadcasting Union; Hamdy Kandil, managing director of the Arab States Broadcasting Union; Josef C. Dine of the Corporation for Public Broadcasting; James Dodd of NBC International in New York and Alistair MacKenzie of NBC International in Mexico City; Fenton Coe of NBC, Burbank; and Richard Connelly of ABC. Barney Keelan at the Independent Television Authority in London kindly allowed me to use the ITA's library, where Linda Coles and her staff were constantly helpful.

The problems of understanding material in many languages were overcome by the multi-lingual talents of Yvonne Milliet, Jacqueline Nicolotti and Irena Podleska. My wife, quite apart from putting up with my spending almost a year away from home to undertake the overseas research, has been an invaluable editor. Pat Chan and Louise Sweeting have typed the book with speed and precision.

T.S.G.

Dulwich, August 3rd, 1971

I

Introduction: The Universal Eye

MAN'S first step on the moon on July 19th, 1969, was watched by an estimated 723 million people in forty-seven countries—rather more than one-fifth of the world's population. No other event in history has ever been so immediately seen by so many of the human race and, as a television critic put it, 'in that one gesture TV's priority at the centre of man's future historic development was symbolically demonstrated.' Never before has the earth been so nearly one community, one village, all gathered together eagerly before millions of glowing screens. Capitalists and communists, rich and poor, all sat down as one to see and hear Neil Armstrong a quarter of a million miles away take his step for all mankind.

The ghostly pictures from the moon must have been rather like the first flickering images that men like John Logie Baird conjured up on tiny screens in the privacy of their workshops less than fifty years ago. Yet today the pictures travel in a micro-second from moon to earth, there to be distributed instantly to a hundred million homes on every continent. Just three satellites, each little bigger than an oil-drum, poised in space 22,500 miles above the Equator over the Atlantic, Pacific and Indian oceans throw an electronic girdle round the globe. (They remain in fixed positions, as they are moving at precisely the same speed as the earth.)

Pictures of a moon launch from Cape Kennedy can be beamed instantly from an 'earth station' at Andover, Maine, up to the Atlantic satellite, which bounces it down again to the giant receiving dishes of earth stations in Europe, Africa or South America; while the same signal, shot upwards from the earth station at Jamesburg, California, radiates via the Pacific satellite to Japan, Hong Kong and Australia. It is the satellite that has truly made the world an 'electronic village'.

Television is so much a part of most of our lives nowadays—in America the average set is on six hours a day, in Japan for five and in Britain four—that we often forget just how young it still is. Although the world's first regular television service started in Britain as far back as November 1936, television has only got into its stride in the last two decades. In 1950 there were no more than five million television sets in the world. The United States, Britain and the Soviet Union had television, but there was none in France, Germany or Japan. Twenty years later more than 250 million sets were scattered around the world in 130 countries. The United States alone had 84 million in 1970, Western Europe had 75 million, the Soviet Union 30 million and Japan 23 million. Only in Africa and much of Asia is television still a curiosity; the whole of Africa south of the Sahara has less sets than San Francisco or Marseilles; China has scarcely 200,000 sets among its 750 million people and India a mere 20,000 for 600 million—one set for every thirty thousand people, compared to one for every two and a half in the United States.

Many might say the Chinese and Indians are fortunate. Elsewhere television is the handy scapegoat for those attacking the ills of our society; it is accused of promoting violence or permissiveness and wasting our time with trivia. Malcolm Muggeridge regards the television camera as 'the greatest destructive force of our time; the great falsifier'—an opinion which does not for a second prevent him from being a tireless and highly entertaining performer in front of it. And an American professor of sociology argues: 'Next to the H-bomb, television is the most dangerous thing in the world today.'

That judgement depends on what use is made of it. I spent

an evening recently in a small village in India with a crowd of farmers who were watching their 'prime time' show—a lesson in sugar-cane planting. The potential for television there, as in so many countries of the Third World, is enormous as a means of education in health, hygiene, farming, as well as reading and writing. Often there are no schools or qualified teachers, so that television can make the difference between some education and none at all. I remember talking to a UNESCO communications expert just back from South America, where a particular project for primary education by television was bogged down in political wrangles. 'The delay', he said, 'means that thousands of children miss out on school completely—they'll be grown up and working before we get started.'

Even when television, either for education or entertainment, does get off the ground in developing countries, its effect is often blunted by the fact that a set costs more than most people earn in one year or that electrification does not extend beyond the main cities.

Despite such drawbacks, television finds its feet in all kinds of out-of-the-way places. Ethiopia has a tiny television station in six rooms of the city hall in Addis Ababa; the whole set-up was installed in nineteen days and the one studio is not much bigger than a family living-room, yet they produce nearly half their own programmes. Their budget for a year is about £80,000—less than the cost of one episode of *Bonanza*. And the most unlikely television station of all, perhaps, is perched on the Rock of Gibraltar. It serves just six thousand television sets and gets by on little over £40,000 a year. Yet the staff of twelve produce almost half the five hours of programmes each evening, using part-time cameramen. Obviously it is not very sophisticated, but at least the local effort is being made. Television programmes may cost over £80,000 an hour in America or £20,000 an hour in Western Europe, but a great deal can be done for far less. Even the commercials, which may cost £20,000 to make in the United States, can be done on the cheap. In the West Indies, for instance, the television announcer sometimes whips off his shoes and holds them to the camera saying: 'Buy fine shoes like these at Joe's Store on Bay Street.'

Setting out at the beginning of 1970 to review television in some forty countries on five continents, I anticipated that I would find that outside the major countries the American package show reigned supreme. That may have been true ten years ago, but is no longer. In television these days everyone is quite determined to do their own thing. They may have little talent and no money, but they all find there is no substitute for local programming. 'You can show them films from other countries for a while,' said a consultant who helped to establish television in the Sudan, Kenya, Aden and Sierra Leone, 'but what they really want to see are their own people debating, arguing, getting in their sly jokes about one another.' When I spent a morning in Nairobi talking to the controller of television for Kenya his phone was abuzz with politicians and businessmen all trying to get on the Voice of Kenya's evening chat show, *Mambo Leo*.

Not that the universal appeal of the western or the *Lucy Show* is over. Nothing can touch *Bonanza*, which is watched week in week out by 400 million people in eighty-two countries, from Poland to the Philippines from Nigeria to Nicaragua. The *Lucy Show* goes out in Cantonese, Spanish, French and German. But only a handful of American programmes are big international sellers. NBC International reckon to earn forty per cent of their income from the sale of *Bonanza, High Chaparral, Get Smart* and *I Spy*. MCA Universal's two trump cards are *Ironside* (known variously as *Der Chef* and *L'Homme de Fer* overseas) and *The Virginian*.

But this hard core of bestsellers cannot fill the screen for more than a few hours a week. Although television is still primarily an evening pastime—only the United States, Canada, Japan and Australia start at crack of dawn—something like sixty to one hundred hours of new programmes are required each week in countries with two or three channels.

Home-grown productions, therefore, are accounting for up to eighty-five per cent of output in many countries. Against them American shows or British exports like *The Saint* and *The Avengers* have a harder time pulling audiences. In South America, nowadays, nothing can rival the *tele-novela* in popularity. These shoe-string soap operas about poor country girls who find fame, fortune and lovers in the big cities often fill the screen for four or five hours an evening, playing out the dreams of the poor. 'Against that competition the chances of selling some stupid American situation comedy are dying,' said an American programme salesman in Mexico City.

The flavour of the top programmes varies, like the cuisine, from country to country. The Japanese passion is for samurai dramas about sword-wielding war-lords in feudal times and 'hard training' dramas depicting team effort to achieve some sporting or business victory. The Germans all sit down together to watch detective stories and a real-life crime series in which the police enlist their aid to catch the crooks. The night that particular programme goes out every wanted man in Germany sits quaking in his hide-out ready to run if he is mentioned. The Norwegians, a rather serious-minded people (they rejected the *Lucy Show* on the grounds that children ought not to speak like that to their mother), came up with a highly original *Idebanken—Bank of Ideas*—that picked the brain of the viewer to solve such problems as to what is the best way to get a handicapped person in a wheelchair off and on a train. One viewer designed a small hydraulic platform with which many railway stations in Norway are now equipped. And the Irish—well, who can beat the Irish at talking? They have a Saturday night *Late Late Show* that is as rowdy as an Irish pub. They simply get a studio full of farmers, bricklayers or even Women's Lib. members, who are needled a little at the start by the host—and they are away. 'Almost every Saturday it's a ding-dong battle,' said Irish television's director of programmes. 'One week we had 120 priests and started asking them what they knew of sex, marriage and how to run a house.

They were almost bashing each other by the end.' The week I was in Dublin there was a slight variation: the *Late Late Show* featured frog-racing.

Television's parochialism is overridden only by a handful of world events—the moon-walks, the Olympics and the Clay–Frazier fight. The fight, in particular, caused the most poverty-stricken of television stations to forget their budgets for a night. Countries like Jordan and Pakistan, who normally pay no more than £20 or £25 an hour for imported shows, lashed out with £800 for the fight, which would normally be their outlay for about a week.

Although the satellites hovering above the Equator have introduced the era of global broadcasting, language barriers thwart much international programming. What has developed, however, is 'electronic imperialism' wherever a common language is shared. Spanish television, for instance, is carving out a market for its programmes through South America. Egypt is trying to establish its superiority in television in the Arab world. And the French earnestly give programmes away free in their former colonies of Africa and Asia. The Americans, in addition to conventional programme sales, often offer, through the United States Information Agency, to pay the satellite costs involved for nations wanting to take live coverage of crucial presidential speeches. Even the Russians are slowly easing into this electronic empire-building; in Cairo, along with westerns, television features Russian folk-dancing and solemn films on industrial safety or productivity.

The headache for everyone, of course, is the cost of television. As Michael Garvey of Irish television put it, 'We get through money at a paralysing speed.' Much as everyone would like to make nearly all their own programmes they have to fall back on cheap, imported shows and, increasingly, on co-productions with other broadcasting services. The co-productions, which tend to be historical spectaculars like French and Italian television's version of *The Aeneid* or the BBC and Time-Life's *History of the British Empire*, may cost up to

£400,000 and would be quite beyond the resources of a single organisation. 'We have to do these joint enterprises to stay in serious television,' said Aubrey Singer, who oversees these epics at the BBC.

The majority of nations now flesh out their budgets with advertising. Ninety of the 130 nations with television accept commercials for all or part of their income. In Europe, the stronghold of public-service broadcasting financed by annual licence fees, everyone except the Scandinavians, Belgians and the BBC top up their budgets with small quotas of commercials. Even the communist countries have advertising pushing new lines in consumer goods or spelling out the joys of a Black Sea holiday. The precaution, however, that most countries take when they go commercial is to seal off the advertiser from the programmes; governments and broadcasters look aghast at sponsorship's cramping effect on American television and determine not to get trapped in the same mire.

The real bogy for many television services is the politician, not the advertiser. In the communist camp television is naturally a tool of the Marxist revolution but, elsewhere, it is also frequently a political preserve. In developing countries television is usually under the umbrella of the Ministry of Information—and anyone trying a *coup d'état* must capture the TV and radio station and transmitter as a priority. Parts of Western Europe face the same threat. De Gaulle kept French television firmly under his thumb as long as he was President, and in Spain and Portugal the screen reflects the wishes of their right-wing dictators.

This political control is likely to increase. Already in South America governments are taking over commercial stations that have previously been privately owned symbols of prestige for wealthy families. Even in Britain politicians, who would otherwise be accounted liberal, stamp the country saying that broadcasting is too important to be left to the broadcasters.

The new era of global television opened up by the satellites is making politicians much more aware of the chance of propaganda from overseas showing up on screens in their domain. Scientists are already forecasting direct broadcast satellites in the 1980s, which will radiate pictures that can be picked up by simple antennae attached to the television set in every home. The prospect of being able to tune in direct from London via satellite to television from New York, Moscow or Peking inevitably means that governments will become more concerned in controlling the airwaves than they were when the television signal only jumped a few miles. As Lew Kuan Yew, the Prime Minister of Singapore, puts it, 'I may be its slave, but it is my lamp.'

THE AMERICAS

2

The United States: The Commercial Colossus

ALTHOUGH television in the United States is unequalled anywhere in wealth and output, the Americans remain a remarkably under-privileged nation in what they are actually offered on the screen. The money, to start with, is enormous. The £1,450 million spent buying advertising time on America's 650 commercial stations each year is more than is available to all the other commercial and public-service television systems of the remainder of the non-communist world combined. Procter and Gamble alone, the largest advertisers on American television spend nearly £80 million a year sponsoring programmes or buying 'spots', which is just about the annual income of the BBC's television service. The three major networks—ABC, CBS and NBC—each earn more from advertising every year than any national television service outside the United States, while their combined profit of £94 million for 1969 was about the same as the entire revenue of French television that year. Yet never was so much spent on so little. American television has not been daring enough to step out and explore the immense opportunities offered by such riches. Instead, it has been imprisoned in a narrow world, whose confines are defined by the advertiser rather than by the broadcaster or the viewer.

There is, of course, nothing wrong with commercial patronage. As one American advertising executive remarked to me, 'After all, Renaissance art was commissioned. Even Rembrandt was commercial: the lace on the doublets in his paintings is perfect—to please the local lacemakers—and the right people have the correct prominence in his groups. He combined all these commercial requests and came up with a work of art.'

But are the American advertisers, the major patrons of today, spurring television on to similar creativity? 'Ah, the advertiser's job is to buy ratings, not to raise the public taste,' said the agency man. 'We want numbers, "tonnage" of homes. Sponsoring the New York Philharmonic as opposed to blood and guts just doesn't work. Television is still making cave drawings instead of painting the Mona Lisa.'

In a nutshell, that is the dilemma and the tragedy of American commercial television. The patrons that feed it so generously are preoccupied with tonnage not with tone. Apart from the fledgling public television service that now blends some two hundred educational and community stations into a 'fourth' network, American television is chiefly in the business of selling goods.

At least no one makes any pretence about it. 'We have to think of our advertisers and shareholders all the time,' said a vice-president of NBC. 'Look, no American network could put on a programme like *Civilisation* for thirteen weeks, they'd take a bloodbath financially. You'd have to put it on in the early evening to catch children and that would kill the whole night.' He added, shuddering at the thought: 'And all our viewers would sample the competition on the other networks; they might like it and stay with them. We're boxed in by the fact that we are a profit-orientated industry.'

Although American television, as a result, is often a 'wasteland' (as Newton Minow, a former chairman of the Federal Communications Commission once dubbed it) there is also much to its credit. In many things, from entertainment specials by Frank Sinatra or Barbra Streisand to coverage of the Apollo moon-walks and documentaries such as CBS's *Hunger in America* or the *Selling of the Pentagon*, the networks have set professional standards that few other television services can match. The western has become American television's classic production: around the world 400 million people in eighty-two countries turn at the end of a hard day's work to relax with *Bonanza*. And it was Edward R. Murrow who, in the 1950s, pioneered the whole craft of television journalism in his remarkable *See It Now* series. The trouble is that these days such programmes are occasional delicacies in fare that is otherwise, as one critic put it, 'as bland as a diet of oatmeal three times a day'.

The audience eats it up obediently. The sixty million American households who own a television set (forty-two per cent had colour and thirty-four per cent at least two sets in 1970) blithely leave it turned on for a slightly longer period each day, year by year. In 1950, sets were on for four hours and thirty-five minutes a day; in 1970 for almost six hours. American women watch television for four hours every day; their husbands for just under three; teenagers also view for about three hours a day; those aged 6–11 for three and a half hours and tots from two to five face the electronic babysitter for four hours. This daily dose means that by the time the average American student graduates from high school he or she has spent 15,000 hours watching television, compared with a mere 10,800 in the classroom. 'Only sleeping time surpasses television as the top time-consumer,' a report on children's viewing remarked.

The addiction is encouraged by the sheer volume of programmes. Turn on your set almost anywhere and you have a choice of half a dozen or more—ten in New York—channels, many of them running eighteen or nineteen hours a day, some nonstop. WCBS in New York, for instance, shows old movies right through the night. The last one comes on around 4.30 in the morning. Once, when I was in Chicago to appear on a talk show, I arrived at the television station in the evening to make an advance tape. I enquired when the show went out. '2.30,' said the producer. 'Which afternoon? Tomorrow?' 'No, no,' he corrected me, '2.30 tonight.'

Talk shows and old movies are a good way of filling up time

at relatively little expense. Indeed, the cardinal rule of many smaller stations seems to be: if in doubt pop on another movie; forget your programme worries for an hour and a half and just collect the money from the commercials. Most weeks there are about 130 old movies shown over New York's television stations alone—a veritable history of the American cinema. In the space of seven days during April 1971, for instance, one had the choice of Errol Flynn in *Dodge City* and *Istanbul*, Marlon Brando in *Viva Zapata*, Gary Cooper in *Friendly Persuasion*, Ronald Colman in *The Prisoner of Zenda* and Bob Hope in *Paleface*. Any passionate admirer of Susan Hayward could have watched her five days in a row in Tulsa at eleven o'clock in the morning.

Since relatively few American stations are geared to originate programmes, with the exception of local news, they are enormously dependent on networked programmes from ABC, CBS and NBC. The choice of fresh material is especially narrow for stations not affiliated to the networks. They have to rely heavily, along with movies, on re-running old network shows or cheap syndicated quizzes and panel games. Shows such as *To Tell the Truth* (an innocuous little guessing game in which a regular panel tries to sort out a real contestant from two pretenders) are available in five half-hour packages every week, costing as little as £17 a time, plus the cost of videotapes. The high cost of programming precludes most producers from turning out anything of better quality for syndication around independent stations. Shows have to be sold in at least eighty to a hundred good markets (everyone in commercial television speaks of 'markets' rather than cities) to break even, and few people take the risk. One notable exception is Group W, the broadcasting offshoot of Westinghouse Electric Corporation, who try to originate both documentaries and talk shows which can go on their own five television stations and then into general syndication. Group W, for instance, launched David Frost's ninety-minute talk show for five days a week and it swiftly became one of the most critically acclaimed new programmes on American television in recent years. Yet even that was barely breaking even in early 1971, although it was on over seventy stations, including important independent ones in New York, Los Angeles and Washington in the golden hours from 7.30 until 11 each evening which everyone calls 'prime time'.

Virtually all the major new programming therefore is seen over the ABC, CBS and NBC networks. The real duel for leadership over the years has been between the Columbia Broadcasting System (CBS) and the National Broadcasting Company (NBC). The American Broadcasting Company (ABC) has always been number three, although recently it has chipped away at the lead of the two giants. Like Avis trying to beat Hertz out of first position in the car-hire business, ABC claim they try harder. But the history of American broadcasting, both in radio and television, is really the growth of CBS and NBC. CBS, under the constant guidance of William S. Paley for over forty years, has grown from a small East Coast radio network in the 1920s to a communications empire with a net income of over £400 million a year. Its television network embraces five owned stations (the most that any group is permitted to own in the United States), in New York, Los Angeles, Chicago, Philadelphia and St Louis and over 190 affiliated stations. CBS's other activities include everything from film-making to book-publishing and owning the New York Yankees baseball team. They have also been a pioneer of the dawning cassette age through their Electronic Video Recording division, which has devised one of the main systems (EVR) for playing cassettes.

NBC is even more closely interwoven with the American business establishment as a subsidiary of the Radio Corporation of America (RCA), which, quite apart from making television cameras and sets, radios and record players, is a major producer of highly sophisticated electronic equipment for defence and satellites. Every new employee at NBC gets a little booklet which tells him proudly 'RCA is a major figure in maintaining the United States defence posture. There is hardly an area of national defence in which one or other of RCA's operating divisions has not played a key role.' RCA also owns the Hertz car-hire business, a publishing house and even an organisation called Banquet Foods, which supplies frozen meals for all occasions. The television network itself covers NBC's five owned stations, in New York, Washington, Chicago, Los Angeles and Cleveland, and over 200 affiliates, together garnering over £250 million each year in advertising revenue.

Only ABC has not yet become a communications mammoth, because a plan to merge it into the mighty International Telephone and Telegraph stable was refused by the U.S. government as being against the public interest. Even so, its television network of five owned stations, in New York, Chicago, Detroit, Los Angeles and San Francisco, plus 170 affiliates, attracts something over £190 million a year of advertisers' money.

Since federal broadcasting regulations, administered from Washington by the Federal Communications Commission (FCC), prohibit anyone from owning more than five television stations, the affiliates of each network spin the distribution web for programmes. Their tastes and prejudices, not surprisingly, have considerable influence on the programmes put out by the network.

Although an affiliate station usually agrees to take a minimum of eight hours of network programming each week, it has no obligation to accept any specific one. It can 'bump' the network whenever it chooses and replace a programme with one of its own. Normally, affiliates are only too happy to take the lot: the full three hours of network programmes in prime time each evening, together with the soap operas and game shows that while away the daytime hours, and the late-night talk shows of Johnny Carson, Merv Griffin and Dick Cavett that keep the patter and chatter going until one in the morning. However, many individual stations, particularly in the South, are more wary even than the networks of controversial programmes and serious documentaries. Often less than half a network's affiliates take documentaries—they just pop on an old movie instead. The rejection of more serious programmes by affiliates is a constant headache for the networks. They have a difficult enough time persuading many advertisers to buy time on a programme not conceived as mass entertainment without affiliates also playing truant.

In the large cities there is normally an affiliate of each network, but in smaller communities with one or two channels the stations often pick and choose their programmes from all three networks. The classic example has been KTBC-TV in Austin, Texas, a highly profitable station owned for many years by Lyndon Johnson and his family (the controlling shareholding is actually in the hands of his wife, Ladybird). KTBC is an an affiliate both of ABC and CBS and can take its pick of the most successful programmes from each.

The affiliates receive a share of the advertising revenue of each network programme they carry, according to the size of their market. The real gravy, however, is the earnings from national or local 'spot' ads placed directly with the stations, which they can pack into station breaks during or between network shows. Strictly speaking, advertising in networked shows in the three hours of prime time in the evening is supposed to be limited to six minutes per hour, with another ceiling of twelve minutes an hour outside prime time. But many stations slip in up to fifteen minutes in the hour. The Federal Communications Commission, the licensor of TV and radio stations and watchdog of the industry, once blew the whistle on a station that was proposing thirty-three minutes advertising in an hour.

The affiliates themselves are often subsidiaries of publishing or industrial groups. Cowles Communications, which ran *Look* magazine, is in TV, so is the Post-Newsweek empire which owns the *Washington Post* and *Newsweek*; Condé Nast —publishers of *Vogue* and *House and Garden* have interests in four television stations, and the publishers of the *Chicago Tribune* and *New York News* have stakes in three. Time-Life owned five stations until 1971, when they sold them out to another major publisher, McGraw-Hill. In all, 106 American newspapers or magazines had major holdings in television in 1970.

The largest non-network group, however, is the Westinghouse Electric Corporation, whose Group W subsidiary controls stations in Baltimore, Boston, Philadelphia, Pittsburg and San Francisco. Although Group W's stations are all affiliated to the major networks (two with NBC, two with CBS and one with ABC) they have been striving in recent years, under the energetic direction of their president, Donald H. McGannon, to emerge as a programming group in their own right. Apart from developing two syndicated talk shows—those of David Frost and Mike Douglas—Group W have embarked on a wide range of documentaries. In 1968, for instance, they established an Urban America Unit to take four or five special reports a year on the problems of America's cities.

But it is one thing to produce programmes, quite another to break the hold of the three networks on prime time so that they can be shown to best advantage. McGannon's real strategy was to persuade the Federal Communications Commission to pronounce a new ruling in 1970 (quickly dubbed the McGannon Rule) that from September 1971 onwards the networks would be permitted to provide only three hours of programming in evening prime time, instead of the traditional three and a half. (Strictly speaking, the new Rule applied only to stations in the top fifty markets, but such is the value of advertising time in the top fifty that it is not worth the networks investing in programmes at all if they cannot be shown there.)

McGannon hoped that, by turning half an hour back from the networks to individual stations each evening, the scope would be greater for Group W and other producers to display their wares. He believed also that the whole spectrum of programmes might be widened. The rewards of winning a slice of prime time are considerable; the earning power of a programme in the evening is about six times that during the day.

Most evenings, when up to forty million Americans are looking at television, advertising costs anything from £17,000 to £35,000 a minute, depending on the rating for a particular show. By day, advertising commands a more modest £4,000 a minute. Prime time, therefore, is the seductive lure which the networks have guarded jealously. The potential advertising revenue to *each* network *every* night of the week is somewhere over £400,000. Indeed, few American television executives seem to spend time thinking about anything except prime time. Walk into any of their offices in the networks' skyscraper headquarters on Sixth Avenue in New York (or any advertising agency office on Madison or Park Avenues) and there, prominently displayed either on the wall or beneath a glass desk-top, is the crucial chart mapping hour by hour the rival offerings of ABC, CBS and NBC during prime time. Everyone's thoughts and energies are on juggling the position of their network's programmes in that schedule to maximise the audience. Moves are planned with concentration worthy of an international chess master. Programming for the less lucrative daytime hours is handled by a separate vice-president with his own department.

Until Don McGannon promoted the new FCC three-hour rule, prime time began at 7.30 (right after the evening news) and finished at 11 when most stations put out their own late-night news. From 1971 onwards network prime time was normally from 8 until 11, leaving individual stations to find their own programmes from 7.30 until 8.

The target, however, is unchanged: the maximum possible audience for every single second and, ideally, as many of the audience as possible aged between eighteen and forty-nine living in an urban area. With that magic formula in mind, the next trick is to devise a series that will so entrance the public that it will be good, not just for twenty or so episodes this year, but for every year in the foreseeable future. Programmes establish a 'track record', which is the number of years they have survived. The record is held by Ed Sullivan, whose Sunday night variety show lasted for twenty-three years before it was finally axed in 1971. Lucille Ball is now bidding for the championship: *Here's Lucy* has been running for twenty years (under various titles) and is still going strong.

Although all the networks do one-shot entertainment and documentary 'specials', which are spaced through the season like occasional oases, the real search is for long-running series of either variety, situation comedy or drama. Except for occasional short summer seasons, the notion of doing a six- or eight-part serialisation of a novel or thirteen parts on *Civilisation* does not come within anyone's thinking. When I asked one executive whether he would have considered buying something like the BBC's *Forsyte Saga*, he explained politely that if they had and it had been a success what would they have done when the twenty-six episodes were finished? So, lacking *Son of Forsyte*, a worthwhile production cannot stand in its own right in America; it does not fit the known formulas. 'The secret of a good series,' said David Victor, one of the most successful of American TV producers, with *Dr Kildare, The Man from Uncle* and *Marcus Welby M.D.* to his credit, 'is that you must be able to see episodes thirty-five or forty-nine clearly before you begin.'

The priority, therefore, is for some central character or group of characters around whom incidents can be created week after week after week. *Marcus Welby M.D.*, the most successful show on American television in 1970–1, fitted this bill perfectly. Dr Welby is a general practitioner and the trials and tribulations of his patients revolve round him. 'The concept is very simple,' said Dick O'Connell, co-producer with David Victor, 'Dr Welby is a nice man. He is presented with a problem each week and he accomplishes it. The general practitioner is the ideal format.'

So, too, are policemen, lawyers, surgeons and cowboys. 'But what could you do with a dentist?' asked a Hollywood producer. When I told him the Japanese had a highly successful series in which a dentist was in love with a lady paediatrician he was not persuaded of the potentialities.

Within the given framework the television dramas go through periodic fashions. During the mid-1960s hospital shows were in vogue. 1970 was the 'year of relevance' with everyone struggling with the issues of drugs, permissiveness and teenage delinquency. For the 1971 season, detectives were the craze, the networks introducing variously a fat private eye called Cannon, a funny police team in *The Partners*, a policeman turned priest in *Sarge* (this show was quickly nicknamed *God Squad*) and a blind insurance investigator called Longstreet.

Once upon a time, the networks ordered thirty-nine new shows for each series per season and completed the remaining thirteen weeks of the year with re-runs of the most successful segments. But the soaring costs of television production, now over £80,000 an hour, has discouraged such massive investments. Nowadays only twenty to twenty-six episodes a year are made of even proven series like *Bonanza* (although this still involves a yearly investment approaching £2 million). For a new series only thirteen or sixteen will be ordered initially. If the newcomer wins good ratings when the new season opens in mid-September with all the flourish of a great race meeting, then a further half dozen or ten instalments may be made quickly. If it flops, it is dropped with no ceremony. A replacement will be hastily shuffled into the schedule about the first of January. Everyone keeps two or three potential replacements on the stocks ready to go on as soon as they see how the season is shaping.

All these new programmes only take the television year through to late March; thereafter the re-runs begin. For the next five months there is little new material on the screen with the exception of 'specials' and some try-outs of series that are considered for mid-season replacements the following January. ABC, for example, tested a Val Doonican variety series from Britain during the summer of 1971 to see if audience response merited giving the singer a fully fledged slot in a more auspicious season of the year. CBS also slipped in the BBC's prize-winning *Six Wives of Henry VIII* during the summer hiatus of 1971.

The initial guides to triumph or disaster are the ratings (determined by special meters on a cross-section of sets) and share of households. A good rule of thumb is that a programme with over an eighteen rating (i.e. eighteen per cent of all television households, which is eleven million homes) and over a thirty per cent share of the audience at that time is home and dry. These proportions depend, of course, not just on the appeal of a programme, but on the competition facing them on the rival networks. A programme may do very well at one time because of weak opposition, and poorly at another because it is matched against the nation's firm favourite. A prime example of a runaway triumph was *Marcus Welby, M.D.*, on the ABC network on Tuesday nights during the 1970–1 season. The competition was the weekly current affairs programme *Sixty Minutes* on CBS, while NBC had a current affairs documentary, *First Tuesday*, once a month at the same time. Neither of them attracted a vast audience, so *Marcus Welby* coasted to success. That kind of one-sidedness did not last long; for the 1971 season CBS cancelled *Sixty Minutes* as a regular Tuesday offering and pitched *Cannon*, their chubby private eye, against the good Doctor Welby; NBC shifted *First Tuesday* to Fridays and weighed in with a situation comedy, *Marriage can be Fun.*

That little manoeuvre called for no great scheduling skill; any entertainment matched against documentaries was bound to do well. The real test of the programme scheduler's art comes when he has to find some answer to a show on a rival network that is knocking spots off his own entertainment. Then he has to take courage—and maybe his job—in both hands. NBC, for instance, were considerably troubled during 1970 on Tuesday nights by ABC's bouncy police series *Mod Squad* which was edging out their own *Julia*, the saga of a well-heeled, well-rounded black widow. *Julia* vanished the next autumn and instead NBC hauled up good solid *Ironside* to take on *Mod Squad* for the ratings at 7.30 on Tuesday nights: a daring move, because *Ironside* was doing excellently in a later period on another evening; all the rules say if a programme is doing well leave it where it is. But NBC felt that *Mod Squad* could be beaten only with the really big guns. 'We have to hurt that *Mod Squad* rating,' said a determined NBC programme vice-president, outlining his battle plans behind clouds of smoke from a six-inch cigar, '*Ironside*'s rating will not be so good, but nor will *Mod Squad*'s. Sometimes you just have to slug it out; both parties will get hurt, but that's the way the game is played.'

While old faithfuls fight it out, new programmes are cosseted like babes in arms. One of NBC's great hopes for the 1971 season, James Garner as *Nichols*, the slightly reluctant sheriff of a small western town in 1915, was placed securely between the *Flip Wilson* and the *Dean Martin* shows. The strategy was that *Nichols* got the benefit both of the millions watching Flip Wilson, who are too inert to switch channels when that finishes, and of further millions who love Dean Martin and will tune in early to be sure to catch him.

Although the networks nurture a new programme from birth and will invest over a million pounds before anything reaches the screen at the September starting-gate, they make very few of the programmes themselves. In fact in 1971 the only prime-time series actually produced by a network was NBC's *Bonanza*. The major television producers today are the old Hollywood movie companies, who have finally come to terms with television. Twentieth Century Fox, Paramount, Warner Brothers, Screen Gems and MGM are all in the game, but the clear champion is MCA-Universal.

'Universal,' said a network vice-president out in California, 'is just a television factory. They roll out the programmes as if they were on a production line.' Indeed, that is just how Universal view their sprawling complex of studios at Universal City in Hollywood. 'Just as General Motors turns out cars, we turn out television shows. It's a business,' a Universal executive remarked unabashed. 'The movie industry is a gamble, you can invest £1 million in a picture and you may get back £4 million or nothing. But with television we know precisely what the networks are looking for. They also put up much of the money and we keep tight control of the costs by strictly limiting the number of days' shooting.' Most television dramas are finished in precisely six days. 'And when we say six days we mean six days,' said the man at Universal, banging his desk sternly; 'we have writers and directors that we know can deliver on time.' Although Universal themselves will invest a great deal of time and money in developing a 'pilot', they will never go ahead on a complete series without a firm network order.

Their formula pays off. They contributed no less than eleven prime-time programmes in 1971, seven of them to NBC and four to ABC. Their nearest rival, Paramount, could muster only seven, while Twentieth Century Fox and Screen Gems had luck with just four each. Small independent producers, who did rather well from television in the 1950s and 1960s, while the movie companies were still fighting shy of television, have finally been squeezed almost out of the market. In the 1971–2 season they managed to woo the networks into buying a meagre eight hours of their programming in prime time.

Actually, the most successful new rival to the major Hollywood companies is Britain's own Sir Lew Grade. His Associated Television Corporation succeeded for the first time in 1971 in winning prime time positions on ABC in the competitive autumn season with Shirley MacLaine in *Shirley's World* and *The Persuaders*, a fairly light-hearted crime series with Tony Curtis and Roger (alias The Saint) Moore.

While the networks pay handsomely, the movie companies reckon to make their real profits on the syndication and re-run business that follows the first network showing. There is plenty to be recouped; very few shows now cost under £80,000 an hour. The *F.B.I.*, for instance, is budgeted at £85,000 per episode, *Gunsmoke* and *Bonanza* cost around £92,000, the

Dean Martin show eats up £96,000 every week. Even with this kind of money to play with, production schedules are extremely tight. All kind of corners are cut to save money. On *Bonanza*, for example, the whole team will go out on location for two or three weeks in a season to shoot miles of stock footage for twenty or more episodes. The Cartwright brothers will be filmed from all angles, riding across plains, through gullies, up hills and across rivers; selected clips can then be inserted as appropriate in future episodes. To ensure continuity, the brothers always wear exactly the same clothes and ride the same horses year in, year out. If the story calls for one of them to be riding by a lake, a snippet of film shot perhaps two or three years earlier can be dug out as their appearance is unchanged.

The hectic production period out on 'the coast' is from April until mid-October, when everyone competes for studio space to get a dozen or more shows complete before the 'off' for the season in September. As everything is pieced together through the summer, the ever-watchful eye of the advertiser is peeking over the networks' and the producers' shoulders. In the early days of television in the United States, almost all shows were sponsored and advertisers scanned scripts with eagle eyes to delete any reference that might either be controversial or tarnish the image of their product. The tales of their red pencilling are legion. Once, on a Groucho Marx show sponsored by De Soto cars, one of the assistant producers was named Ford; the advertiser insisted the name be deleted from the credits. Car manufacturers are notoriously shy of their cars being involved in accidents in police dramas. 'They get very touchy,' conceded a network executive in Hollywood, who acts as a diplomatic go-between. 'No accident may imply any fault on the part of the automobile. If there really has to be an accident, then they prefer the car to be hit by a train.' Before cigarette commercials were banned on American television from January 1971, the tobacco companies were equally fussy. When Dr Marcus Welby was once required by the script to recommend one of his patients with a serious lung complaint to stop smoking, an advertiser who had bought time on the show was outraged; as it happened the episode was already shot when the ad agency saw the script, and the producers refused to delete what was clearly essential medical advice. Cigarette advertisers were also always unnerved by Dean Martin, who chain-smokes on his show, but is inclined as he tosses a cigarette away to put his fingers in his ears as if it might explode.

These are examples of trivial obsession, but underlying it all is the advertiser's expectation that any programme with which his name is associated will not only display his product in the most favourable light but will fit into the neat, sanitised view of life displayed in the commercials. Procter and Gamble's editorial policy, for instance, states: 'There will be no material that may give offence, either directly or by inference, to any commercial organisation of any sort ... There will be no material on any of our programmes which could in any way further the concept of business as cold, ruthless and lacking all sentiment or spiritual motivation.'

Erik Barnouw, in the third volume of his history of broadcasting in America, notes that the advertisers nipped in the bud the flowering of good drama on television in the 1950s because the plays then being written by Paddy Chayefsky and others clashed head-on with the sponsors' view of the world. 'Most advertisers were selling magic. Their commercials posed the same problems that Chayefsky's drama dealt with: people who feared failure in love and business. But in the commercials there was always a solution as clear-cut as the snap of a finger: the problem could be solved by a new pill, deodorant, toothpaste, shampoo, shaving lotion, hair tonic, car, girdle, coffee, muffin recipe or floor wax. The solution always had finality. Chayefsky and other anthology writers took these same problems and made them complicated. They were for ever suggesting that a problem might stem from childhood and be involved with feelings towards a mother or father. All this was often convincing—that was the trouble. It made the commercial seem fraudulent.' (Erik Barnouw, *The Image Empire*, Oxford University Press, 1970, p. 33.)

Down in Madison Avenue one afternoon I asked the executive vice-president of a leading advertising agency what his attitude to the relationship between advertiser and programme was. His reply was candid: 'If my client is paying £25,000 a minute for advertising associated with a programme, the least he can expect is that it is friendly towards his business.'

This close liaison between advertiser and programme-maker is, of course, the main difference that distinguishes commercial television in Western Europe and the United States; in Europe programmes are insulated from the advertiser's control because sponsorship is not permitted.

Potential advertisers may be sounded out at a very early stage in planning a new series. When NBC, for instance, was kicking around ideas for a series in the fall of 1971 involving Jim Garner, they decided that Chevrolet might like to sponsor a part of it. So, a high-powered NBC team, consisting of Don Durgin, the president of the network, Mort Werner, the vice-president for programming, and Jack Otter, vice-president in charge of advertising sales, sallied forth to Detroit. 'At that stage we had two versions of what the show might be,' recalled Otter later: 'either Garner as a detective in a big city or as sheriff of a town out west in the early 1900s, but really we were just selling Garner.' Chevrolet bought. They agreed to pay £1.8 million for three minutes of advertising a week on each of the first twenty-six episodes.

Full sponsorship of programmes by a single advertiser is now rare. The other three minutes of time available on the Garner programme (which was eventually called *Nichols*) was taken up by other advertisers. Most advertisers prefer to scatter their favours around: a minute on *Walt Disney*, a couple of minutes on *Ironside* or *Hawaii Five-O*, another minute in CBS Friday night movies or on the *Evening News* with Walter Cronkite. This avoids the sponsor being caught with a complete disaster on his hands. Frequently in recent years, advertisers have waited very late to book their minutes, hoping that the network at the last moment, with unsold minutes on its hands, will sell them time at a 'distress' price. But cautious advertisers get into trouble too. Those who wisely bought time early in the *Flip Wilson Show*, one of the biggest hits of the 1970 season, paid only a little over £17,000 a minute. When the programme fast became the most fashionable of the year, NBC soon pushed up the rates to £33,000 a minute for advertisers who came late. And they opened the bidding for the 1971 season at £36,000 a minute. It pays the advertiser to spot a winner early.

The advertiser's initial concern, of course, is the number or 'tonnage' of homes that a programme can attract. But he wants to know also what kind of people are watching; are they young adults, middle-aged or old people? Are they college-educated? Do they live in rural or urban areas? So the network provides him with the 'demographics' of each show; that is to say a profile of the age, sex, educational background and living habits of the audience. The demographics of the network evening news, for instance, indicates that many of the audience are people in their thirties and forties of fairly good education and income. They turn on the news as soon as they come home from the office. So, what better time to promote the aspirin and the anti-acid stomach settlers that will soothe the harassed executive after a hectic day in the office and a three-martini lunch?

The preferred demographics for most programmes is that they should be seen by people aged between eighteen and forty-nine living in urban areas—for the simple reason that they usually have more money to spend. Woe betide any programme whose main audience turns out to be over fifty and living in the country. That lesson was punched home firmly in 1971 when CBS threw out a whole clutch of programmes including *Beverley Hillbillies*, *Green Acres* and *Mayberry RFD* whose ratings were still healthy but whose demographics were senile. The advertisers had told CBS in no uncertain terms that there were too many elderly countryfolk watching their shows. Similarly NBC chopped *The Man from Shiloh* (née *The Virginian*). 'That western still had a very satisfactory rating,' Dr Thomas Coffin, NBC's director of research explained, 'but we took it off because it was focussed too sharply on the older, non-urban audience.'

Luckily for western fans, the grand-daddy of all westerns, *Bonanza*, which has been running since 1959, still cuts a dashing city-orientated demographic profile and has survived for the entertainment of fifty million Americans and 350 million other people among the eighty-two nations where it is seen each week.

The pressure of trying to tailor every programme to appeal to the largest possible audience of eighteen- to forty-nine-year-old city-dwellers is, of course, the factor that stultifies American commercial television. The formula allows no leeway for experiment or controversy. It is only by conscious decision of the networks to run certain programmes at a loss that many documentaries and current affairs programmes get on the air at all. Although the news divisions of the three major networks employ some of the finest television journalists to be found anywhere, they rarely have the opportunity to stretch themselves to full advantage. It is almost impossible to compare the amount of regular current-affairs and documentary output of public-service organisations like the BBC in Britain, ARD in Germany and NHK in Japan with the American commercial networks' serious programming in prime time; the ratio is more than twenty to one. Briefly stated, in the autumn of 1971 both NBC and CBS had just one hour of prime time per month clearly set aside for current affairs or documentary programming; ABC had no regular slot. In addition, occasional documentary 'specials' were dropped into the regular schedule pre-empting series. But these were often dressed up with movie stars doing the commentary and even the interviewing in an attempt to ingratiate them with a larger audience. While I was in New York NBC did an hour-long documentary on Scotland Yard in which David Niven of all people interviewed the Commissioner of Police.

This state of affairs has not come about without the stoutest rearguard action from the news divisions of the networks. For almost twenty years, ever since Ed Murrow pioneered television journalism at CBS with *See It Now*, the network news directors have laboured to keep at least an hour a week in prime time for serious current-affairs programming. One can only report that they have not succeeded. Fred Friendly, in perhaps the most publicised resignation ever in American television, walked out in disgust as president of CBS news in 1966 when the network chiefs overruled his request to pre-empt daytime programming for live coverage of a crucial Senate Foreign Relations Committee hearing on the Vietnam War. Instead, they insisted on keeping in that famous fifty re-run of the Lucy Show, explaining that they stood to lose £70,000 in advertising revenue if the Vietnam hearings replaced it. Money is the key.

In the spring of 1971, I asked a CBS vice-president why his network was moving the weekly *Sixty Minutes* current-affairs programme from prime time and was reported to be relegating it to Sunday afternoons. He said: 'Of course it's outrageous—but it's a great money-loser.'

The pity of it is that on the rare occasions when the television journalists are allowed to make a worthwhile documentary—as CBS has done in recent years with two memorable reports, *Hunger in America* and the *Selling of the Pentagon*—they show just how fine American television could be. The technical and professional skill and the money are available in abundance to create masterly programmes, given freedom from the stranglehold of the advertiser.

Happily, over the years some advertisers, notably companies like Xerox, Mobil Oil, Alcoa, Borg Warner and Dupont, have accepted the responsibility of buying time on current-affairs programmes that they know may be controversial or in sponsoring documentaries that do not have mass appeal. And in these instances it is a cardinal rule of the network news divisions that the advertisers have no control over subject or content and see the programme for the first time when it goes on the air.

But this kind of institutional advertising is not always looked on kindly by advertising agencies advising their clients how to spend money. Once when a leading oil company suggested to their agency—one of the top half dozen in New York—that they would like to undertake a campaign on television sponsoring worthwhile programmes to improve their image, the agency's chairman responded 'Institutional advertising is like a man in a blue serge suit peeing in his trousers. He gets a nice warm feeling all over, but nobody notices.' The oil company, to its credit, switched its account elsewhere.

The hurdles to be surmounted by the television documentary have not been lessened over the last two or three years by the outrage with which Vice-President Agnew and others have responded when the networks—CBS in particular—have tried to tackle some of the pressing problems facing the United States. The *cause célèbre*, in the spring of 1971, was the outcry against CBS's *Selling of the Pentagon* which took a swipe at the methods the Pentagon had been using to explain—or rather sell—its Vietnam War policy. Agnew charged CBS with 'propagandist manipulation'; one congressman complained that it was 'the most un-American thing I've ever seen on the tube'.

'The tragedy of this kind of reaction,' one former network news president remarked to me, 'is that CBS are actually getting attacked for doing their *best*. No one says a word all the time they are doing their worst with the usual run of comedies. And the fuss created over that programme means that everyone from Dick Salant (president of CBS News) down will have to spend weeks replying to all the criticism instead of getting on with making good television. The producer will be so busy explaining himself he won't have a chance to make another documentary for months.'

Yet for all the resistance to documentaries and current affairs in prime time, television news gets ample allocation every day—albeit outside prime time. The sixty percent of Americans who claim that television is their prime source of news are well served. Most of the major city stations run at least an hour of local or combined local and national news in the early evening and follow this with the half-hour network news at 7. These news shows—the *CBS Evening News* with Walter Cronkite, the *NBC Nightly News* with David Brinkley, Frank McGee and John Chancellor and the *ABC Evening News* with Harry Reasoner and Howard K. Smith—are flagships of network prestige. The anchormen, like Cronkite, are all distinguished journalists, not mere news readers, who are closely involved with the day-to-day writing and editing. Cronkite sees his role on the *CBS Evening News* like that of the managing editor of a newspaper. His calm, reassuring style has made the *CBS Evening News* the top rated of the nightly news shows for many years. The box office appeal of the best announcers brings them substantial rewards; Cronkite is said to earn up to £100,000 a year, while ABC, seeking to bolster the ratings for their news, lured Harry Reasoner away from CBS for a five-year contract reportedly worth £400,000.

In addition to a total of one and a half hours' news on many stations from 6 until 7.30 each evening, there is normally a further half-hour news round up at 11 p.m. In Los Angeles, widely regarded as being a 'news crazy' city, the network-owned stations run between three and four hours of news daily. The CBS station, KNXT, even goes so far as to pre-empt commercials outside regular news time to report briefly on a major breaking story.

Many stations also run daily editorials at the end of the evening news. Their news staff will include a special editorial writer—just as newspapers employ leader writers—whose remarks will always be prefaced with a statement that they represent the views of the management of that particular station. The editorials are normally concerned with local issues; they will tax city government, for instance, about delays in mass transportation improvements, inadequate schools or pollution hazards. ABC, CBS and NBC leave editorialising to the discretion of their local owned stations, which may even express differing views. When the American supersonic transport plane was cancelled early in 1971 the NBC station in Los Angeles ran an editorial deploring the action, while the NBC stations in Chicago and Cleveland applauded it.

In fact, once the high-powered world of the networks is left behind, it is possible to find individual stations who take their broadcasting role seriously. 'As I see it the networks are in show business, but we are in broadcasting,' said the programme director of CBS's KNXT in Los Angeles. Although the station carries the normal network output, it does report extensively on the problems facing Los Angeles. 'Television in my opinion largely ignores its opportunities to inform and educate and make people smarter on how to conduct their lives,' said the general manager, Ray Beindorf, 'but here we are trying to provide information in a palatable, upbeat way. Nearly half our programmes are local and we try to pre-empt the network for at least half an hour of prime time each month for important public-service programmes.' They have a regular half-hour magazine programme, *Insider Outsider*, for the black population of Los Angeles and another, *The Siesta is Over*, for Mexican-Americans.

One of KNXT's most ambitious local programmes in 1970 was an hour-long report on the danger of drugs called *If You Turn On*, which was uninterrupted by commercials. The public reaction was so favourable that immediately afterwards, not just the station's switchboard, but the entire Hollywood telephone exchange was jammed for hours as viewers tried to phone their compliments. The telephone company, when they finally untangled the lines, estimated that 170,000 people had tried to phone the station at once. 'This is the way that television should go,' said Beindorf.

The difficulty is that local stations, however public-spirited they may be, inevitably have to fall back on mass entertainment from the networks for much of the time in order to earn their keep. *If You Turn On* cost KNXT nearly £20,000; relatively few stations are prepared to invest that kind of money in public service documentaries.

The greatest castigator of U.S. television's weakness, is a bright young man named Nicholas Johnson, one of the seven commissioners of the Federal Communications Commission. Nick Johnson has become the *enfant terrible* of the American television scene—for ever damning the networks for serving up 'chewing gum for the eyes'. 'Television tells us, hour after gruesome hour,' Johnson complains, 'that the primary measure of an individual's worth is his consumption of products, his measuring up to ideals that are found in packages, mass produced and distributed to corporate America.' He has proposed, therefore, what he calls 'the one-third time rule', which would affect every network-affiliated television station. 'Each station,' he explains, 'would have to provide one-third of its "prime time" for purposes other than profit-maximising programmes, That's to say public affairs, cultural, educational programmes, anything other than the lowest common denominator—"commercially laden fare"—we're now offered.' But Nick Johnson is a voice crying in the wilderness of the FCC; his six fellow-commissioners are not likely to vote for his rule.

There are signs, however, that the FCC, which for years was regarded as a lapdog of the networks, is beginning to bark. Under a new chairman, Dean Burch (the man who ran Barry Goldwater's campaign in 1964), who was appointed by President Nixon in the autumn of 1969, the FCC is demanding that the networks improve their children's programming, which for years has consisted of little but cat-chasing mouse cartoons (a highly profitable exercise: CBS nets £4.6 million a year from Saturday-morning cartoons). Burch has told the networks categorically that things must improve 'regardless of whether cereal or toy sales' (the main sponsors of Saturday cartoon shows) 'reach new heights or not.' 'I am appalled at a lot of what my own children watch,' Dean Burch told me, 'we've got to have a higher proportion of beneficial programmes.'

The real impetus for better children's programmes came, however, not from the FCC but from the Children's Television Workshop, established in 1968 by the public-service National Educational Television (NET) in partnership with the Carnegie Corporation. Backed by a £3.3 million grant, Joan Cooney, the Workshop's president, set about devising a programme for pre-school children that would teach them the basic skills of reading and counting. The result was *Sesame Street*, an oasis of originality, vitality and colour amid the desert of American television. Sesame Street 'situated' in East Harlem, is peopled by grown-ups, children, a seven-foot canary known as Big Bird and assorted puppet interlopers, such as Oscar the Grouch, who lives in a dustbin. and the Cookie Monster, whose sole aim in life is finding yet another excuse to down a cookie. The programme ranges over ideas with all the free-wheeling imagination of a child's mind. A casual drive up the street in a make-believe car leads to a kaleidoscope of brisk, visual adventures; the car's licence-plate has the letter V in it which triggers a cartoon about the letter V and shows ten words beginning with the letter. Then back to the car pulling up at a red light, waiting for go. What letter do Stop and Go have in common? ... O ... and off into a fantasy on the letter O.

The bright little thirty-second cartoons juggling with letters and numbers are, in fact, *Sesame Street*'s commercials. 'We use the brief episodic technique of commercials to sell not products but letters and numbers,' Joan Cooney explains. And at the end of each show a voice announces that it was presented by the letters J and N or A and E, after the custom of programme sponsorship.

Sesame Street opened five days a week in the autumn of 1969 on nearly two hundred educational and community-owned stations across America. That first season, some seven million children looked at it regularly; it was the first resounding hit for the blossoming public television service. The programme also became an inevitable yardstick against which to measure the performance of the commercial networks' children's shows. The networks reacted quite promptly to *Sesame Street*: they appointed their own vice-presidents for children's programming and began to conjure up something more original than *Tom and Jerry*. ABC launched *Old Curiosity Shop*, designed to widen the horizons of children up to the age of eleven. But this and other new programmes are still for ever interrupted by those 'Be the first on your block ... Ask Mommy to get some now' commercials for candy and toys. I watched an excellent NBC children's documentary which tackled the delicate subject of explaining the dangers of drugs to under-tens, but which was completely ruined by the intrusion of commercials for toys; there were two commercial breaks in the first ten minutes and four in the first half-hour.

But *Sesame Street*'s success in prodding the commercial networks to rethink their children's programming is a landmark in American television history. Moreover, it has made millions of Americans aware for the first time that a fourth non-commercial network is slowly maturing.

As far back as 1952 the FCC set aside 242 television channels for educational television stations across America. Gradually over two hundred stations have been established, either as offshoots of universities and colleges or community-run channels in cities like New York, Boston, San Francisco, Los Angeles and Chicago. Most of them have lived—indeed, still live—a very hand-to-mouth existence; until the end of the 1960s they were not co-ordinated in programme planning and had no actual network. Programmes were 'bicycled' by post from one station to another.

At first central inspiration came only from National Educational Television (NET), which began in the 1950s primarily as an organisation advising local community stations how to incorporate themselves and collect funds. Gradually, NET evolved into a national programme-producing group, distributing about five hours of programmes a week to affiliated non-commercial stations. The Ford Foundation, the largest single benefactor of educational television in America over the years (£80 million up to 1971), was its main source of income.

Then, in 1967, the Carnegie Commission on Educational Television, a detailed enquiry into the prospects for public television in the United States, reported: 'We have reached the unqualified conclusion that a well-financed, well-directed educational television system, substantially larger and far more persuasive and effective than that which now exists in the United States, must be brought into being if the full needs of the American public are to be served.'

The Commission recommended that Congress establish a federally chartered, non-profit-making, non-governmental corporation to oversee the whole development of educational—or public, as it is increasingly known—television. President Lyndon Johnson supported the Commission's view. Accordingly, the Corporation for Public Broadcasting was set up in 1967 to knit together the assortment of educational and community stations into a strong public television system. The Corporation is financed both from Government and private sources. Essentially, the Corporation is a dispenser of funds to programme-makers; it is not in the production business itself. 'We are the catalyst, the stimulator in developing the whole system,' said John Macy, the Corporation's president. An offshoot of the Corporation, the Public Broadcasting Service (PBS), is charged with developing the actual network—the fourth network as it is now being called—linking together more than two hundred non-commercial stations in the United States. PBS also co-ordinates a network schedule comprising programmes made by its member stations or acquired from overseas (mostly from the BBC). From October 1971, PBS networked thirteen hours in prime time each week, plus three hours each morning, including *Sesame Street* and a new children's reading programme.

Despite this auspicious beginning, public television in America still has to overcome the crucial hurdle of its long-term finance. In 1971 the combined income of the Corporation and the non-commercial stations (many of whom receive grants from state or city authorities and universities) was just over £40 million (compared, for example, to the BBC in Britain with £80 million and NHK in Japan with £104 million). The Corporation itself had a grant from Congress of £14.7 million for the year 1971–2. 'What we really need is £40–£50 million a year,' said John Macy. His goal is to persuade Congress to grant the Corporation guaranteed long-term financing, ideally provided by a two per cent tax on the sale of television sets. But pushing that kind of legislation through Congress may be an impossible task, for if the Corporation had permanent funding, as opposed to annual grants, Congress would no longer have any direct control over it. 'Politicians here are not in the mood to give that kind of freedom to a medium as powerful as TV,' said Ed James, executive editor of the Washington-based *Broadcasting Magazine*.

In wooing the politicians Macy himself stresses the educational potential of the fourth network. Politicians are more likely to respond with hard cash if they feel that television can overcome some of the America's education deficiencies. But he also says proudly: 'We are attracting for the first time the thirty-five per cent of Americans who normally don't watch commercial television.'

This is the real potential of the new network; it is gradually widening the whole spectrum of American television. Apart from *Sesame Street*, three of its first big triumphs have been imports from the BBC—*Forsyte Saga, The First Churchills* and *Civilisation*. They have been greeted and devoured with a delight that makes one realise just how under-nourished Americans have been in their television fare. 'My wife and I now watch public television all the time and so does everyone we know socially,' said one executive vice-president of a commercial network, 'but don't write that or I'll kill you!'

But public television's real task for the seventies is to create a strong track record in its own programme-making; so far too much of its reputation is built on its BBC purchases. The network draws primarily on four production centres: National Education Television, which has been merged with Channel 13 in New York to form the Educational Broadcasting Corporation; WGBH in Boston, an educational foundation supported by, among others, the Boston Symphony Orchestra, Harvard and Yale Universities and the Massachusetts Institute of Technology; and two California stations, KQED San Francisco and KCET Los Angeles, both financed by their local communities.

All have already established their credentials with a variety of programmes of much greater originality than is customarily encountered on the commercial screen. Boston and Los Angeles has jointly produced *The Advocates*, a weekly hour-long debate that has tackled such topics as gun control, marijuana, abortion and the Calley verdict. An 'advocate' for each side, supported by the testimony of expert witnesses, argues the case, and at the end of an hour the moderator asks the viewing audience to write in with a 'yes' or 'no' opinion. One debate on the Middle East crisis drew 80,000 letters.

San Francisco's KQED presents a weekly review of the world's press, in which journalists compare the coverage of events in newspapers as diverse as *Pravda, The Times* and *Le Monde*. And two programmes from NET and Channel 13 in New York are the first on American television to be produced by and for the black community. *Black Journal* is a visual magazine on issues of importance to black Americans; *Soul* is a variety show. The latter has proved so popular in New York that an estimated sixty per cent of black households tune in.

Yet, even now, public television still teeters on the brink of bankruptcy. The secure financing that would enable it to flex its programming muscles is still missing. When I called on KQED in San Francisco, the general manager, Richard Moore, and the programme director, Jonathan Rice, both of whom have been with the station from its birth in 1954, were in the midst of a perennial debate on whether or not they would have to cut staff in a month's time. 'We are still flying by the seat of our pants,' said Rice. 'Once I actually had to borrow £800 from my mother and a friend to keep the station open. Just this morning I got a phone call saying that someone will put up the money that will enable us to televise a concert.'

KQED was the first non-commercial station in the United States to draw its main support from its viewers. Fifty thousand people subscribe either £6 as individual members or £10 for family membership. This brings in about £400,000 a year; the rest of the station's £2 million annual budget comes from donations, chiefly from foundations, and an annual television 'auction' to which viewers contribute everything from a used Rolls-Royce to a week's free treatment at a beauty parlour. In 1970 the auction raised £150,000.

KQED's main facilities are in a converted warehouse, where the sole studio has egg-boxes stuck to the walls in an effort to soundproof it from the traffic outside. This limitation has not stopped KQED pressing ahead with some of the most original television I have encountered anywhere.

During the newspaper strike in 1968 the station offered the city's journalists the chance to continue their reporting on the air. The result was, and still is, an hour-long evening *Newsroom.* The report is presided over by a managing editor who sits in the centre of a horseshoe desk, in the style of American newspaper offices, with the reporters seated around the outside. Each reporter in turn reads his story. The editor then asks him for clarification on any point or leads into a general discussion of the story, bringing in the other reporters for their opinions. The result is a very informal and sometimes verbose news report; items are not strictly timed and may run on longer than planned if the managing editor feels discussion is going well. On fast-breaking stories, reporters come in breathless with their reports while the programme is on. The format was so well received that *Newsroom* outlasted the strike. The

Ford Foundation then chipped in an annual grant of £300,000 to keep it going. Although *Newsroom* lacks the wide national and international coverage of news on the commercial networks, more than a third of the families in San Francisco watch it at least once a week. The non-commercial stations in Dallas and Washington D.C., have picked up the idea and now have their own editions.

So far local programmes like *Newsroom* and networked programmes on public television are not making any dent in the commercial networks, because their main attraction is to people who normally watch little television. But a Lou Harris public opinion poll in October 1970 showed that the national weekly audience for the fourth network had risen thirty-seven per cent in one year; 33 million Americans were looking at non-commercial television at least once a week. President Nixon showed his recognition of its achievement early in 1971 by including a correspondent from the fourth network in a televised *Conversation with the President*, thus giving PBS new status alongside the commercial networks.

The newcomer, however, is not likely to undercut the commercial networks or cause them to alter their policies in the foreseeable future. Although some commercial broadcasters will admit privately that they watch *The Advocates* or *Civilisation*, no radical change in the networks' programmes is brewing in response to PBS. Actually, they are more concerned about the potential threat of cable television.

Initially, cable or community antennae television (CATV) developed haphazardly in small towns that were just beyond the range of conventional television signals. Some local entrepreneur, often the man selling TV sets, set up a tall mast on a nearby hill to catch the distant signals, which were then carried into the home by coaxial cable. The habit caught on fast and by 1971 at least 5½ million homes were linked into 2,700 CATV systems. The largest system—in San Diego, California—was hooked into 50,000 homes, bringing a perfect signal from Los Angles stations more than a hundred miles to the north. Most CATV companies charge about £8 for installation and a monthly fee of £2. To begin with, everyone sat back happily and watched the profits roll up. But the coaxial cable opens all kinds of new programming horizons, for it can carry a dozen or more channels into the home. Some CATV companies soon embarked on their own programming—nothing ambitious, usually a time clock, a weather chart, a news ticker and a few interviews with local celebrities. One CATV company in Grand Junction, Colorado, even started television bingo. However, CATV programming has been given new impetus by an FCC ruling that from 1971 all systems with over 3,500 subscribers must originate some programmes of their own.

By now the real possibilities of CATV in bringing multichannel television into every home in the United States have been realised. Suddenly everyone wants to get in. Time-Life have sold their five television stations and invested in fifteen CATV systems, the most important being Sterling Manhattan, one of the fast developing systems in New York City. In mid-1971 Sterling Manhattan had 33,000 subscribers and estimated there were a potential 370,000 within their cable franchise area in mid-town Manhattan. The system carries all the main New York television stations and originates its own programmes on two spare channels, with live coverage of all ice hockey and basketball games at Madison Square Gardens and a regular evening bulletin of local news. So far, none of the CATV systems have the money to produce programmes on the scale of the networks but, by concentrating on very simple coverage of local events of interest, they can start to erode the networks' markets.

The commercial broadcasters, therefore, are considerably worried by the challenge of CATV over the next decade. The advent of twenty or thirty channels for every home could fragment that precious mass audience in prime time which they have striven so hard over the years to coalesce. 'The networks have had a hammerlock on air time for twenty years,' said the director of one New York CATV system, 'now it's being challenged.'

Although cable by itself will not force an overnight revolution on American television a combination of circumstances have suddenly come together to throw up all kinds of options for the future. Quite apart from the birth of public television and the swift growth of CATV, everyone is waiting to see how cassettes will change the cards. At the same time the FCC, which long seemed the handmaiden of the networks, has been debating the new 'McGannon' prime-time rule and muttering about forcing newspapers to dispense with their television holdings. 'There is a ferment today, just as there was in the late 1940s when television was getting established,' said Barry Zorthian of Time-Life's broadcasting division. 'The first television era is almost over and the whole audio-visual field for the next generation is being established.'

3

Canada: The Giant's Neighbour

THE village of Pembina in North Dakota seems a strange place to have a powerful television station. Only a couple of hundred people live there and the nearest American town of any size is many miles away. But the advertisers who queue up to buy time on KCND-TV Pembina have their eye, not on Americans, but on the half a million Canadians living just north of the border in the city of Winnipeg. The investment pays off; the people of Winnipeg spend a fifth of their viewing time watching the Pembina station. Furthermore, Pembina is one of twenty-five television stations scattered along the American–Canadian border whose signal reaches easily into Canadian homes. Consequently, Canada's two home-grown television networks operate constantly in the shadow of the American giant. The challenge facing Canadian television in the seventies is to preserve its own identity and avoid engulfment from south of the border.

The majority of Canadians, who spend an average of four hours a day before their sets, have displayed little loyalty to their own services, the part-commercial Canadian Broadcasting Corporation (CBC) and the independent commercial network, CTV. They devote up to two-thirds of their time looking at American channels, whose pictures are received just as clearly as the Canadian output because many homes in the major Canadian cities are wired by cable to powerful community antenna. Only ice hockey, that enduring Canadian passion, which is televised every Wednesday and Saturday evening throughout the long, harsh winter, can lure them by the million to their national channels. At other times even these rely heavily on imported American shows; for years the Canadians have been the best customers of the American network.

Amidst the American onslaught the lone outpost of Canadian television has been the French-speaking province of Quebec, where the language barrier has forced both CBC's French network and private commercial stations to create, rather successfully, their own programmes. CBC's French-language network proudly claims that it makes more French-language programmes than ORTF in France. But elsewhere every television executive is haunted by the American spectre at his shoulder. 'We have absolutely no cushioning from the Americans,' said the programme director of CBC's English network. 'I spend sixty seconds of every minute thinking about their challenge in making up my schedule.'

To compound the problem, Canada is about the most awkward country in the world to provide with a comprehensive television system. Quite apart from having two official languages, requiring dual programming, the geography is a nightmare. As James Finlay, CBC's man in London, put it, 'We are twenty-one million people rattling around in half a continent; a thin line of people spread across four thousand miles through seven different time-zones. Our network would reach from London to Moscow and far beyond.'

Yet for that reason broadcasting in Canada assumes great importance as a lifeline holding the nation together. Canada has no national newspapers and precious few magazines; while the theatre and films have always been overshadowed by the United States, responsibility for maintaining a distinct Canadian identity has fallen to radio and, increasingly, to television. 'I don't think Canada could survive without CBC,' a television news director told me in Toronto.

Faced with this problem, the Canadians are now scrambling to preserve their television from what one TV critic called 'wall-to-wall Hollywood in prime time'. The impetus came from an investigation into the future of broadcasting, the Fowler Report, which declared in 1965: 'The Canadian broadcasting system must never become a mere agency for transmitting foreign programmes, however excellent they may be. A population of twenty million people surely has something of its own to say, and broadcasting is an instrument by which it must have an opportunity to express itself.'

Following this report, a Canadian Radio and Television Commission was established in 1968 under the energetic guidance of a French Canadian, Pierre Juneau. He has wasted no time in attempting to Canadianise broadcasting. He has insisted that at least sixty per cent of the programmes put out both by CBC and the private commercial stations must be of Canadian origin; moreover, this sixty per cent must be maintained in prime time from 6.30 until 11.30 each evening. And to prevent the networks running American programmes for the remaining forty per cent, he has also set a ceiling of thirty per cent for programmes from any one country.

Yelps of protest, especially from the commercial stations, greeted this pronouncement. 'They are telling us to produce more Canadian programmes, but they are not giving us any money to do it,' complained Murray Chercover, president of the CTV network, 'and it's a fact of life that the further we have to make our money go, the less we're going to get for it in the way of quality.'

Juneau is unmoved. He realises that it will take time to build up Canadian talent, the best of which has traditionally been lured away by the coffers of the American networks. The real question, however, is whether these fine intentions are viable. Although CBC, for instance, is conceived as a public service with a clear mandate to 'contribute to the development of national unity and provide for a continuing expression of Canadian identity', it depends on advertising for a quarter of its income. Advertisers are not known to be impressed by high-sounding phrases about 'national unity'; they want big audiences. In cities where the CBC faces competition from both the local CTV network and American stations, it has rarely gained more than fifteen or twenty per cent of the audience. Canadianisation could mean, initially at least, an even smaller share of the audience, making CBC even less attractive to advertisers. Not an appealing prospect, especially as the Canadian Government is reluctant to step up the official grant which provides the rest of CBC's income; it 'froze' the grant during 1970–1.

CBC's declared intention that its 'prime objective for the seventies is the repatriation of the Canadian air waves' is further complicated by another local quirk. CBC does not own all the stations in its network. It owns about a dozen stations in major cities, but the majority of stations on both the English and French networks are privately owned affiliates, whose income is dependent entirely on advertising since they do not share directly in CBC's government grant. The advantage they have is that they get all CBC's networked programmes (about forty hours a week) free; and if CBC has sold a networked programme to a national advertiser, then they receive a slice of that income.

Inevitably, there are incompatabilities in a network that comprises both public-service and commercial stations. 'We are uneasy bedfellows,' admitted a CBC executive in Ottawa. The affiliates always want network programmes that will attract maximum audiences to boost the price of their own local ads. Devising an acceptable programme schedule is like trying to walk a tightrope that is being tweaked from both ends at once. 'Mickey Mouse could make up an American network schedule,' said Norman Garriock, programme director of CBC's English network, 'it's all numbers and dollars, but I defy him to come and make up mine.'

But CBC is not deterred from trying to originate as broad a spectrum of programmes as its £85 million a year budget allows. In an attempt to nurture young Canadian writers, it has set up a special fund to devote time and thought to producing television plays. No one expects miracles overnight. 'It's going to take a long, long time to build up Canadian drama,' admitted a senior drama producer, 'but at least we are giving writers the chance.' Also to its credit, CBC devotes at least one hour of prime time on four nights a week to serious documentaries and current affairs—which is precisely sixteen times longer than is allocated regularly by American networks over the border. One of the best in recent years was *The Magnificent Gift*, a dramatisation of the founding of the Hudson's Bay Company, which eloquently showed the downfall of the Indians as they confronted the fur-traders and were swept aside in the relentless pursuit of gain. CBC's overseas reporting has also been aided by Canada's political determination to remain independent of the United States on such issues as the recognition of communist China. CBC teams have been able to visit China and North Vietnam for first-hand objective reports. 'We are certainly not insular,' said John Kelly, the deputy director of information programmes, 'we try to look at every part of the world through Canadian eyes.'

Inevitably, the dominance of the Americans has some influence on the nightly news. CBC news cannot afford to use satellites regularly for its own news coverage, but, if NBC, for example, is using the Atlantic satellite for pictures of riots in Belfast, CBC can pick up a feed of those pictures at little cost out of New York. However, if NBC decides not to use the satellite, CBC will wait for its own filmed report to be flown across the Atlantic and will show it a day later.

The Canadians also have to bow to the Americans in making up the evening's schedule. The secret is to place all the American entertainment programmes early in the evening, in the hope of winning viewers who will then remain faithful throughout prime time. With the exception of ice hockey, which can hold its own against all-comers, most Canadian programmes are held back until nine o'clock, after such American goodies as *The Partridge Family*, *Laugh in* and *The Dick Van Dyke Show*.

The commercial CTV network of twelve stations, which

covers all the major cities of Canada except Quebec but does not penetrate deeply into rural areas, presents an equally Americanised front. Looking over its schedules, it is hard to believe that it is not an American station. With the exception of ice hockey on Wednesday night, no Canadian show gets a look-in before 9, by which time everyone will have been mesmerised by *Bewitched, Andy Williams, Dean Martin, Carol Burnett* and *Here's Lucy*. Not that CTV seems to be hiding many Canadian gems away. Their most popular local programme, known as *Pig and Whistle*, is a variety show set in a pub with a singing landlord. As I watched it, I wished he'd stick to serving beer.

The most heartening viewing in Canada comes from CBC's French network of six owned stations and nine affiliates, with its headquarters in Montreal. Apart from two stations for French-speaking communites in Winnipeg and Edmonton, all are in the province of Quebec. Although Montreal and much of Quebec are within the range of American television stations, the French-speaking Canadians have shown enormous loyalty to their own network, which has responded with a remarkably wide range of programmes. 'What I'm aiming at is a real divorce from the normal North American way of scheduling,' said Jean-Marie Dugas, the director of programmes for the French network. 'We may live in North America but we are an island of French-speakers. I want to capitalise on that.'

He has established a close working relationship with the French-language television services of France, Belgium and Switzerland, joining with them in co-productions. The late-night movies are culled from all over Europe. The week I was in Montreal one had the choice of good films from France, Italy, Hungary and Britain. But the network has really established its reputation on its own local production. In 1970, only two of the top fifteen programmes were not made in Canada. Moreover, in complete contrast to CBC's English-language network, the most popular programmes were not ice hockey or variety, but local comedies or drama series—*télé-romans*, as the French call them. The *télé-romans* are normally about family life in and around Montreal. One of the most successful, *Rue des Pignons*, is a rather more cosmopolitan version of *Coronation Street*. 'Our viewers feel a great affinity for these programmes,' explained Dugas, 'because three-quarters of the people in Quebec province live in and around Montreal. They have a great feeling for this city—there are about twenty-five news sheets every week full of gossip of who is sleeping with who and everyone knows about everyone else. So characters in our *télé-romans* set in Montreal are very familiar to them. We have this great advantage that we are making programmes for one city.'

Blended with the *télé-romans*, which are good, lightweight entertainment, is a considerable amount of more serious documentary and drama programming. Every Sunday evening, a two-hour programme *Les Beaux Dimanches*, from 8.30 until 10.30, presents concerts, ballet, operas and plays. During the 1970–1 season *Beaux Dimanches* presented twelve original plays by Canadian authors, a dramatisation of Steinbeck's *Of Mice and Men* and two full-scale operas, Gounod's *Faust*, Humperdinck's *Hansel and Gretel* (the competition for bilingual viewers from the American channels over the border at that time was *Bonanza* and the *Ed Sullivan Show*). Not that CBC's French network is a heavyweight channel; it has its own share of imported American programmes—*Bewitched*, charmingly retitled '*Ma Sorcière Bien-Aimée*', is the most popular—and such British fare as *The Avengers*, rechristened *Chapeau Melon et Bottes de Cuir* (Bowler Hat and Leather Boots). 'I'm trying to be purist *and* commercial,' said Jean-Marie Dugas.

The French-Canadians' hard work at their own programming has been duly rewarded by the building in Montreal of a £27 million television centre, with twenty-six radio and seven television studios, which comes into full use in 1972. CBC are proudly heralding it as the most modern television centre anywhere—improving, they hope, even on NHK's impressive facilities in Japan. From the top of the 320-foot hexagonal tower that rises above the studios you have a fine view not only of the whole of Montreal but out across the St Lawrence River to the hills of Vermont and upper New York state. However, despite the view from the roof, television in Montreal is standing firmly rooted on Canadian soil.

The English-language networks are not so solidly placed. Their new determination to withstand the American avalanche and match the French in establishing their own identity now faces a more demoralising threat, cable television, which is spreading faster in Canada than anywhere else in the world. A quarter of all Canadian homes had cable TV in 1971, bringing in not just the Canadian channels but at least three, and sometimes six or seven, American stations. In cities like Vancouver (British Columbia) and London (Ontario) two-thirds of the homes have cable TV with a choice of ten channels.

The Canadian Radio and Television Commission has been racking its brains as to how best to counter the growth of CATV. It insists that all cable systems must carry Canadian stations as a priority, but, as the basic systems being used can fit in twelve channels, that is no problem. Any threat to stop the development of CATV is greeted by loud complaints from communities not yet connected that the Commission is depriving them of their civil rights in denying them access to programmes which are already piped into many other Canadian homes.

Thus within a very few years it is likely that almost every Canadian will be able to tune into ten or a dozen TV channels. This will fragment the existing audiences for CBC and CTV, seriously undercutting their attraction to advertisers. 'Just look at the top ten advertisers in the U.S. and Canada,' said the managing director of one leading Canadian commercial station; 'they are the same and are all controlled out of New York. Quite soon the Americans will be able to place their advertising for the Canadian market on *American* channels, which will be seen in every home here. What is the future for us?'

CBC, with its large government grant, clearly stands the best chance of survival in this bleak scene. The dismal commercial prospect is not interfering with its determination to improve Canadian television in the seventies. Furthermore, a new stimulant will arise in 1972 when Canada launches a domestic communications satellite, the first in North America. Operated by the Telesat Canada Corporation, it will have ten operational channels, of which three will be used exclusively by CBC. Two of the channels will distribute English-language television programmes, the third will extend the coverage of the French network. The satellite will also extend the television network throughout the far north, bringing the Eskimos and miners living in those barren lands into the Canadian fold. But even this, while giving a few thousand more the opportunity to watch television, will not roll back the American giant, whose shadow will continue to dog every effort to Canadianise Canadian TV.

4

Latin America: *Tele-novela* Land

TELEVISION in Latin America can be as uncertain as local politics. Stations mushroom overnight, flourish for a year or two and then vanish in bankruptcy or in a cloud of dust from a guerrilla's bomb. One station in Guatemala, with an American general manager, gets a brisk burst of machine-gun fire every few weeks from a passing car as an anti-American *billet-doux*. In Venezuela a new channel, heralded as the most modern in Latin America, opened with great promise, but, unfortunately, the transmitter had been placed on the wrong mountain. A few villages in the jungles of the interior, if they had had electricity and TV sets, would have received a fine picture, but the two million population of Caracas barely had a glimmer on their screens. The station lost £5 million. In Costa Rica engineers erected a transmitter on top of a volcano, beaming excellent pictures throughout the country; then the volcano erupted and the transmitter was engulfed in lava. A station in Buenos Aires must have established a record by having forty-three director-generals in less than twenty years.

Along with other mishaps, political revolutions are coped with as briskly as the weather forecast. 'Our last revolution was very gentlemanly,' said an executive of Teleonce—Channel 11—in Buenos Aires. 'Three soldiers came along from the palace and just told us to broadcast the takeover by the new president.'

Despite the prompt arrival of soldiers at the hint of a coup, television is owned and operated by the state in only three

Latin American countries—Cuba, Chile and Colombia. Elsewhere it is hard to find the programmes among the commercials; many countries allow sixteen minutes of commercials in one hour. That is not quite as profitable as it sounds, because too many stations are chasing too little advertising. The entire television advertising kitty in Latin America is no more than £75 million a year (which is just about the same as the BBC television budget in Britain), yet many of the major cities have five or even six channels. Both Lima and São Paulo had seven until 1970, when one channel in each city quietly faded away. 'There are so many stations,' remarked a European programme salesman after touring the continent, 'that you feel there is one on every corner, just like the tobacconist's.'

Although television has a mass audience in Latin America, a set is still beyond the means of millions of families. In Brazil, for example, there is one television set for every fifteen people (compared with one set for every 2.5 people in the United States), while in Peru the ratio is one set for thirty. The problem is not just the cost of the sets; it is that large rural areas have no electricity supply. 'What we need,' said a director of Channel 5 in Lima, 'is a kerosene-powered TV set.'

Actually, even if one existed, many people would still be outside the range of television, for it is concentrated almost entirely in the centres of population. Major cities within a country are often not linked by microwave; video-tapes and films travel from one local station to another by bus. Only in Mexico, Cuba and Colombia has there been a concerted effort to build a nationwide microwave link. The Brazilian government is slowly linking up the main cities, but the whole country will not be hooked in for several years. In Buenos Aires, when I asked the general manager of Teleonce if Argentina might have a complete network in this decade, he replied a little sadly: 'Perhaps in this century.'

The issue, of course, is not a simple one. The distances involved are enormous; Western Europe could be lost comfortably in the jungles of Brazil. The real answer, many experts feel, is a Latin American satellite, which would not only give complete coverage of individual countries but would link them together. The existing Atlantic satellite, which the Latin Americans already use for international football games, moon-walks and a daily news film exchange with Europe, does not help their distribution problems, and for the moment a Latin American satellite is beyond both budgets and political co-operation. Although television organisations are now co-operating much more closely, political agreement between regimes as diverse as those of Brazil and Chile, or Argentina and Peru, is hardly likely.

Moreover, the concept of public-service broadcasting is only now emerging; the few government educational channels that exist are starved of money and expertise. 'The trouble is,' lamented an executive of the Argentine government's own Channel 7 in Buenos Aires, 'that we never have a government in power long enough to formulate a broadcasting policy. The aims of the channel as a result are something of a mystery.'

Television-operating licences in the past have been granted mostly to wealthy supporters of governments. A friendly political attitude, rather than broadcasting skill, has been the main requirement for winning the right to open a TV station. In Costa Rica a dentist ran a TV station for a while until it lost so much money that he had to accept expert help from a Panama channel. Latin American families who first made their wealth in rum, sugar, oil, cattle and newspapers have frequently tried to extend their empires into television. Indeed, it seems to have become quite fashionable in countries like Venezuela for the most powerful family businesses to operate a TV channel. Family rivalries may be perpetuated in the competition between their private channels. The clash between the Chiari and Elata families in Panama to win the highest ratings for their respective stations reminded an American adviser there of the Montague–Capulet feud in *Romeo and Juliet*.

The ease with which people had previously made great profits in radio in Latin America, where stations multiply like amoebas (there are 365 in Brazil and 200 in Peru) convinced many innocents that TV offered equally easy loot. 'People operate radio stations here almost from their bath-tubs,' remarked an American television executive in Mexico City. 'Commercials are often paid for in merchandise. It's highly profitable.' Television programmes, however, cannot be paid for solely out of free cases of whisky or soap-flakes from a sponsor.

Nevertheless, the most successful television entrepreneurs in Latin America have been, without exception, men who graduated from running radio networks. There are only a handful of them. Goar Mestre gave Cuba the world's first complete TV network in the 1950s before departing for Argentina, after Castro's arrival, to become the *Czar* of television in Buenos Aires. Emilio Azcarraga controls the three channels of Telesistema in Mexico. In Peru, Genaro Delgado Parker, president of Panamericana Radiofusion, has produced the most successful soap operas in Latin America, while in Brazil the late Francisco de Assis Châteaubriand Bandeira de Mello founded Diarios Associados, which controls fourteen of the country's fifty-two stations. Two other men are bidding for leading roles—Alexandro Romay, a brash former disc-jockey in Buenos Aires, whose Channel 9, which runs mainly live variety shows, is giving Goar Mestre tough competition, and Dr Roberto Marinho of Brazil's new TV Globo network, which, after several years of considerable losses, has finally become the most popular channel in Rio de Janeiro and São Paulo.

The wealthiest empire founded on the profits of television in Latin America is undoubtedly that of Emilio Azcarraga in Mexico. 'Azcarraga,' says one of his friends genially, 'is the Metro lion of Mexican TV.' He began his career in the 1930s as a representative of RCA records in Mexico City. While plugging RCA, he also recorded local Mexican artists and migrated into radio to promote his records. Early in the 1950s he applied for a licence to open a television station, although the credit for opening the first channel in Mexico (indeed, in

Latin America) goes to another successful radio man, Romulo O'Farrill. O'Farrill's XH-TV opened in Mexico City on August 31st, 1950. Azcarraga's station opened shortly afterwards. For two or three years the two men fought a bitter rivalry to win audiences and advertising. Finally, President Aleman suggested tactfully that it was time to stop squabbling and concentrate on developing television. He urged Azcarraga and O'Farrill to merge.

They took his advice and, absorbing a third station in Mexico City, formed Telesistema Mexicana, with Emilio Azcarraga as undisputed leader. Telesistema is still the most formidable television combine in all Latin America. It operates three channels in Mexico City, owns stations in Monterey, Guadalajara and Tijuana and has nineteen affiliates in other cities. The main channel in Mexico City is networked throughout the country. Azcarraga has also moved into cable television by the simple expedient of picking up signals from American stations near the Mexican border, relaying them to the capital and feeding them into homes by cable. He has built a television production centre in Mexico City, which he conveniently leases out to his three channels. The programmes produced there are also ideal fodder for the myriad little TV stations in Guatemala, Nicaragua and Costa Rica that cannot afford to make their own programmes.

The profits from all these enterprises have been substantial. Over the years Azcarraga has branched out into numerous other activities (158 different companies according to one count) including car sales, real estate and a grand hotel in Acapulco. He even owns a football team, whose matches may be televised only on his own channels. This enthusiasm for soccer led to some highly embarrassing moments for Azcarraga just before the 1970 World Cup football competition in Mexico. Azcarraga's son, without his father realising it, secured all the television rights to the competition and then set about making a deal individually with each country that wanted Telesistema's pictures. Much to the dismay of the BBC in Britain he sold the British rights to Independent Television. Only after many spirited exchanges was the commercial network forced to back down and agree that on an event of such importance the BBC must also be able to carry the pictures.

Telesistema's monopoly has been challenged since 1968 by several new commercial stations, backed by a group of Monterey businessmen. The newcomers, whose money has been made largely in breweries, do not yet appear to understand that making television is a different process from making beer. For Emilio Azcarraga, whose fortune is founded in television, they are no great threat.

While Azcarraga's energies have been concentrated in Mexico, Goar Mestre has been roaming at large in Latin America. He is a big, avuncular man in his late fifties who chain-smokes Romeo y Julieta cigars in his blue-carpeted office on the top floor of the television centre he has built in Buenos Aires for Proartel—his TV production company. After graduating from Yale, Cuban-born Mestre went into business in Havana, in the early 1940s, as the local agent for Kolynos toothpaste and Jello. Quickly becoming dissatisfied with the commercials made for these and other products on the radio stations then existing in Cuba, he went into radio in 1942 to improve matters. He built up the CMQ radio network throughout Cuba, and also operated two local stations in Havana, one giving non-stop news and time-checks interspersed with commercials, the other broadcasting classical music to satisfy his own taste. In the early 1950s he stepped naturally into television. The relatively small size of Cuba enabled him to establish two networks, each of seven stations. They were linked together by eighteen microwave hops. Mestre thus takes credit for being the first man to create a television system covering the entire population of a country—an achievement which played conveniently into the hands of Fidel Castro after the fall of Batista.

'When Castro came into Havana we simply turned television over to him lock, stock and barrel,' Mestre recalls. 'He was in my office all the time. While he was in the hills as a guerrilla he had never realised the power of TV but, once he became President, he saw that this was the one way to reach the Cuban people in their homes. Then you couldn't keep him off. He was the prime-time show. He never spoke for less than four hours, and his record was six hours and fifteen minutes non-stop. He just chatted on and on, repeating himself, hammering home his points about improved social services, better education, no more corruption. He had the style of a star performer, with that big beard and his olive-green uniform; all through he'd smoke away at his cigars and sip coffee and cognac.'

A Swiss journalist, Jean Ziegler, visiting Cuba in those early days noted: 'I have seen the Bouglione Circus, Cinerama atrocities by Cecil B. de Mille, Arab festivals and Broadway parades, but never have I witnessed a show to hold a candle to Fidel Castro's television marathon ... What is government by television? A cheap newspaper gimmick? No, for with his non-stop TV show Fidel Castro has actually created a new form of government that is just as original and will prove no less significant in its historic effects than the Greek invention of the ballot ... For six million Cubans the sole expression of their government's will is the television speech.' (Quotes in International Press Institute, 1960.)

The joke in Havana then was that one could only rely on the electricity supply on the evenings when Castro was due to make another harangue.

Castro's command of television quickly left Mestre out in the cold. 'I bailed out and came to Argentina.' There he started his own television production company, Proartel, and won a licence for Channel 13. Since the only real rival was the chaotic government channel, he had little difficulty in making Channel 13 the prime station in Buenos Aires, on the air fifteen hours a day, with almost eighty per cent of the programmes produced locally. He also established a limited network of ten stations in other cities. However, the blanket coverage he achieved in Cuba has not been repeated, because there is still no microwave network throughout Argentina. The government will not let him build one, although it keeps promising to build its own.

His success in Argentina prompted Mestre to embark on a variety of television forays in Peru, Colombia and Venezuela. They were much less rewarding; the Venezuelan expedition, in particular, was disastrous, for it was there that the transmitter was placed initially on the wrong mountain.

Beyond the Andes in Lima another would-be television empire-builder, Genaro Delgado Parker, is employing all his ingenuity to prevent Peru's left-wing military regime from taking over his and the other four commercial stations. His father has long been established in radio in Lima, but Genaro and his two brothers, Hectora and Manuel, have graduated into television. Manuel runs Channel 5 in Lima, Hector looks after their overseas operations, while Genaro heads a holding company, Panamericana Radiofusion, which co-ordinates all their activities. When the brothers first went into television they found that their ambitions were thwarted by very restricted budgets. The total television advertising revenue in Peru is a mere £3 million a year, shared among five competing stations. 'We decided the only way for us to develop was to make our programmes for all Latin American markets,' said Genaro. 'We've been very lucky. We started in 1966 and so far we've sold our programmes in fourteen countries, which isn't bad for a small Peruvian company.'

Encouraged by this success, the brothers have been moving into television outside Peru. They have a stake in one station in Argentina and another in Puerto Rico, where they have also established a production company. In Lima, Genaro Delgado Parker proudly shows visitors to his office a large model of the new television centre he planned if he could obtain guarantees from the government not to nationalise television. That plan, however, was thwarted in November 1971 when the Peruvian government announced they were taking over fifty-one per cent of all commercial television stations.

The takeover marks an accelerating trend of government intervention in broadcasting throughout the continent, which has helped to speed the retreat of the three major American networks and Time-Life, who all embarked on a great, but unhappy, flirtation with Latin American television in the early 1960s. The Americans were tempted into Latin America, not just to find a market for their programmes but to sell stations equipment and television sets in the belief that television could be just as profitable as in the United States. The broadcasting law in most countries forbade them actually owning a television channel, but they found a local partner who obtained the licence, and then they pumped in capital, equipment and know-how. The prospect seemed most attractive. A network like NBC, which is owned by RCA, could fit out the station with RCA equipment, have a ready outlet for its programmes and reap, they thought, great advertising profits. In Venezuela the American networks bought into every single TV station; NBC joined the local Phelps family in Channel 2 in Caracas; ABC went into Channel 4 with the Cisneros family (which had made its fortune bottling Pepsi-Cola), while CBS and Time-Life linked up with Goar Mestre from the Argentine and the Vollner family, whose main interests were sugar and rum, to open Channel 9.

Down in Argentina, CBS and Time-Life worked with Mestre on his own Channel 13, NBC invested in Channel 9 and ABC joined a group of local Jesuits who were hoping to propagate the faith over Channel 11. Further investments were made in stations in Brazil (where Time-Life backed the developing TV Globo network), Peru, Panama and Guatemala. Everywhere it was the same story—huge losses.

'We simply over-estimated the market,' said an NBC executive, who spent several years helping his network bail out of Latin America as gracefully as possible. 'For a while everyone thought it was the new frontier. We quickly found out it wasn't. There were just too many stations.'

In Venezuela, for example, the advertising revenue available was about £9 million a year, but the combined budgets of the three stations in which the Americans had stakes came to £10 million. Once they realised their mistake the Americans tried to retreat, but often the losses of the stations were so great that no one locally would buy out their interest. They have either had to retain the investment, hoping for better days, or sell out to their existing partners on extraordinarily generous credit terms.

A simple miscalculation about revenue was not the sole cause of the American failures. Their Latin American invasion began just as nationalist feeling was gaining momentum; Argentinians, Peruvians and Brazilians resented the American domination. 'The Americans failed to realise that television here is a different animal from television in the United States,' said Goar Mestre. 'People in Argentina don't mind the occasional American programme, but what they really like are shows with local flavour. We make seventy-eight per cent of our own programmes.'

Local programmes, in fact, are pushing American imports right out of Latin America. Moreover, because the whole continent, with the exception of Brazil, speaks Spanish there is a fine pool of programmes in Spanish which can be conveniently swapped between individual countries. Peruvians can watch Mexican programmes, Venezuelans can understand shows from Colombia or Argentina. Prime time everywhere is now given over entirely to local programmes or those produced in neighbouring countries; American shows are relegated to the afternoons or late at night. 'Programme directors know they can beat any American series hands down by putting their own *tele-novelas* against it,' said an American programme salesman sadly in Mexico.

The life-blood of Latin American TV is the *tele-novela*. Two or three of these soap operas frequently follow each other right through prime time. In Mexico, Telesistema's Channel 2, the main network covering the whole country, runs *novelas* back to back every day from 4.15 until 7.45. In Panama, 8 till 10 every evening is *tele-novel*a time. In Argentina they prefer them in the afternoon; Goar Mestre's Channel 13 carries non-stop novelas from 3 until 6. Every one has the same essential theme: a poor but beautiful country girl comes to the big city, works as a maid in a rich household, is seduced, has an illegitimate baby, but prospers and opens a chic boutique or marries a millionaire playboy. Variations on the theme are endless. TV Globo in Brazil scored a great success with *Pigmalião 70*, which simply reversed the normal Pygmalion roles, so that poor country boy comes to the big city, is taken up and educated by rich, beautiful, sophisticated, sports-car-driving lady.

'The story of a successful *tele-novela* must be the story of many people in Latin America,' explains Genaro Delgado Parker 'It's not melodrama, it's not crime. It's like the lives of many of the viewers—or how they would like their lives to be. The dialogue is simple and unsophisticated. The characters aren't all bad or all good.'

Delgado Parker's own Panamericana Radiofusion has been responsible for two of the most successful *tele-novelas*—*Simplemente Maria* and *Natacha*. Both of them have the same poor-country-girl-starts-as-servant-in-big-city-home theme; the only real difference is that Natacha marries her lover and Maria does not. *Simplemente Maria* has been seen in every single Latin American country and also on Spanish-language stations in New York, Los Angeles and Miami; Brazil, Argentina and Venezuela have all made their own versions. At the latest count around 400 episodes had been made. *Natacha*, which started rather later, easily notched up 260 episodes and Delgado Parker told me: 'Maybe we'll make 400 in the end.' *Simplemente Maria* has also been made into a film; when I was in Lima the queues stretched all round the block from the cinema.

The production of *tele-novelas* has been honed down to the barest essentials. Most half-hour episodes cost between £500 and £800, depending on how little the producers can get away with paying the stars. Location scenes are almost unknown; the *novelas* are normally churned out in one studio with a couple of sparsely furnished sets. Three episodes are shot in an eight-hour working day. The secret of such swift productions is a midget radio receiver plugged into the ear of each actor, which dispenses almost entirely with the time-consuming business of memorising lines thoroughly or learning detailed stage directions. As the action proceeds before three cameras, a prompter in the control room reads the script and stage directions into a small radio transmitter so that the actor hears his lines in his tiny earplug. He just follows orders or repeats what he hears.

The Mexicans are particularly brisk at this business. One morning I stopped by a Telesistema studio where they were making about the hundredth episode of a saga called *La Cruz de Mariza Cruzes*, in which a poor country girl goes to work as a maid on a Mexican ranch, gets pregnant etc.... Work on making three episodes that day had started at 10 and by 11.15, when I arrived, they had already completed one in its entirety. Now the director, a splendid Mexican with a short, clipped beard and a frock coat, was busy briefing his cast for the next chapter. He ran over the main points of the script for a while but, by 11.30, they were all set to shoot the second half-hour episode of the morning. The prompter hunched over his microphone, everyone adjusted their earplugs and they were away. 'Mariza stand up, move to your right and say "I am yours for ever." ' The actress responds accordingly. In another corner of the set a man in white tie and tails holds a woman in a low-cut evening gown in his arms and, on instructions, they start jogging up and down before a camera to simulate dancing. Cut to an empty set. An old man comes wandering slowly on, looking puzzled and confused. To me it is not clear if that is how he should look or if his earplug has broken down. Never mind. Minor errors are overlooked. The important thing is to finish the episode before lunch. At least they only do three episodes a day here. At Channel 8 in Caracas, Venezuela, they reckon to do three episodes on weekdays and four on Sundays.

The mass audiences for the *tele-novelas* are, however, hardly stern critics of production techniques; for them a story with which they can identify is all-important. 'The secret is a good, strong script,' said Goar Mestre. In the slums of Rio, Buenos Aires or Lima the tale of local-girl-makes-good is far more compelling than *Ironside* or *Bewitched*, which are completely beyond the experience of simple and frequently illiterate people. '*Novelas* keep them mesmerised,' said a young television producer in Buenos Aires. 'For an hour or two they forget the conditions in which they are living—perhaps it even stops them making revolution.'

Beside the *novela* the other hallmark of Latin American television is live variety on Saturdays and Sundays lasting anything from six to twelve hours. These marathons are a potpourri of singing and comedy acts, quiz games and interviews, normally compèred by a breezy host who becomes, almost inevitably, the number one television personality. The Argentinians have the greatest passion—and stamina—for these non-stop programmes. Goar Mestre's Channel 13 offers a seven-hour Saturday show, *Sabados Circulares de Mancera*, hosted by a chatty, slightly aggressive young man with unruly hair, called Nicholas Mancera. Alexandro Romay's Channel 9 offers eight and a half hours of *Sabados de la Bondad*, introduced by Hector Coire, but Romay himself, a slim brisk figure with a toothbrush moustache, can rarely resist the temptation of stepping down from his director-general's chair on Saturday evenings to participate, often without warning, in the show. He has been known to stroll into the studio, hold out a commanding hand into the camera lens, call, 'Wait a moment,' and launch into a series of outlandish anecdotes about mythical adventures that have befallen him. This unexpected arrival of the boss gives the show a spontaneity that makes up for the technical gaffes which are inevitable in such a test of endurance.

One night when I was watching the show (and being vastly entertained by it) a leading Argentine pop singer, Sandro, got lost behind the scenes during the commercial. Hector Coire, meanwhile was leading into an elaborate introduction heralding his entrance. Trumpets blared, the cameras switched to the top of a staircase. 'Sandro,' yelled Coire, as teenagers in the studio audience squealed with delight. No sign of Sandro. Coire cued him again. Still no Sandro. Coire taken aback, turned and walked over to the teenagers and started interviewing them to gain time. While he was in the midst of that, Sandro finally strolled, unnoticed, down the stairway.

The eight-and-a-half-hour Saturday show is really just a warm-up for Sunday, when *Feliz Domingo* (Happy Sunday) lasts a straight twelve hours, from 11.30 in the morning until 11.30 at night. The formula of quizzes and pop singers is the same. While this exhausts the host, Orlando Marconi, the camera crews and even the studio audience, the ordinary viewer simply tunes in once in a while, as if he were dipping into a Sunday colour supplement.

The popularity of these shows has pulled Alexandro Romay's station back from the brink of financial disaster. When he took over, he inherited such a pile of debts that he had no money to buy outside programmes and precious little to make his own. Undaunted, he rounded up a pool of local out-of-work actors and pop singers and started building live studio shows around them. The lack of polish was more than compensated for by everyone's enthusiasm. By 1969 Romay was seriously challenging Goar Mestre's Channel 13 for top audience ratings in Buenos Aires. Not only was Mestre forced to respond with live shows; the habit is now spreading fast throughout Latin America. In Mexico Telesistema has started *Siempre el Domingo* (Always on Sunday) which lasts seven and a half hours; in Brazil you can watch the *Silvio Santos Show* for five and a quarter hours on TV Globo each Sunday afternoon, and the moment that finishes switch to *Diarios Associados*, where Flavio Cavalcanti is just beginning his four hour stint.

The Brazilians have also launched the one international variety programme in Latin America—*The Rio Song Festival*, a close cousin of the Eurovision Song Contest. Staged as a grand spectacle in a stadium in Rio, it has all the excitement of a football game and is the television event of the year. In 1970 more than forty countries from Europe as well as Latin America entered songs and singers in the contest, which was broadcast live by satellite throughout the continent. Globo even imported colour cameras so that the finale could be sent in colour by satellite direct to Europe.

But the era of endless song and dance on Latin American television is drawing to a close. Rather belatedly, politicians there are beginning to realise the power of television both for good and bad. Castro has efficiently demonstrated in Cuba how to bring a country to heel by television; but Colombia has set the best example in Latin America by opting out of the *tele-novela* circuit in favour of programmes designed to counter illiteracy and disease. The Colombian television service is one of the poorest on the continent (it has to get by on £2 million a year) and is closely government-controlled, but it has attempted to provide some form of public service. When I visted Abraham Zalzmann, the director of television at the National Institute for Radio and Television (Inravision), he was reading the Pilkington Report, seeking further guidelines. Inravision controls all the studios and transmitters in Colombia, but leases out time to commercial programme companies in the evening. By day, however, the network is used for programmes for schools, financed by the evening commercials. Inravision has established one of the most complete networks in Latin America, covering almost ninety-five per cent of Colombia's population of twenty million scattered through the foothills of the Andes. It has achieved this by building the highest television transmitter in the world, perched over 13,000 feet up on an Andian peak, and by establishing the longest jump between microwave links in the world—260 miles between two mountain-tops.

One full network is already in operation, plus a second local channel in the capital of Bogota which puts out adult education programmes in the evenings. A second national network should be complete by 1973: this will broadcast educational programmes non-stop from eight in the morning until midnight 'Without television,' Abraham Zalzmann explained, 'it is quite impossible for us to educate everyone. Education is not compulsory in Colombia because there are not enough teachers or schools. Television can fill that gap.'

The major task is to ensure that every community is equipped with a television set; in 1971 there was only one set for every twenty-five people in Colombia. The £170 needed to buy one is quite beyond the means of millions. The government and overseas aid agencies are therefore proposing to establish community receivers around which all the children or even the adults in a village or a street can gather. The United States has supplied 1,500 sets for schools to receive daytime programmes, while several hundred more have been distributed to local teleclubs for adult education programmes each evening on the local Bogota station. 'These teleclubs are not only to teach people to read and write,' the director of educational programmes pointed out, 'but to explain to people the basic facts about public health and hygiene, housing construction and agriculture.'

Everywhere, however, the pressure is on to increase educational broadcasting. All commercial stations in Brazil now have to broadcast at least five hours of educational programmes each week and the government is building its own network of forty educational stations. The new tone of television was evident when I called on the CBS representative in São Paulo, who for years have happily sold *Gunsmoke* and *Hawaii Five-O* to Brazilian stations. I found him busy writing a new catalogue of all educational and documentary programmes available from CBS. 'Until now the stations here have been concerned only with ratings,' he said, 'but they've had it made clear to them that if they don't change their programmes the government will.' He was sending out, as a gentle hint with his new catalogue, the full text of a speech by President Medici chiding the television industry for being so slow to mend its ways. 'This is not the first time I have had to speak like this,' the President pointed out sternly. 'I have reminded you before that it is not enough just to have five hours weekly of educational programmes, but essential to raise the whole level of programming; poor quality programmes must be forbidden; the creative talent of Brazilians must not be destroyed by television.'

The cry for educational television is, of course, often a convenient cloak to cover government manoeuvres to strengthen their hold on the medium. Stations whose editorial policies are embarrassing to the government can quietly be nationalised as educational channels. But most of them are fully aware of the dangers and steer an obsequious course rather than risk losing their income from commercials. Open censorship is not always necessary; news editors are well drilled in what not to cover. 'We practise self-censorship,' a television news editor, who once worked for the BBC, admitted in Buenos Aires. The Mexican government, who were incensed by television coverage of student riots in Mexico City just before the 1968 Olympics, have since enacted a law that enables them to claim twelve and a half per cent of all television time to explain their own policies to the people.

Clearly the happy-go-lucky age of television in Latin America is past. The days when any rich family with good political connections could bid for a television-operating licence are finished; the Americans are bowing out, trying hard to forget the losses they have made. 'Television in Latin America is at the crossroads,' said Alistair McKenzie, who has spent more than fifteen years representing NBC interests there. 'The beginning of 1970 was really the turning point. Now the politicians are stepping in everywhere. Chances of selling some routine comedy are dying. In future the preoccupation will be the moral and educational content of programmes.'

WESTERN EUROPE

5

Eurovision

THE nerve centre of European television is concealed high up in the roof of the Palais de Justice in Brussels. Outside, the broad flight of steps up to the cavernous entrance hall are bustling with lawyers, policemen and witnesses, but tucked away in the far corner of the entrance is a tiny lift which soars non-stop towards the roof. The door slides back to reveal a narrow gallery running round inside the roof of the entrance hall. At the end of the gallery—quite a nerve-racking walk, for there is only a metal handrail—a door leads into first a kitchen and then a warren of attic rooms. There half a dozen young men in their shirt-sleeves sit before a panorama of television monitors that glow with the call signs of Europe's stations. Very shortly, the screens will come alive with film of that day's happenings all over Europe—an avalanche in the French Alps, a riot in Belfast, a football match in Italy, a disarmament conference in Vienna. Just now, the young men, who come from the Netherlands, Britain, Belgium, West Germany and Sweden, are busy checking their circuits with television stations as far-flung as Dublin and Lisbon, Tunis and Belgrade, Rome and Copenhagen. They talk in English or French, alternating easily. Occasionally, when some capital is slow to respond, they show a moment's irritation: 'Can't the twit switch that circuit?' There is no time for delays; precisely at five o'clock they must have the whole of Europe and three North African countries hooked in together for what they call EVN 1

—the first session of a twice-daily exchange of news film. Another exchange, EVN 2, will follow at seven o'clock. Before that, however, they have to funnel all over Europe live coverage by satellite of the landing in the Pacific of an Apollo spacecraft back from the moon. They must also cope with special transmissions between individual European capitals as various foreign correspondents make their personal reports home for the evening news. Later in the evening they will relay an important football match from London to half a dozen other television services across Europe.

The hide-out beneath the rafters in the Palais de Justice is the control room for Eurovision, the European Broadcasting Union's (EBU) unique multi-national programme exchange. Twenty-seven television stations in twenty-two European countries are linked to this network, which extends also to Morocco, Algeria, Tunisia and to Intervision, Eurovision's counterpart in Eastern Europe and the Soviet Union. Yugoslavia, although a communist country, is an integral part of the Eurovision, not the Intervision, network. The lone European nation not on the network is Iceland, which is too remote. Iceland does have television—broadcasting for about three hours a night six days a week (never on Thursdays)—but has to rely on its imported programmes coming in by air freight.

Brussels became the technical centre for Eurovision from the beginning because, when the network started to evolve in the mid 1950s, Belgium was a convenient hub for European telecommunications to converge on. Moreover, most of the early multi-national programme exchanges were between Britain, France, Belgium and the Netherlands (for Queen Elizabeth's Coronation in 1953, for instance). The Palais de Justice, then the tallest building in Brussels, its dome rising to 360 feet, was ideal, as antennae placed inside the dome could pick up television pictures over great distances.

Nowadays, the pictures from the crossroads at Brussels can be relayed instantly to all the seventy-five million television sets in Western Europe. By 1970 there was one set among every five people. Only in Spain, Yugoslavia, Portugal and Greece was television not a commonplace in the home; Portugal, for example, had one set among twenty people, Greece one in fifty. Television in these countries is still a rarity outside the cities. Villages in the north of Portugal have only one or two sets in bars and cafés. 'The people here have still not got accustomed to watching television in their homes,' said Dr Antonio Bivar, director of international relations for Portuguese television. 'For centuries they've gone out to bars every evening and they still prefer to go there and watch the television among their friends. It's just the same in the south of Italy, people don't like sitting at home.'

Everywhere in Europe television is primarily an evening attraction. No one yet has programmes with breakfast, although many start up at lunch-time with entertainment for housewives. In small nations like Norway and Denmark part of the evenings viewing is considerately repeated during the next day for night-shift workers. Italy has one major feature programme each evening starting at 9, while in Portugal there is virtually no entertainment before 10 in the evening.

The Portuguese, incidentally, have the most curious legislation regarding television programming. All public entertainment has to be licensed as being suitable either for ages up to six, up to twelve or up to seventeen. Since television viewers cannot be segregated by age-groups, *all* programmes must be deemed suitable for viewing by twelve-year-olds. This drastically limits their output. As a Portuguese television executive lamented: 'Can you name me a modern play that is suitable for twelve-year-olds?'

A limitation that most European countries have in common however, is on television advertising. Television almost consistently earns its living from annual licence fees; the advertiser is kept at arm's length. While there is plenty of entertainment to attract large audiences, the public-service concept prevails. The statutes of broadcasting organisations invariably require them to 'inform, educate and entertain the public'. Only two countries, Spain and Monaco, have wholly commercial television; while Britain alone has the dual system of one commercial network earning its living from advertising and the two networks of the BBC supported by licence fees. The cheapest licence fees in Europe are in Ireland and Portugal, which charge about £6 a year, the highest is £14.50 in Sweden. Several countries charge extra for licences for colour sets—the Swedish colour licence, for instance, costs £22.50. Licence income, however, cannot always meet the rising costs of television. Gradually many of the public-service broadcasting organisations have come to accept strictly limited blocks of commercials between programmes to supplement their budgets. West Germany allows twenty minutes of commercials in four blocks between six and eight o'clock each evening and none thereafter. France permits a mere eight minutes per evening. The advertiser, therefore, is privileged to get any advertising time; he may get only a quarter of the spots he applies for, as the networks are quickly overbooked. Direct sponsorship is usually forbidden.

The pace of development has been set primarily by the British and the West Germans. The British were the moving force behind the establishment and expansion of the European Broadcasting Union, and their professional standards have set targets for others to match. Moreover, their programmes have been shown more widely throughout Europe than those of any other nation except the United States. Since many of the smaller countries, such as Holland and Sweden, do not bother to dub they are also seen in English, thus contributing to breaking down the language barriers. The West Germans, on the other hand, have set the main pattern of development for colour in Europe, by devising the PAL system, an adaptation of the NTSC colour system used in North America. PAL has been almost universally adopted by their European neighbours with the notable exception of the French who, with typical Gallic independence, have opted for their own colour-system, SECAM. The British and the West Germans, together with the French and Italians, dominate the programme scene. Only they have the resources to mount large-scale productions or series. In any overseas crisis, for example, one of these 'big four' will inevitably move swiftly to book satellite time for news film transmission. The Belgians, Finns or Swiss—with much less money—normally wait until one of the four has booked the satellite and then take a feed over the Eurovision network, splitting the satellite charges.

The smaller nations almost always operate in the shadow of their big neighbours. Since European television is unconfined by political frontiers, all kinds of international overlapping occurs. The ordinary family in Brussels can, with a good aerial and a modified television set, view no less than eleven channels in five countries. Besides Belgium's own two channels—one broadcasting in French, the other in Flemish—Belgians have a choice of two channels from ORTF in France (three from 1972 onwards), three from Germany, two from the Netherlands and one from Luxembourg. The Danes, the Dutch, the Swiss and the Irish are also swamped by foreign television, although the choice of channels is never so extensive. This encroachment certainly stimulates small nations to improve their own programmes and technical standards, but it may also precipitate them into second channels or colour before they can really afford it. The Dutch, for instance, have to try to match the West Germans, since their viewers demand the same quality. However, most of the time, viewers remain fairly loyal to their own national channels, with perhaps only ten or fifteen per cent of viewers regularly tuning to foreign ones. The exception is Ireland, where Radio Telefis Eireann (RTE) in Dublin have to compete with two strong British signals beaming down from Belfast and across the Irish Sea from Wales. Where reception is best, two-thirds of the Irish homes watch British commercial television, the remaining third being split between the BBC and RTE. Irish television was originally started in an attempt to distract the Irish from British television. 'We were set up as a shield against incoming material—to stop people watching programmes from across the water,' said Michael Garvey, RTE's controller of television, 'which is a rather negative way to start.'

The reaction of the smaller services is often to link up with the major networks next door for the more costly entertainment programmes, provided that languages are compatible. The Austrians, for instance, undertake many co-productions with the second German network, ZDF. The Irish have a deal with the BBC, whereby they can show programmes from the second BBC network, BBC 2, which has little coverage in Ireland, before the BBC repeats them on its powerful first channel. Complications set in when a single country has television services operating in more than one language. In Belgium, where the French- and Flemish-language services operate quite separately, each with their own staff, the French network works closely with ORTF in France while the Flemish side co-produces with the Netherlands and repeats many of their plays. Switzerland is even more diverse, having a French-speaking network operating from Geneva, a German network from Zurich and an Italian network from Lugano. The Geneva station regularly co-produces with ORTF—whose programmes can easily be picked up in Geneva—and Zurich works with the Germans and the Austrians. This does not mean that the smaller nations do not produce their own programmes—most of them are making sixty per cent or more locally—but simply that they lack the budgets to embark alone on expensive series. Irish television, for example, has a budget of only £4.2 million a year compared with £180 million available to television in Britain.

Europe's three smallest stations, Télé-Monte Carlo in Monaco, Télé-Luxembourg and Gibraltar Television exist mainly by running old films and American series interspersed with commercials. Moreover, many of their viewers are in the surrounding countries. Télé-Monte Carlo covers the French Riviera east to the Italian frontier and west to Marseilles; Luxembourg's pictures radiate to France, Belgium and West

Germany. Although they all kick off the evening with local news and magazine programmes, and Télé-Monte Carlo and Télé-Luxembourg undertake some joint quizzes with ORTF in France, their chief attraction is old movies and series. They are the only stations in Europe which still rely heavily on American material. Télé-Luxembourg and Gibraltar Television receive a small part of their income from licence fees, but essentially all three rely on commercials for survival.

The freedom from advertising pressures enjoyed throughout most of Europe is frequently offset by government control. The restrictions vary from country to country. French television was tightly regulated under President de Gaulle, but has an easier time under President Pompidou. In Finland, where television reporting lurched to the left under one director-general in the late 1960s, a conservative government made its own party secretary his replacement after a general election. General Franco's government in Spain keeps a firm grip on television which, although it earns all its income from advertising, is actually a part of the Ministry of Information and Tourism. The Ministry keeps close control over television news; there is plenty of film of General Franco and his heir apparent, Prince Juan Carlos, but strikes or demonstrations by university students pass unmentioned.

With or without political control, broadcasting organisations in several countries, including West Germany and Italy, try to present an impartial front by a system of checks and balances. If the director-general is a socialist, his deputy will be a conservative—and so on down the line. Promotion, therefore, can sometimes depend on the party affiliation rather than ability. News and current affairs reporting under such circumstances often lack objectivity, as each side busily tries to edit out points that might offend its own supporters.

The most unusual attempt to break out of the straitjacket of political checks and balances was made in Austria. For many years radio and television there were organised strictly on party lines; if one job was held by a conservative, the next went to a socialist and, as the joke used to go, a third man was also required to do the work. 'Both radio and television were sterile and insignificant,' Alfons Dalmas, the chief editor at Austrian television, ORF, told me. 'We didn't risk anything at all on the news—even a story about British socialists would be banned because it might help our socialists.' Then in 1963 a young Viennese newspaper editor, Hugo Portisch, published a violent attack on this stifling system and, beneath his editorial printed a coupon asking those in favour of broadcasting reform to complete it and send it to him. The paper received 300,000 replies. Thus encouraged, Portisch decided to take advantage of a clause in the Austrian constitution which says that if 250,000 signatures in favour of a new law can be obtained in a plebiscite Parliament must debate the reform proposed. He organised a plebiscite which drew 832,353 signatures. This pressure led to a new broadcasting act decreeing that in future ORF and the persons employed by it were to be independent. Since then Austrian television has blossomed into all kinds of news coverage. Portisch himself, having inspired the revolution, became a leading television personality overnight—a cool soothsayer for all seasons, travelling the world making documentaries and giving his personal view of the week's events every Saturday night in peak time. His programme draws some seventy per cent of the Austrian audience, rivalling *What's My Line?* and *The Man from Uncle* in popularity.

Such a revolution, however, is hardly likely to deter politicians in Austria, or elsewhere, from meddling in television affairs wherever they get the chance. Moreover, they all love appearing on the box. Party public relations men keep score to the nearest second of the amount of time their leaders are given on television to ensure that they are on at least as often as—and preferably more often than—their rivals. Political reporting is expanded in West Germany, the Netherlands, Sweden, Denmark and Norway by regular television coverage of important parliamentary debates. The West Germans, in particular, often run the debate all day and through the evening if the Bundestag is discussing a major issue of economic or foreign policy. The real outsiders are the British; Parliament has consistently refused to allow either radio or television access to the House of Commons. The campaigners for televising Parliament regard this as a weakness of British television, which otherwise enjoys a reputation for its freedom from political control.

Every European country, however, firmly resists advertising by politicians or parties at election time. They view with dismay the millions of dollars spent on American television by politicians in search of power. The usual procedure is to allocate time for party political broadcasts, every party being granted time according to some prearranged formula—either the number of candidates it is fielding or its registered support. The Dutch, whose television is organised entirely by farming out so many hours a week to a variety of political and religious pressure groups, have this down to a fine art. The twelve political parties represented in the Dutch Parliament are entitled to ten minutes each four times a year, with extra time at elections. The British parcel out party political broadcasts at a secret conference of party leaders and representatives from the BBC and the commercial network; all broadcasts are shown on all channels, so the viewer cannot escape.

Just how effective such broadcasts are is another matter. A careful survey by the Television Research Unit at the University of Leeds has shown that election television fulfils a mainly educational role in providing voters who have already made up their minds with information about party policies. 'There was no evidence to show,' the study concluded, 'that the viewing of party broadcasts has affected voting or the attitudes of electors to the Labour and Conservative parties.' (Jay G. Blumler and Denis McQuail, *Television in Politics: Its Uses and Influence*, Faber & Faber, London, 1968.)

Television journalists with whom I have discussed this conclusion in several European countries agree. What every television editor wants, but can rarely achieve, is to persuade party leaders to sit down together face-to-face during elections, or at least for interviews with leading journalists. Most European leaders, however, have learnt the lesson of the Kennedy–Nixon debates in the United States and decline to confront their opponents on TV. At the time of the Kennedy–Nixon debates, Harold Macmillan remarked to a senior BBC executive that any premier who exposed himself to argument with the leader of the Opposition was a fool; it was bound to be to the Opposition's advantage.

Harold Wilson tried a different tactic during the 1966 general election: he timed many of his public speeches to coincide with the BBC's main news at 8.50 each evening. Knowing that the BBC were covering them live, he arranged for an aide to signal to him the moment he came up live on the news, then, regardless of what he was saying, plunged into what he wanted the television viewer to hear, sometimes leaving the local audience floundering at the transition. The BBC finally circumvented this by recording all his speeches and editing the section they wished to show. As one of their governors told me, 'We couldn't tolerate this news editing by the Prime Minister.'

Considering the political pressures brought to bear on many European television organisations their international activities through the European Broadcasting Union are remarkably free from politics. Within the EBU, broadcasters from right-wing dictatorships like Spain and Portugal work side by side with colleagues from socialist Yugoslavia and Sweden. Right from its birth, at a conference convened by the BBC at Torquay in February 1950, the EBU has prided itself in being a non-commercial, non-political, non-government outfit serving the needs of professional broadcasters. Its staff is multi-national; the administrative director is a Swede, a naturalised Frenchman runs the legal department, a Yugoslav directs the programme co-ordinating centre and a Belgian is in charge of the technical operations. Although Brussels serves as the technical centre, the EBU's headquarters are in Geneva. Along with thirty-three members from thirty countries in its own broadcasting area, the EBU has fifty-four associate members in thirty-four other nations as far away as Japan, Australia, Nigeria and Peru, which makes it the world's premier broadcasting union. Indeed, outside the communist bloc there are relatively few major broadcasting organisations which do not belong.

The prime role of the EBU has always been as a 'clearing house' for its members' programmes, particularly in sports and news. The real incentive for the original establishment of the Eurovision network was the European passion for sport; every television organisation needed coverage of major football games, international skiing, boxing championships and, of course, the Olympics. The EBU, speaking for all its members, was able to co-ordinate these arrangements. During 1970, for instance, 518 out of 645 programmes handled by Eurovision were of sport and over ninety per cent of all programmes were news or sport. Nowadays, the EBU sends a team, composed of producers and technicians drawn from various television services, to negotiate for all Europe over Apollo moon-shots or the Olympics. A handful of men—Vittorio Boni and Ernst Braun from Italy, Thomas Garcia from Spain and Richard Francis from the BBC in Britain—have established themselves as the EBU's top troubleshooters for these occasions. Consequently, instead of a host of individual broadcasting organisations all scrambling to secure their own arrangements, the EBU's team fixes coverage for everyone. If satellite transmissions are required, the EBU books the satellite and distributes the pictures through the Eurovision network from Brussels. Thus only one satellite charge is applicable and it is shared by all. The EBU bills its members for satellite time or other special circuits on what is known as the Rossi scale. This was devised by Richard Rossi, a Swiss banker, and is based on the number of television sets per country; small nations appropriately pay less then large ones. Its great advantage is that it enables countries like Switzerland, Belgium or Norway to receive exactly the same calibre of coverage as the wealthier Germans or British, who could, if necessary, afford to go it alone. 'The strength of the

EBU,' said Vittorio Boni, director of international relations for Italian television, 'is that it has won the very best coverage of world events for *all* European viewers.'

The value of the EBU as a clearing house is demonstrated daily by the news exchange, which enables even the poorest European countries—and North Africa—to be given a wide view of that day's events not only in Europe but around the world. The major news film agencies of Visnews, UPI-ITN and CBS are all linked into the news exchange, so that they contribute film from all five continents.

The daily exchange begins at 10.45 each morning, when the Brussels technical centre links up Geneva with all Europe's television services for a story conference. The conference, in sound only, is conducted by an EBU co-ordinator in Geneva and a news editor of one of the participating countries. Each country shares this job in turn, a fresh editor taking over every two weeks. When I was in Geneva the EBU co-ordinator was a bright-eyed Irish girl, Katie Kahn-Carl, who had previously worked for RTE in Dublin. She began by saying, 'Good morning, *bonjour, tout le monde*' to the newsmen listening all over Europe. She briefly mentioned that there were no satellite bookings that day and handed the conference over to a Belgian in Brussels, whose turn it was to handle the conference that fortnight. He proceeded to ask each country in turn what news film they could contribute that day. Germany offered floods on the Rhine, Italy had a cycling race, Switzerland came up with world skiing championships, France had floods and President Pompidou leaving for the United States. Next the agencies made their offers: UPI-ITN had guerrilla activity in Jordan, Visnews had demonstrations in Chicago against the Vietnam War and a speech by Spiro Agnew in Minneapolis. Then came a list of stories available from Intervision in Eastern Europe, including what was described as 'report from a tank farm on the occasion of the day of the Soviet army' and a Polish congress of Christian youth from Warsaw. As each item came up the news editor would enquire, 'Anyone interested?' Organisations who wanted to could stake their claim. Normally if only one country requested a story it would be turned down for lack of interest, but if two or three responded 'yes' it was at once accepted. Finally, the conference was thrown open for anyone to request coverage from another organisation of a story *they* had not proposed. The Italians wanted to know if the BBC had film of Mia Farrow's twins in London, several people asked the BBC if they had a report on a Scottish doctor who was experimenting with test-tube babies. The BBC said they would find out and advise Geneva later.

The conference over, the Geneva co-ordinator worked out a formal story list, which was then telexed to everyone with a request that they advise Geneva by 13.45 which items they required. The conference merely established that there was sufficient interest in a story; the full list of who wanted what came later. As the day proceeded there were some changes on the list: the guerrilla film was scratched because of a delayed flight from Beirut; the Germans came on the line with a late offer of armed police surrounding a plane at Frankfurt airport that was suspected of having a bomb on board. Fast-breaking stories can always be slipped in at the last moment before the first exchange of film takes place at five o'clock. An important story may warrant a special link-up of its own late in the evening, but as most of Europe's television services put out their main news before eight o'clock it has to be an event of exceptional significance. If a sudden newsbreak requires a satellite booking, Geneva will at once ask the British, Germans, French and Italians if they are interested. The moment one or other agrees, Geneva books the satellite and advises everyone by telex that they too can participate if they wish. The final list for EVN 1 and EVN 2 normally totals eight or nine stories; most are transmitted at EVN 1 at five o'clock, while EVN 2 is really a late edition for film that is delayed getting to the studios in the originating country or for events in the early evening. During 1970 a total of 3,798 news stories were transmitted on the news exchange, of which 275 items were contributed by Intervision from Eastern Europe and the Soviet Union. The biggest users of the exchange were the small nations with no foreign-based correspondents or cameramen; in 1970, for example, Yugoslavia took 2,810 of the 3,798 stories sent on the exchange. Austria took 2,808 and Switzerland 2,569; the rich ARD network in Germany, by contrast, accepted only 528.

Normally the exchange gives a good panorama of the day's major events but political pressures in some participating countries mean that film of strikes, riots or other happenings reflecting unfavourably on that country are not offered. The Italians and the Spanish do not contribute reports of strikes, the French, during the de Gaulle period, never covered any demonstrations against the General; even the British withheld film of a soccer riot in Scotland after pressure from the Football Association. If a country does not offer coverage of a riot, others will sometimes ask if it is available; when they are told, 'Sorry no,' the matter rests. Actually what often happens is that one of the agencies will have covered the trouble, so that from London Visnews or UPI-ITN will offer film of strikes in Madrid, when Spanish television has nothing to contribute. Alternatively, there is nothing to stop one country sending its own team to cover trouble in another, but it will have to send the film home by plane, not via Eurovision link-ups.

The news exchange was extended early in 1971 by the addition of a link-up with television stations in South America on five days a week. Co-ordinated through Spanish television in Madrid, this exchange makes the Eurovision pictures available by satellite to Brazil, Colombia, Peru and Venezuela and receives in return their top stories of the day, which are 'injected' into the Eurovision network. Although language barriers limit programme exchange mainly to news and sport, the EBU also co-ordinates such assorted multi-national activities as 'The Largest Theatre in the World' and the Eurovision Song Contest. For the theatre series, well-known European playwrights are commissioned to write an original play for television. This is then shown, more or less simultaneously, by all the guaranteeing nations, as separate productions in their own language. The first play was Terence Rattigan's *Heart to Heart*; others have included *Rainbird* by Clive Exton, *Enclave* by Ingmar Bergman and *Pitchi-Poi* by Billetdoux. 'Largest Theatre' also commissioned Benjamin Britten to write an opera for television and he responded with *Owen Wingrave*, based on a Henry James short story. Thirteen countries, including Britain France, Germany and Sweden, backed this commission. The advantage of such co-operation is that it enables the playwright or composer to be tempted by a substantial guarantee and the satisfying prospect that the production will reach an immense audience all over Europe. *Owen Wingrave* was seen by an initial audience of three million people, more than could see it in an opera-house in half a century.

What makes most people of Europe sit down together before a television set is the annual Eurovision Song Contest to choose a popular 'song for Europe'. Something like 250 million viewers, including five nations of Eastern Europe, watched Monaco win with '*Un banc, un arbre, une rue*' in 1971.

The only rival to the Song Contest for popularity is another international contest (arranged directly among broadcasting organisations, not through the EBU), *Jeux Sans Frontières* or, as the British prefer to call it, *It's a Knockout*. This caper begins with heats between towns in each country and then, in midsummer, becomes international. The contest is essentially a series of obstacle races over the most ingenious courses that television producers can devise; there are tests along greasy poles over swimming pools, wall-scaling, trying to pitch footballs through impossible combinations of hoops or into buckets. In Britain the programme attracts nearly as many viewers in August (the traditional worst month for television) as the most popular series in winter. I recall walking down the Champs Elysées on a hot July evening and being attracted to an enormous crowd goggling at a shop window. Struggling through, I found they were looking at *Jeux Sans Frontières* on a colour receiver in a showroom.

The attraction of these international programmes is that costs are shared. Even the wealthiest television service in Europe has fallen on difficult days as production expenses soar. Drama now costs up to £20,000 an hour, an opera nearer £60,000. The trend towards co-productions, therefore, is expanding rapidly, although most are being negotiated outside the framework of the EBU. The Italians, French and Spanish have established a particularly close working relationship on a host of historical series from *The Odyssey* to *Caligula*.

Even though these co-productions split expenses, budgets are sorely tested. Most countries have now reached a plateau in sales of television sets, so that licence fee income does not rise much each year. The licence fee can be increased, but this is often a touchy political issue. If advertising is already accepted in some limited way, then the temptation is to meet rising costs by stepping up advertising time from, say, fifteen to twenty minutes a day. Belgium, Sweden, Norway and Denmark, the only countries not yet to capitulate to the advertiser, all have strong advertising lobbies; many people believe that financial pressure in the 1970s will force them to yield. That would leave the BBC in Britain as the lone European broadcasting organisation in which the advertisers have no toehold.

6

Britain:
An Enviable Reputation

BRITISH television is in the enviable position of being widely regarded as the best in the world. Although at home the two channels of the British Broadcasting Corporation and the commercial network of Independent Television face broadsides for serving up trivia and pap, encouraging violence and fostering the permissive society (to cite but a few of the evils laid at their doors), overseas they are seen as examples of what television should be.

There are, I believe, two reasons why people admire British television: first, its relative independence both from political and advertising pressures; and secondly, the breadth and high standard of programmes available, ranging from *The Saint* to *The Forsyte Saga*, *Civilisation* and hard-hitting plays like *Cathy, Come Home* on the plight of Britain's homeless.

American movies caricaturing the British way of life often include a scene of a television announcer saying: 'And now Professor Throstlethwaite will give an illustrated lecture on the development of the bagpipe in Glencoe.' Actually, what one is more likely to see from Glencoe is the former Olympic runner, Christopher Brasher, now a BBC producer, introducing a live coverage by five colour cameras of a bunch of British mountaineers challenging some formidable crag there. That may be boring for non-mountaineers, but it shows how British television, and the BBC in particular, hauls its cameras all over the country to catch something of the action and flavour of life.

(They also recently sent a camera team on a Mount Everest climb.) British television offers something of interest to almost everyone some of the time. It is not constantly in pursuit of the mass audience.

The programme spectrum, within a single typical week in June of 1971, besides that Glencoe climb, encompassed an hour-long profile of Ingrid Bergman, the final instalment of a dramatisation of Guy de Maupassant's novel, *Bel Ami*, a report from the United States, *The Black American Dream*, about the Negro civil-rights movement, four new plays written for television, documentaries about a Hovercraft journey across Africa, Harrods, the Paris Commune of 1871, and Brazil's passion for football. Although these were sprinkled through prime time, they still left plenty of room for the customary medley of simple entertainment—comedy series, police dramas and a few American imports such as *Flip Wilson* and *Alias Smith and Jones* on BBC, *Hawaii Five-O* and *Peyton Place* on ITV. (Imported programmes are voluntarily limited to around fourteen per cent of programme time by the BBC, while ITV is required to keep to that quota, which is one reason why there are such flourishing home-grown productions.) The British passion for sport was fully indulged: the BBC gave most of one evening to the European Cup Final between Amsterdam and Athens, both BBC and ITV went horse-racing for the Derby (neither channel ever seems to trust the other to cover the major sports events adequately), there was plenty of daytime cricket and even a visit to the European Karate championship in Paris.

This broad base of programming has been achieved because the British have brewed, like a fine blend of tea, a formula for their television that is unique (the nearest parallel is Japan). The subtlety of the concoction lies in the fact that, while competition exists between the BBC, supported by about £100 million a year from licence fees for television and radio, and ITV, supported by a similar sum from advertising, there is at the same time complementary programming between the

BBC's first and second channels. The complementary programming means, as the BBC's managing director, Huw Weldon is always putting it, 'boxing on one channel and non-boxing on the other. The two channels are central to our operation. With them you can please quite a lot of the people a lot of the time. The success of television in Britain is that we've got both complementary and competitive networks.'

The two great stimulants have been the introduction of commercial television in 1955 to challenge the BBC's monopoly and then, nine years later, the opening of the BBC's second channel. Both have forced programme-controllers to rethink their whole approach—something that has never happened, for instance, in American television.

In the beginning there was the BBC. Long before the days of television it was already a formidable institution, moulded by its first director-general, Lord Reith, to be a moral force in the land. It gave the public what it thought was good for them, not what they wanted. Furthermore, Reith kept the corporation, established by Royal Charter, sternly out of the hands of politicians. When Winston Churchill as Home Secretary tried to take over the BBC as a medium of propaganda during the General Strike of 1926, Reith rebuffed him.

Thus the BBC, although regarded as a part of the Establishment, became entrenched as an independent institution. As Lord Hill, the present chairman, states: 'The BBC espouses no causes; it tries to hold the ring in argument.' Naturally its impartiality has been assailed many times. Sir Anthony Eden, as Prime Minister during the Suez crisis in 1956, murmured about controlling the BBC but was ignored. The violence between Protestants and Catholics in Northern Ireland since 1969 has sorely tested the BBC's impartiality; and Harold Wilson, both during his years as Prime Minister and in Opposition later, often complained that the BBC was pursuing a personal vendetta against him. But although individual reporters and producers sometimes allow their personal opinions too much weight, the image is still one of reasonable neutrality.

Furthermore, the British broadcasters enjoy a degree of freedom rarely shared by their colleagues in France, Italy, Spain, Portugal or Austria. The lack of political restraint in Britain makes the BBC (and ITV) a lively forum and attracts to its staff many of the most intelligent and progressive people in the country. It has become fashionable to work in television and, roaming the corridors of the BBC and ITV, one meets few people over forty. In Britain television is clearly a medium of the young.

The BBC is presided over by a chairman and eleven governors, all officially appointed by the Queen in Council and chosen for their achievements in various walks of life—the governors in 1971 included a city merchant banker and the secretary of the Union of Post Office Workers. None of them need have any prior knowledge of broadcasting. The chairman of the governors since 1968 has been Lord Hill of Luton (who was previously chairman of the Independent Television Authority, which rules the commercial network). Although many people saw his appointment as a political one designed to curb the BBC's bias to the Left, it should be remembered that Lord Hill, though a Tory, was appointed by a Labour government. The executive power of the BBC, however, lies with the director-general and it is he who sets the style of the corporation. Hugh Greene (now Sir Hugh), director-general from 1960 until 1969, and Charles Curran, who succeeded him, are both professional broadcasters who worked their way up through the BBC. Their basic guide is the Royal Charter which stipulates that the BBC should disseminate 'information, education and entertainment'.

Regularly scheduled television programmes were first started by the BBC, then still under Lord Reith's guidance, as far back as November, 1936. The first live outside broadcast was the coronation of King George VI in May, 1937. All television operations were suspended during World War II, but resumed in June 1946. After that the BBC's television monopoly was preserved until, in 1955, commercial television burst rudely upon the scene. The lobby that fought and won the battle for commercial television was a small but dedicated one, essentially a triumvirate of Norman Collins, a former controller of BBC television, Sir Robert Renwick and Charles Orr Stanley of Pye, the TV and radio manufacturers. Collins was the moving spirit; he had been passed over for promotion at the BBC and had resigned. He determined 'out of sheer bloody-mindedness' to attack the BBC's entrenched monopoly—and won. Lord Reith, although no longer director-general of the BBC, was appalled at this assault. 'Somebody introduced Christianity into England and somebody introduced smallpox, bubonic plague and the Black Death,' he said in the House of Lords at the time. 'Somebody is trying now to introduce sponsored broadcasting . . . Need we be ashamed of moral values, or of intellectual and ethical objectives? It is these that are here and now at stake.' As it turned out, commercial television was not the plague Reith feared. The programmes for a start are not sponsored; advertisers simply buy spots and are carefully fenced off from any association with programming. Moreover, ITV was like a bucket of cold water thrown at the BBC; for a while the corporation staggered back, drenched, to catch its breath, then, vastly refreshed, came out fighting.

From a monopoly position, the BBC tumbled. By the late 1950s it was barely getting thirty per cent of the television audience. Television advertising jumped from £2 million in 1955 to £64 million by 1960. As Lord Thomson said, in a famous phrase that both he and others have since regretted, 'A television licence is a licence to print money.' While ITV counted the money, the BBC was at first inclined to fall back upon a pompous attitude 'Come what may, we will not change our principles.' But a corporation that takes the public money for licence fees cannot do so with good grace if most of the public are not looking at it. By great good fortune, in 1960, the tall, slightly ungainly Hugh Greene shouldered his way into the scene as the new director-general. A professional journalist and broadcaster since the 1930s, Hugh Greene had no doubts about what must be done. 'I wanted to open the windows and dissipate the ivory tower stuffiness which still clung to some parts of the BBC,' he wrote later. 'I wanted to encourage enterprise and the taking of risks. I wanted to make the BBC a place where talent of all sorts, however unconventional, was recognised and nurtured, where talented people could work and, if they wished, take their talents elsewhere, sometimes coming back again to enrich the organisation from which they had started. I may have thought at the beginning that I should be dragging the BBC kicking and screaming into the sixties. But I soon learnt that some urge, some encouragement, was what all the immense reserve of youthful talent in the BBC had been waiting for, and from that moment I was part of the rapidly flowing stream.' (*Third Floor Front*, Bodley Head, London, 1969, pp. 13–14.)

While Hugh Greene was busy cultivating the soil that enabled the BBC to blossom in the 1960s, there came a television milestone, the Pilkington Report. A special Committee on Broadcasting was established in 1960 under Sir Harry Pilkington, to review the broadcasting scene and make recommendations for the future. It reported in June 1962. The history of British television can be divided into two clear eras: before Pilkington and after Pilkington. Sir Harry and his colleagues came down very firmly on the side of the BBC. 'The BBC know good broadcasting,' they reported; 'by and large they are providing it. Our broad conclusion is this: that, within the limitations imposed by a single programme, the BBC's television service is a successful realisation of the purposes of broadcasting as defined in the Charter.' By contrast, there was hardly a good word to be said for ITV. 'We conclude,' said the Report, 'that the dissatisfaction with television can largely be ascribed to the independent television service. Its concept of balance does not satisfy the varied and many-sided tastes and interests of the public. In the field of entertainment—and not least in light entertainment—there is much that lacks quality . . . The service of independent television does not successfully realise the purposes of broadcasting as defined in the Television Act.'

The BBC's reward was to be granted its second television channel, BBC 2. The chastised Independent Television was more tightly regulated under a new Television Act in 1964 (the commercial network is authorised by Act of Parliament as opposed to the BBC's Royal Charter from the Queen). In future ITV schedules were subject to much closer scrutiny. Moreover, an increasingly stiff tax levy was imposed on television advertising; by the end of the 1960s as much as a quarter of advertising revenue was being siphoned off by the government. The rosy days of commercial television's profits were numbered.

Pilkington, therefore, has set the pattern for British television at least until 1976, when both the BBC's Royal Charter and ITV's Television Act come up for renewal. In retrospect, the Report was rather too harsh on ITV, for, whatever its faults, it gave the BBC a much-needed jolt into the second half of the twentieth century. The tonic administered, the BBC, with Hugh Greene giving it its head, came back to win the audiences it had lost. During the mid-1960s the BBC climbed in popularity until it could claim that viewing was roughly half BBC and half commercial. The precise share depends on whose figures are accepted: the JICTAR audience survey of sets in use prepared for ITV (and based on special meters attached to about 2,400 selected sets), normally shows ITV a nose ahead—about fifty-five to forty-five per cent; the BBC's own audience research department, basing its calculations on over two thousand personal interviews a day to determine the number of viewers as opposed to sets in use, indicates the reverse. The balance is in fact very fine and shifts from day to day and week to week. The JICTAR calculations show that the average British set is tuned to ITV for 2·7 hours a day and to the BBC for 2·3 hours during the winter, the chief viewing season. The crucial point is that the BBC feels that it is justifying the annual licence fees of £7 for black-and-white and £12 for colour, and that it is fulfilling its responsibilities to the public at large. 'I couldn't give a damn whether we are getting forty or sixty per cent of the audience on average over a month,' said David Attenborough, the director of programmes for BBC television, 'but if we had only twenty-five per cent—which would mean we were on the way to even less—I'd be worried. Equally, at seventy per cent I'd think we were not being daring enough, not trying out enough new ideas.'

Attenborough sees the BBC as an electronic publishing house that selects from the community 'the voices that are most interesting, most amusing, most prophetic, most gifted, most informed and most significant'.

Although the BBC may draw upon many talents it prefers to keep the major part of its programme-making to itself. So much so that the 'television factory' of seven studios at the BBC Television Centre at Shepherd's Bush, turns out, along with three other studios near by, almost eighty per cent of all BBC are proud of their efficiency in programme-making. A 604 original productions in 1970. The BBC have never adopted the widespread European and American habit of contracting out programmes to independent production companies. Only NHK, Japan's public service broadcasting corporation, matches the BBC in generating its own material. The BBC are proud of their efficiency in programme-making. A report by McKinsey, the international management consultants, revealed that 'BBC television programmes are produced more economically considering cost and quality, than anywhere else in the world'. Money, of course, is a constant worry. The Corporation received about £100 million from licence fees in 1970, of which television was allocated £75 million. But producing six thousand hours of television a year soon eats into that.

The two channels, BBC 1 and BBC 2, are presided over by a controller with his own budget, who has responsibility for programming and scheduling. BBC 1, being the original channel and the only one covering the whole of Britain, is designed as the more popular channel and naturally carries major sporting and news events. The annual Miss World Contest, which is often the single most popular programme of the year, attracting half the British population, is a natural for BBC 1; so was the Clay–Frazier fight, which was watched by 27½ million people. BBC 1 is the channel to which one automatically turns, without even bothering to check, for great soccer matches, royal occasions or moon-walks.

BBC 2, which by 1972 had achieved about ninety per cent coverage of the population, remains a minority channel; it reckons to be doing well if it gets a twenty per cent share of the audience for some programmes, but mostly gets under ten per cent. Its audience is inclined to be educated and middle-class and its programmes reflect their tastes. BBC 2 also carries the television programmes of the Open University, which began in 1971. The Open University is a separate institution from the BBC, but both its radio and television courses are prepared in partnership with the Corporation. The second network, however, is not conceived either as an educational or minority channel (unlike the purely educational channel of NHK in Japan). BBC 2's role is to provide an attractive alternative to what is on BBC 1. Therefore if BBC 1 has a serious programme drawing a small audience, BBC 2 comes up with lively entertainment attracting millions of viewers. Every Monday night, for instance, BBC 1 puts out *Panorama*, the flagship of its current-affairs programmes, at eight o'clock, while BBC 2 shows a western. Furthermore, programmes such as *Forsyte Saga*, the *Six Wives of Henry VIII*, *Elizabeth R* and *Civilisation* which have consolidated the international structure of the BBC in recent years, were all born on BBC 2. They were transferred later to BBC 1 for re-runs (the controllers of both BBC 1 and BBC 2 hotly deny that they use the second channel as a test-bed, but the record suggests otherwise). Robin Scott, the controller of BBC 2 told me: 'I see BBC 2 as a companion walking slightly behind BBC 1, rather like the Duke of Edinburgh following just behind the Queen. But both are personalities in their own right.'

BBC 1's personality, especially with Paul Fox as controller since 1967, is a blend of show business and journalism. Fox, who came up the BBC ladder via sports and current affairs, is sensitive to accusations that his channel is 'too popular'. He likes to point out that BBC 1 spends forty-seven per cent of its total budget on drama, news and current affairs and that in the peak evening period serious programmes, excluding drama, take up twenty-two per cent of the time. News and current affairs are particularly important; they take twenty-five per cent of the budget and provide thirty per cent of the total programmes.

Robin Scott at BBC 2 puts more emphasis on drama, less on current affairs. 'I give a higher proportion of my budget to plays than BBC 1,' he told me; 'we're doing twenty-eight plays a year and I spend readily on them because in drama the more money you spend the better the returns.' He also sees the second channel as an ideal platform for occasional lengthy assessments of British or world problems. 'You cannot be profound in the short form,' he said. 'I want us to do more programmes of ninety minutes or more. We've already done this on the issues of London's third airport and the Common Market.'

Scott and Fox work closely together in mapping out their schedule to achieve maximum contrast hour by hour and to ensure that most of the programme changes occur at the same moment and that on the air each channel promotes the other. 'Just starting on BBC 2 . . .' says the announcer, 'while here on BBC 1 . . .' 'Robin and I have no secrets from each other,' said Fox, 'our competitor is ITV.'

Some critics complain that competing with the commercial network should be beneath the Corporation's dignity and that it should ignore commercial television. The BBC fields that charge easily enough by pointing out that what they are really doing is indulging in the art of competitive scheduling. Over the last few years they have become adept students of the Inheritance Factor. 'This,' Huw Weldon points out, 'is the fact that one of the main ingredients in the size of any audience is the size of the audience which was watching the programme which preceded it.' The understanding of this factor was one of the reasons for the BBC's climb back to parity with commercial television. ITV had long kicked off prime time at 7.30 two nights a week with *Coronation Street* and similar popular series the remaining evenings. To prevent lazy audiences staying with ITV throughout the evening, the BBC responded with its own popular comedy series at 7.30 to try to snatch their own audience at the beginning of the evening and hold it. 'By doing so,' Huw Wheldon pointed out, 'we were actually able, with popular competing against popular, to claim half the audience available at 7.30 and in consequence (and it is this that matters) half the audience available for the range of programmes which followed during the evening.' The classic example was *Panorama*, which was getting a six-million audience in 1965. Then the popular *Steptoe and Son* was launched immediately preceding it, and *Panorama*'s audience soared to ten million.

Steptoe and Son and, later, *Till Death Us Do Part* were the two popular comedy shows that really helped the BBC to pull back audiences. *Steptoe* began as a single drama about a crochety old rag-and-bone man and his son Harold, but blossomed naturally into a series. The Steptoes' junkyard, with the old cart-horse in its shed, and their living-room dominated by a skeleton amidst mountains of other useless bric-à-brac became the forum for glorious verbal (and sometimes physical) sparring matches between father and son, in which the writers, Alan Simpson and Ray Galton, caught the genuine tang of family bickering. From Steptoe's yard it was a short trip to Alf Garnett's rowdy little terrace house in the East End in *Till Death Us Do Part*. Warren Mitchell as Alf Garnett, the loudmouthed, balding little cockney, saying 'bloody' every other word, calling his wife 'a silly old moo', castigating the permissive society, berating the 'wogs' and beating his breast patriotically at any mention of the Queen became a national figure. The series, written by Johnny Speight, who had grown up in the East End himself, became required viewing throughout the land.

The originality of Steptoe and Garnett was matched by another radical departure—Ned Sherrin's satirical review: *That Was the Week that Was* (TW3), presented by David Frost. As M.P.s jumped regularly to their feet in the House of Commons every Monday to protest at TW3's latest irreverences about them or the Church the previous Saturday night, the image of the BBC as 'Auntie' vanished for ever. TW3 in fact had a relatively short life; it was killed off just before the 1964 general election, but it had set a vital precedent that enabled other novel ideas to develop.

The momentum has been maintained by the surrealist humour of Marty Feldman and *Monty Python's Flying Circus* and, in very different vein, the bawdiness of Frankie Howerd in *Up Pompeii*, a weekly Roman orgy. These and many other comedy shows had sought to explore a new humour rather than accepting the cosy formulae of the *Lucy Show* or *Bewitched*. 'The real achievement of the BBC,' an Australian broadcaster remarked to me in Sydney, 'is that it has been like an icebreaker, always pushing back the barriers.'

The same down-to-earth approach is apparent in many things the BBC does. The long-running police series *Z Cars* and *Softly Softly* take at times an almost documentary form. They do not attempt to fulfil some magic formula of tackling a problem and solving it tidily each week. Often the ending is indeterminate, as is much police work. The calibre of writing in both series is high, because the writers themselves have the freedom to develop their themes, to explore family tragedies without the necessity to tie up all the loose ends in fifty minutes.

This does not mean that the BBC has devised some infallible recipe for drama series. They have plenty of flops, like

Ryan International, the saga of an international lawyer based in Paris. The BBC boldly invested some £250,000 in thirteen episodes (they reckon to spend about £20,000 an hour on drama series) only to find after half a dozen that they had a disaster on their hands. They shot four more, hoping it might get better and then called a halt. 'We were then faced with nearly a quarter of a million pounds' worth of programmes on our hands which we didn't believe in and didn't want to put on,' a senior BBC executive told me. What to do? 'We had no spare money to mount another programme, we had just about £1,000 an hour we could spend putting on a third re-run of *Ironside* instead. In the end we ran *Ryan*.'

The opening is there for good writing, whether in series or single plays. Over the years the BBC has nourished such playwrights as Harold Pinter, Alun Owen and David Mercer, who have developed their craft through radio and television. Week in week out the standard may not be consistently high, but this is simply one of the hazards of television; it gulps more plays in three months than the London theatre gets through in a year. The important factor, compared with television in many countries, is that writers know that the BBC and ITV have regular weekly slots for new plays. In New York I talked with a vice-president of NBC who lamented that he had been trying to find some good young playwrights for a specially projected series, but had had little luck. 'They all prefer to write for the theatre,' he said, 'and anyway it's all four-letter words and the themes are wrong.' The point is that for the last decade the American networks have given no encouragement to the apprentice playwright, so it never occurs to him to write for television. In Britain, television is a natural market. Writers are not the only ones to benefit; directors like Ken Russell established themselves first on television. Russell's film biographies of Isadora Duncan, Richard Strauss and Delius for the BBC paved the way for *Women in Love* and *The Music Lovers* for the cinema.

While biographies are obviously an inexhaustible vein for

television, the novel is another. Galsworthy's *The Forsyte Saga*, with its twenty-six episodes, set the fashion. After a moderately quiet first showing on BBC 2 it became a national passion when it was repeated on Sunday evenings on BBC 1. Pubs were empty and churches advanced their evening services to enable the congregation to get home by 7.30 to join the Forsytes (only the choirboys objected, they missed *Tom and* Jerry earlier). The serial was widely regarded as 'the most habit-forming discovery since tobacco'. More than fifty other countries developed the habit. In the United States it was one of the vital programmes that established the reputation of the fourth 'public' television network; even the Russians bought it, although it was not until two years after the sale was concluded in Moscow that they actually showed it (they pleaded 'technical problems' with dubbing).

Hard on the heels of the Forsytes, BBC 2 has kept up a steady raiding of the novel—Henry James' *Portrait of a Lady* and *The Spoils of Poynton*, Thomas Hardy's *The Woodlanders*, George Eliot's *Daniel Deronda* and Jane Austen's *Sense and Sensibility*. These were not dramatised at such length (most were in four, five or six parts) as the *Forsytes* and not all made such good television; Henry James transferred well, Jane Austen's subtleties were more difficult to capture. Novels have to be carefully selected, for there is always the danger of trying to repeat a successful formula for ever. The BBC has run into this difficulty in its historical series. The prize-winning *Six Wives of Henry VIII*, comprising a distinct ninety-minute play about each wife, was television at its very best. *Elizabeth R*, which was a natural sequel, lacked the same impact despite Glenda Jackson as the Queen; perhaps her reign did not divide so neatly into six episodes which could illustrate a single theme.

Nevertheless, the BBC is finding history an eminently visual topic. Kenneth Clark's personal view of *Civilisation* is to be followed by Alistair Cooke delivering *America—a Personal History of the United States*. *The History of the British Em-*

pire was unveiled early in 1972 in thirteen instalments. In both the last two undertakings the BBC is co-producing with Time-Life (who now handle the sale of BBC programmes in the United States), but is retaining editorial control. 'We insist on one editorial mind,' said David Attenborough; 'ideally on co-productions we prefer our chaps and their money.' The BBC's reputation makes that kind of deal feasible, but they are much less involved in co-productions than many European television networks.

Apart from the dramatisation of novels and recourse to history, the BBC have also developed a variety of programmes that fit into no precise slot. There is the occasional *One Pair of Eyes* series on BBC 2 in which journalists, actors, actresses, politicians and playwrights present personal reports on any subject they choose. I remember a vivid one in which one of the men who helped to build the Bridge over the River Kwai went back there and poked around the ruins of the camp and the railway line in the jungle a quarter of a century later. Malcolm Muggeridge is always turning up, ambling into odd corners of India to recall his life there thirty years earlier, reminiscing about his socialist childhood or conducting a lively Sunday evening series *The Question Why*, on everything from Why Marriage? to Why Evil? Once or twice a year there is a testing quiz, *So You Think You Can Drive*, which analyses road accidents, questions a panel and viewers about new driving regulations and generally shows how sloppy most of our driving is. Cliff Michelmore, the kindly uncle of TV, conducts an annual series in which he and a squad of reporters take package-deal holidays and come back with frank reports on the value they got for their money—something that no commercial network could tackle. Finally there are regular programmes like *Horizon* and *Tomorrow's World* that are highly intelligent reports on science and medicine today, and the *Money Programme*, a fifty-minute weekly review of the business scene.

The broad scope of the BBC's programmes is an object lesson to many television organisations around the world who counter any suggestion that they do too much popular entertainment by saying: 'You can't do opera and ballet all the time.' There are plenty of alternatives. Of course the BBC put on both opera and ballet, but relatively infrequently. BBC 1 normally does two operas a year and the audience is modest. But productions such as Benjamin Britten's *Peter Grimes* have attracted an audience of one and a half million. As Huw Wheldon remarked afterwards, 'To have three per cent of the entire population watching a Benjamin Britten opera on a Sunday evening is a startling phenomenon.' Although no one expects or demands that the audience be larger, this does not prevent the BBC from spending a great deal of money on opera—most productions cost nearly £60,000 (three times the cost of drama). Sometimes they take the short-cut of televising performances at The Royal Opera House or Glyndebourne. Yet in 1967 the BBC, together with ten other European broadcasting services, commissioned Benjamin Britten to write a full-length opera, *Owen Wingrave*, for television. When it was shown on BBC 2 in May 1971 an estimated 250,000 people watched the world première.

This is the true advantage of public-service broadcasting: a small audience can be tolerated quite frequently. No one expects or requires opera or other programmes appealing to special tastes, whether snooker or archaeology—both of which BBC 2 serves—to draw a huge rating. Naturally there has to be some cut-off point. 'You can't do programmes regularly for 50,000 viewers,' said BBC 2's Robin Scott, 'but you can for 500,000.'

That decision is inevitably much harder for ITV, for, although programmes are not sponsored, the advertisers are breathing down the necks of the programme companies pleading for larger audiences. At least there are some built-in safeguards that prevent it maximising the audience all the time.

Commercial television in Britain is rather like a pyramid; at the top is the Independent Television Authority (ITA) and everything radiates down from it and under its sanction. The

ITA wears a variety of hats. It owns and operates the microwave links and the transmitters of the entire commercial network—which gives it the power to veto any programme. Then it makes contracts with the fifteen programme companies that make up the mosaic of ITV; each contract normally runs for six years, but the Authority can legally withdraw it any time it feels a company is not living up to its obligation under the Television Act. It has never withdrawn a licence in midstream, so to speak, but it did assert itself in 1968 by refusing to renew two contracts. The ITA also draws up codes of programme and advertising standards, and presides over network schedules. It can and does require current affairs and other serious programming to be shown in prime time. Many people argue that it is not nearly stern enough in fulfilling this obligation, but at least there are two current affairs reports, a documentary and a play networked each week in prime time, plus the half-hour *News at Ten* five nights a week.

The ITA has to use its judgement here. The Television Act of 1964 specifies that it should 'provide the television broadcasting services as a public service for disseminating information, education and entertainment'. It must ensure 'a proper balance and wide range in subject-matter' and 'secure a wide showing for programmes of merit'. But that still leaves much to its discretion. The Authority is presided over by a chairman, deputy-chairman and at least five other members appointed by the Minister of Posts and Telecommunications and selected from many areas of public life. The first chairman was Sir Kenneth (now Lord) Clarke, the art historian, and the chairman since 1968 has been Lord Aylestone, a former cabinet minister in the Labour government. However, as with the BBC, the executive command really rests with the director-general. The ITA has had only two director-generals in its history: Sir Robert Fraser, a quiet-spoken Australian who was the original architect of the organisation, and Brian Young, who replaced him in 1970. As a newcomer to television, Brian Young (formerly headmaster of Charterhouse and director of the Nuffield Foundation) still has to put his stamp on the medium; the present system is very much the brainchild of Sir Robert Fraser.

Shortly before Sir Robert retired I spent an afternoon with him at the ITA's headquarters in Knightsbridge, across the street from Harrods, and asked him about the network he had created. 'We were entering the unknown at the beginning,' he said. 'For thirty years there had been the monopoly of the BBC, but we were starting a new service from scratch and we couldn't be a second BBC. There were two cardinal differences. First we had to earn our living—the BBC gets it from licences. The importance of that distinction about earning a living is that ITV must ask itself more carefully whether it can take programme risks or not. The second point is that the BBC is a programme company and we are not. The BBC, therefore, is in executive command of the production of programmes and is responsible for their standard; we are not in that position.'

The ITA, therefore, built the technical network and contracted out all the programme-making and advertising sales to a number of programme companies. 'We wanted to avoid concentrations of power,' Sir Robert recalled, 'and we decided not to have a centralised network.' Accordingly, the ITA carved up Britain into thirteen (later fourteen) regions and made contracts with a programme company for each region. Four of the original companies, Rediffusion, Associated Television, Granada and ABC, covering London, the Midlands, Lancashire and Yorkshire, were approved as major network groups, providing between them the bulk of programmes for the commercial channel. The remaining ten regional companies were envisaged, according to Sir Robert Fraser, 'as being in a sense local newspapers'. They produced a few local news and magazine programmes, and contributed only occasionally to the network from whom they took the bulk of their programming. This system prevailed until 1968 when a reshuffling of contracts due to be renewed threw up five network companies and ten regionals. The new network groups are Thames (London, weekdays), London Weekend (London, Friday from seven in the evening through Sunday night), Associated Television (Midlands), Granada (Lancashire) and Yorkshire (Yorkshire). The regionals are Anglia, Border, Channel, Grampian, Harlech, Scottish, Southern, Tyne Tees, Ulster and Westward. The list is completed by Independent Television News, which is jointly owned by all the programme companies.

The fact that ITV is so geographically diversified has given rise to more regional television coverage than was ever attempted by the BBC. With the coming of ITV, cities like Norwich, Aberdeen, Carlisle, Newcastle and even places like the Channel Islands suddenly had their own television station putting out a nightly news magazine of local events. ITV consequently touched more directly on their lives. Sir Robert Fraser in the early days always spoke of ITV as 'the people's television', partly for this reason and partly because he felt it was giving them the programmes that they wanted and enjoyed. One might call ITV the working-man's television, the BBC being more middle-class in its flavour. Indeed, over the years there have really been two types of viewer in Britain: the BBC viewer who occasionally looks at ITV and the ITV viewer who occasionally looks at BBC (probably for sport).

The commercial network tries to be more informal and relaxed than the BBC, particularly in news presentation. Independent Television News has always used its journalists as 'newscasters'. 'Our newscasters are all reporters,' said Nigel Ryan, the editor of ITN, 'and I think this lends authority to our news. We like the newscasters to be lively and to address themselves to the man in the street in his language.' ITN lacks the vast resources of the BBC's news division and has only one overseas staffer in Washington D.C., but Ryan believes ITN responds faster to the news. 'The BBC,' he remarked cheerfully, 'is rather like an octopus, but we are a fast-flying wasp.' At the insistence of the Independent Television Authority ITN now rates a half-hour *News at Ten* on weekday evenings.

The audience figures are highly gratifying; *News at Ten* normally notches up one or two places in the Top Ten programmes every week. ITN has also given the BBC very tough competition on Apollo moon-walks. Both naturally have covered these exhaustively, but ITN is often just a little brighter and more inventive.

The co-ordination of ITV's programme schedules around *News at Ten* and other serious programmes required by the ITA is a matter of hard horse-trading. Each of the five major companies contributing to the network is always trying to get the best times for its programmes, while the ten regionals are clamouring for an occasional opening. Officially, the juggling is handled by the Network Programme Committee, made up of representatives from all the companies, ITN and the ITA, which meets six times a year. The real bargaining, however, takes place in a much smaller cabal, the Programme Controllers' Group, composed of the programme controllers of the big five and Frank Copplestone, the controller of the network secretariat. The framework for the schedule is drawn up many months in advance and requirements for plays, drama series and documentaries mapped out. Then each network stakes its claim. Some time-slots are sacred, such as Monday and Wednesday evenings at 7.30 for Granada's *Coronation Street. Coronation Street* celebrated its tenth anniversary in August 1970 and its thousandth episode early in 1971; it shows no signs of flagging in popularity, regularly notching up the No. 1 position in the Top Ten and sometimes first and second spots. No one challenges its position; the bargaining is more concerned with whose new series gets accepted. The toughest battles are about the weekend; no one seems to be able to agree what the network should put out. While London Weekend puts up ambitious plans for more culture, Sir Lew Grade at ATV clamours for more variety and films, especially on Saturday afternoons when the commercial network tries to outdo the BBC in sport. Since the BBC have long been the prime network for sports, Sir Lew would happily leave the games to

BBC and offer a movie on ITV. 'We've never really resolved it,' admitted one network controller. 'Our plans for Saturday have never come off, which is one reason the BBC does so well at weekends.'

Once the network line-up is thrashed out by the big five, the regionals have their nibble. Of the 104 plays the network needs during an average year, the regionals normally produce ten (eight of them from Anglia). But it is difficult for these small companies to get programmes written into the schedules in advance. 'They really have to take a gamble and make the programme,' said Frank Copplestone, 'then we'll look at it for the network.'

The final schedule must meet with the approval of the ITA; the target is that about one-third of the programmes should be serious. The Authority also keep a watchful eye on specific programmes to ensure that they stay within required programme standards. A synopsis of every play is studied by the Authority before it is made and, in conjunction with the Independent Television Companies Association, they grade every film series and movie. Each gets a certificate indicating when it may be shown; the crucial hour is nine o'clock. 'After nine o'clock,' said the ITA's programme censor, 'the responsibility goes to the parents.' The ITA's toughest rules are on violence. They forbid, for instance, hanging scenes before 9.30 in the evening. Both *The Avengers* and *The Saint* have occasionally been toned down for British audiences. A scene in *The Avengers* of a man being chased with an axe along a seafront was snipped out because it looked 'too real'. A Granada series, *Big Breadwinner Hog*, about a gang leader in the East End of London also ran foul of the Authority, who insisted that it be moved to later in the evening. Several ITV companies dropped the programme. Most series, however, are made with the ITA's regulations in mind. The trouble comes with old Hollywood movies. *Tarzan* needed ITA scissors to cut occasional scenes of natives being whipped. *Blackbeard the Pirate*, with Robert Newton, had scenes of men hanging from yardarms, being flogged, heads and hands being chopped off—all had to come out.

The Authority is equally watchful of advertising. Commercials are limited to an average of six minutes an hour over the day, with a maximum of seven minutes in any clock hour; usually there are three breaks for advertising per hour. The ITA has established a Code of Advertising Standards and Practices designed to prevent misleading advertising—particularly of food and medicines. The scripts of many ads are approved in advance, while the finished commercials for nationwide campaigns are previewed at 9.45 each morning in closed-circuit sessions linking the ITA with the programme companies. Each year the ITA insists on about 800 amendments to commercials and rejects up to 150 as being misleading.

Among the five network companies the programme pace is set by Thames, the London weekday company, ATV in Birmingham and Granada in Manchester. Yorkshire and London Weekend (LWT), both newcomers in 1968, have had to fight hard to win places for their programmes on the network. Yorkshire, with great hopes for their current affairs output, found they had difficulty competing with Thames' *This Week* and Granada's *World in Action*, which enjoyed established reputations. One of their best assets has been the redoubtable Alan Whicker, an indefatigable reporter who left the BBC to help found Yorkshire. He is constantly seen leaping aboard a jet and soaring into the sunset to question Bluebell Girls in Paris one week, some South American dictator the next and then the people of a remote island in the Pacific.

London Weekend, of which David Frost is one of the mainstays (at one time he had his own programme every night), has been beset by successive crises and palace revolutions. LWT was launched amidst promises to add a new dimension to weekend television with programmes on the arts and hard-hitting current affairs reporting. This aim did not match the ambitions of the rest of the network, which wanted good, solid entertainment. By early 1971 barely any of the original LWT executives remained, although Frost was still a powerful shareholder behind the scenes. Then Rupert Murdoch, the Australian newspaper entrepreneur who had already breathed new life into the *News of the World* and the *Sun* since coming to London, bought a major holding. He and Frost persuaded John Freeman, formerly editor of the *New Statesman*, High Commissioner to India and ambassador to the United States, to take over as chairman of the ailing company. Freeman himself is no newcomer to television: his BBC series of *Face to Face* interviews is remembered as one of the best things on television in the 1950s.

While London Weekend under Freeman is still in search of a style, Granada and ATV long ago established distinctive characteristics.

Granada, based in Manchester, has always reflected the socialist beliefs of the Bernstein brothers, Sidney (now Lord) Bernstein and Cecil, who founded it. Lord Bernstein, as chairman, has always presided personally over every aspect of programme-planning, so that he and Granada are really one and the same thing. 'He is the nearest that television has to a Northcliffe or a Beaverbrook,' Anthony Sampson observed in *Anatomy of Britain Today* (p. 661). 'Originally I was opposed to commercial television on social and political grounds,' Lord Bernstein told me, recounting his early days in television, 'but when I saw that it was coming anyway I said, "We can't let the big boys get away with all of it." So we looked at the map. We decided that the *Daily Mail*, under Rothermere, would get London, so we tried for Manchester and got it. We had no big money and we turned down several newspapers—we didn't want to confer with anyone. I like to do something on my own and to my liking.' While other programme companies based in provincial cities have often remained heavily London-orientated, Granada—although regarding itself as a national television company—has nourished and been nourished by Lancashire talent. Their programmes, whether *Coronation Street* or *Family at War*, the account of a Liverpool family's experiences throughout World War II, reflect the harsh life of the industrial north. *World in Action*, their weekly current affairs report, is brisk and brash compared to the BBC's prestigious and rather ponderous *Panorama* which competes with it; the editing is so tight that it often packs more into half an hour than *Panorama* manages in the full hour. The sense of responsibility that Bernstein sought to instil in the programmes attracted socially aware writers, producers and reporters who developed a loyalty for the company not usually found in ITV. 'You stay with Granada out of a sense of loyalty,' said one of their executives, 'and because it isn't run by committee. You may fight to get a programme approved but, once it is approved, you can go ahead and make it free from committee control.'

In contrast with Granada's firm Manchester roots, the ATV Network, a subsidiary of the Associated Television Corporation, which is officially based in Birmingham and responsible for programmes in the Midlands, often seems to have emigrated to New York; its managing director, Sir Lew Grade, is for ever jumping on planes to America to conclude a new deal with ABC. Sir Lew always hastens to point out to those who suggest that he is concerned only with 'mid-Atlantic' entertainment that his company does its full share of documentaries and serious plays. This is true, but its reputation is certainly founded on international film series like *The Saint, Department S* and *U.F.O.* And no one outside America can compete with Sir Lew when it comes to cracking the networks there. Quite apart from having had Tony Curtis and Roger Moore in *The Persuaders* and Shirley Maclaine in *Shirley's World* on prime time on the ABC network in the autumn of 1971, he has also achieved network showings for variety series with Marty Feldman, Des O'Connor, Tom Jones and Val Doonican, and for Millicent Martin in *From a Bird's Eye View*, the travails of an air hostess. In 1970, Associated Television earned more than £15 million from overseas programme sales, including over £10 million from the United States alone. The BBC, by comparison, earned a modest £2·5 million.

Sir Lew is immensely proud of the international appeal of his programmes. Before he launched into the international market, he says, no one realised that British television existed. And the money from the overseas contracts enables the programmes to be far more lavish than if they were conceived simply for the British screen. *The Persuaders* is costing £100,000 per episode. 'We can't earn that from advertising here,' he pointed out. 'Moreover,' he added, 'people ignore the fact that our responsibility is to the majority, though we do not ignore the minority.' Sir Lew regards himself as 'the average person in this country' and sees no reason to fill the screen with documentaries all the time. 'I want to be entertained by good dramas, by variety shows, by good escapist adventure series.'

Sir Lew's technique of selling a series in America before it is even made may be good for Britain's balance of payments (it has earned Associated Television three Queen's Awards for industry), but it inevitably means that programmes made by a British commercial television company for a British audience are being tailored to American requirements. 'The great danger of getting the American sale first is that it colours how you make the programme,' said the managing director of a rival ITV company. 'We believe our first responsibility is to people here.'

Amid the big battalions, the ten small regional companies wage a constant campaign to win the occasional network showing. Although they recognise that their prime job is local programming, a networked play or documentary is good for the budget and morale. Two regional companies, Anglia and Southern, have been particularly successful at cornering special subjects and treating them well. Anglia, based in Norwich, specialise in natural history and drama. Their natural history unit under Aubrey Buxton has made a remarkable wildlife series, *Survival*, and several one-hour nature specials which have been distributed world-wide. *The World of the Beaver*, narrated by Henry Fonda, was shown on network television in the United States in prime time (in Britain it was first shown at 10.30 at night). Anglia are also the only regional company to have a regular position in network drama—they rate eight plays a year.

Southern, based in Southampton, have concentrated on children's programmes, which the ITV network long neglected. As the largest of the non-network companies Southern often feel frustrated at not getting more nationwide showing. Like many of the other companies, they have unused studios. 'The trouble is we come last in everyone's consideration,' said David Wilson, Southern's managing director. 'If Lew Grade suddenly comes up with a series we lose our place in the network. I could double the output of our studios given more network time.'

Life has not been easy for Southern or any other regional company. During 1969 and 1970 advertising revenues fell from just over £100 million to £94 million and the bite of the special tax levy went deep. Although the levy was eased early in 1971 and advertising looked more promising, this did not save several companies from merging their sales forces. Scottish (once Lord Thomson's crock of gold) joined with Grampian in Aberdeen, Yorkshire teamed up with Tyne Tees in a new joint holding company, Trident, and Westward in Plymouth got together with little Channel out in the Channel Islands. Each company, though, retained its individual programming identity.

Hard times, however, did not stop the commercial companies, especially the major ones, lobbying vigorously for longer programme hours and a second commercial channel. In 1971 both ITV and BBC 1 were limited to 53½ hours of programmes each week, plus special outside broadcasts; BBC 2 did thirty-eight hours. Both Sir Lew Grade and Howard Thomas, the Managing Director of Thames, pressed the government to allow programmes to start earlier in the day and finish later at night (television normally finishes by midnight). The BBC has resisted this, because they would have to match such an increase and their budget is tight already. They could cope with longer hours only if the licence fee went up substantially; the commercial companies, of course, would simply rake in more advertising, while a second, more selective, commercial channel might draw in fresh advertisers, those who at present use the Sunday colour magazines.

Howard Thomas of Thames argued: 'The only fair division is for ITV to have a second and complementary system so that we too can balance a serious programme with light entertainment. Only by having two simultaneously planned channels can we maintain our present edge on the BBC.' The extra channel could be started relatively cheaply—possibly operating on £15 million a year to begin with—because of all the studios now sitting idle, and would be less popular than the present ITV. 'If ITV 1 is like the *Daily Express*,' said Howard Thomas, 'ITV 2 would function like the *Daily Telegraph*, offering a different range of programmes to a different audience and attracting new kinds of advertising. This does not mean that ITV 2 would be in any sense a minority service. There would need to be a full quota of entertainment, although we should use ITV 2 as a try-out ground for programme experiments.'

A new channel would certainly enable ITV to cope with the challenge from BBC 2, which is slowly eating into their audience. 'We are in a stagnant situation', David Wilson of Southern complained. 'We cannot increase our audience or our advertising rates. An extra channel would give us room to manoeuvre.' Whether one will be granted before 1976, when both the Television Act and the BBC's Royal Charter come up for review, is a matter of speculation. Just as the Pilkington Report in 1962 provided one watershed in British television, the new legislation due in 1976 is likely to produce another. If a fourth channel is awarded then—or even earlier—it could provide the same tonic as did the original advent of commercial television and BBC 2.

Such a stimulant is likely to be essential by the mid-1970s. Already there are signs that the BBC's great leap forward of the 1960s has lost momentum. The Corporation, like ITV, has its money troubles. The number of television sets has now more or less levelled off at just under sixteen million, so that the only increase in revenue is from the sale of colour sets, a colour licence costing £5 more than a black-and-white set. The BBC is pinning its faith for more money on an accelerated sale of colour sets (there were nearly half a million in 1971). 'One of the best things Hugh Greene did at the BBC was to ensure that colour licences cost more than black-and-white,' said one programme controller; 'that is our bread and butter for the future.' The limited budget, however, means that the BBC, like ITV, is reluctant to take risks. It simply cannot afford a £250,000 investment in a series that fails. The tendency, therefore, in these days of tight purse-strings is towards the 'safe' programme. Yet it was exactly because the BBC did not have financial worries in the 1960s (when soaring television sales ensured more money each year) that their programmes had so much vitality. Their reputation of being the best in the world was possibly justified then; the difficulty in future is going to be to sustain it. One way to do it might be to charge a more realistic price; the British licence fee is the cheapest in Europe except for Ireland's and Portugal's, (Sweden's is twice as expensive). It would be a pity to lose the reputation of being the best just for the sake of being the cheapest.

7

West Germany: The Wealthy Patron

WEST GERMAN television sits in the heart of Europe like some great octopus, its tentacles spreading all around. Go to Brussels or Zurich, to East Berlin, Luxembourg or Amsterdam and with a tolerable aerial you can watch the lavish colour programmes of both the main German networks, ARD and ZDF. Add this strategic position to the fact that they are the richest public-service network in the world and you have a formidable system. The Germans have been major trend-setters in Western Europe—they were first to accept a limited quota of commercials (twenty minutes a day) to boost the considerable income from licence fees on their public service networks, while their colour system, PAL, has been widely adopted by other European countries.

Television's disdain of frontiers has often caused viewers in Germany's smaller neighbours to nag their television services to follow suit and to complain of programmes made purely for German consumption. 'Because we are smack in the centre, we have to consider reactions to our programmes, not just among our Common Market partners but in Eastern Europe,' a current-affairs producer in Cologne pointed out. 'People get upset by what you might consider the most trivial things.'

Even the weather, shown nightly after the news, can cause diplomatic outrage. For several years the networks screened a map on which the word 'Germany' stretched across both West and East Germany and even into parts of Poland that were

German-occupied before World War II. The Poles protested frequently. Eventually, when the networks switched to news and weather in colour in 1970, the map was quietly changed. Now it shows only the major cities; names of countries and border designations have been eliminated.

The responsibility of being the television heart of Europe weighs a trifle heavily on West Germany and makes their television terribly earnest. It is thorough, developed with superb professional and technical skill, and immensely reliable, but can be dull to look at. One reason, perhaps, is a slight case of middle age spread. Travelling round a number of the German stations, I was struck by how few young people were in positions of seniority, and how few one saw on the screen. After Britain, this came as something of a surprise. 'There's hardly anyone on the executive floor here in their thirties,' a senior programme planner at ZDF admitted, 'there are just too many old people in television—and it's difficult to get them to make way for the young.' Were there any bright young German David Frosts or Dick Cavetts? 'No—we haven't really encouraged the development of that kind of personality.' The popular television star who immediately came in mind was a middle-aged actor-comedian, Hans-Joachim Kulenkampff—known throughout Germany as Kuli—who ran a very successful quiz show for several years. 'Kuli is just a charming comic whose jokes are straightforward and inoffensive,' explained a programme controller in Frankfurt.

Reluctance to pursue the cult of personality is understandable in the nation where Hitler used radio with such devastating effects, and this legacy has fostered the determination to keep central government at arm's length from broadcasting. Apart from the German post office providing transmitters and circuits, television is firmly entrenched in the hands of the regional governments. Any attempt by the federal government to establish its own television service has been sternly rebuffed. Chancellor Adenauer tried hard in the early 1960s to set up a national commercial television channel, but the constitutional court threw out the proposal. The judges stated categorically that, under the terms of the post-war German constitution, the federal authorities were not authorised to regulate broadcasting. 'The provision of a broadcasting service is a public function,' they declared. 'If the state assumes this function in any manner, it becomes a state function.' The division of Germany after the war into four military zones encouraged this sentiment, as the British, Americans, Russians and French each permitted the separate development of radio in their domain. From these radio stations, first approved by the occupation forces, television gradually emerged.

Today it is the Länder, the regional governments, who authorise radio and television stations to operate within their province. They draw up the constitutions and establish watchdog broadcasting councils. They also approve the licence fee of £11.60 from which broadcasting derives its main income. The revenue from the fifteen and a half million sets in the Federal Republic, combined with the money from a maximum of twenty minutes' advertising a day on each of the two main channels, makes the service the wealthiest in Europe, indeed the richest public service system anywhere. The annual income is over 2,000 million marks (£225 million). Only in the United States and Japan, which have their commercial networks, is the total advertising revenue greater.

The first German network, ARD (short for Arbeitsgemeinschaft der öffentlich-rechtlichen Rundfunkanstalten der Bundesrepublik Deutschland—Standing Committee of Broadcasting Corporations in the Federal Republic of Germany), comprises nine television stations, each being a public corporation established by the Länder. Norddeutscher Rundfunk (NDR), the Hamburg station, for example, was jointly created by three local Länder of Lower Saxony, Schleswig-Holstein and Hamburg; Westdeutscher Rundfunk (WDR), the powerful Cologne station, was authorised by the Government of North Rhine-Westphalia. (Immediately after World War II, NDR and WDR ran jointly as Nordwest-deutscher Rundfunk

[NWDR] covering the British zone of Germany. The original reorganisation of NWDR in the post-war years was handled by Hugh Greene, later director general of the BBC.)

Both these stations are immensely powerful in their own right. WDR's transmitters alone reach at least five million sets in North Rhine-Westphalia; only nine other *nations* in the world have as many sets as that. NDR serves over three millions sets—more than in the whole of Holland or Belgium. So although they are regional stations, they should really be judged on a par with national broadcasting organisations. After all, in the whole of Africa and Asia only Japan has more TV sets than exist in the Cologne area alone.

The third station in the ARD hierarchy in Bayerischer Rundfunk (BR) in Munich. Among them, the troika of NDR, WDR and BR provide precisely sixty-two per cent of all the programmes on the ARD network. A strict quota system, based on the number of TV licences in each region, determines each station's contribution to the national network. WDR's slice is twenty-five per cent, NDR contributes twenty and BR seventeen per cent. Four other ARD stations—in Baden-Baden, Berlin, Frankfurt and Stuttgart—each contribute eight per cent to the network, while small stations at Bremen and Saarbrücken chip in with three per cent.

No one is permitted to specialise in fulfilling their quota. All must share the output of documentaries, light entertainment, plays, the arts and religion. The only exceptions are the weather reports, which Frankfurt handles, a central sports desk in Cologne, and *Tagesschau*, the news unit—rather like ITN in Britain—which is attached to NDR in Hamburg. Otherwise there are nine documentary, nine drama, nine current affairs and even nine religious departments within the ARD network.

The Germans argue that this is a fine way to maintain a balance in programming. In drama, for instance, the viewer has the chance to see plays reflecting the tastes of nine different directors. NDR tends to put on plays of social protest, WDR has a penchant for Francis Durbridge detective thrillers, Munich prefers historical dramas.

An evening's viewing, therefore, is rather like a round-Germany tour. The announcer keeps saying: 'Now we switch to Hamburg for the news, then to Berlin for a play, and later to Munich for boxing.' The task of fitting together the jigsaw of programmes from nine stations is handled by a co-ordinating office in Munich. Normally, everyone accepts the programmes of others without qualms, but occasionally the primmer stations are reluctant to screen a controversial play or documentary. Only once, however, has a lone station refused point-blank to screen a programme after all the others had agreed to show it. Bayerischer Rundfunk in Munich, well known as the most conservative station in the ARD system, rejected a modern version of *Lysistrata*. 'They considered it was underdressed,' said ARD's programme director, Lothar Hartmann.

Whatever advantage the ARD quota system may have in ensuring that viewers see a wide variety of programmes, it is very costly. 'It just isn't a sensible division of labour,' Dietrich Schwarzkopf, director of television programmes at NDR complained. 'It doesn't make sense for every station—especially the small ones like Bremen and Saarbrücken—to maintain a complete staff for every type of programme. Here, in Hamburg, we would like to concentrate on public affairs and documentaries, with the occasional comedy series, like that marvellous British show *Till Death Us do Part*. We'd happily leave all the light entertainment and quiz shows to Frankfurt or Cologne, who are very good at them.'

Costs apart, the medley of ideas from many stations may confuse the viewer. 'I deplore the dividing up of religious programmes,' said WDR's religion editor in Cologne. 'How on earth can we present our viewers with a coherent discussion of the main points of modern theology and relate them to today's social conditions when there are nine religion editors on the network, often with completely different outlooks? No wonder viewers are bewildered about religion.'

There is no such problem for the second network, ZDF (Zweites Deutsches Fernsehen). It is a centralised network based at Mainz and born in 1963 out of Chancellor Adenauer's abortive attempt to create a commercial federal-government station. Once the courts had ruled that project illegal the regional governments got together and agreed to start a communal network designed to offer the public a clear alternative to ARD. ZDF was founded by an interstate treaty signed by all the Länder.

The younger network, like ARD, derives much of its income from licence fees (the actual split is twenty-eight per cent to the Federal Post Office for technical facilities, fifty per cent to ARD and twenty-two per cent to ZDF). But, because ZDF gets a smaller slice of the fee, it is much more dependent on advertising, which provides nearly half its income. The advertising revenue, however, is limited because the maximum time allowed for commercials is twenty minutes a day, all between 6 and 8 in the evening; they are not permitted after 8 p.m. and never on Sundays.

The only way to increase advertising revenue is through high ratings, which enable the price for those precious twenty minutes to be pushed up. Chasing the ratings, therefore, ZDF set out to build its image as a breezy channel of family entertainment in contrast to ARD's rather stern diet of news, current affairs and documentaries. 'We are the entertainers,' said Dieter Stolte, ZDF's head of programme-planning, unashamedly.

Entertainment, as usual, pays off. ZDF frequently win seventy to eighty per cent of the audience in prime time; occasionally they even hit ninety per cent. Their greatest successes have been thriller serials.

Since the Germans, unlike most other nations, run their serial instalments on successive nights, rather than one episode each week, the audience is often held captive in its armchairs for three or four evenings in a row. A particularly successful international spy thriller, shown by ZDF on a Thursday,

Friday and Sunday night during the winter of 1970, almost caused the rival ARD network to abdicate from the screen. On the first night ZDF had eighty-two per cent of the entire German TV audience. At work next day everyone was talking about the thriller, so that night those who had missed the first episode hurried home to tune in for the second—and ZDF had eighty-four per cent of the audience. Meanwhile, ARD, realising that their existence had almost been forgotten, hastily reorganised their programmes facing the Sunday evening final instalment of the thriller. They delayed the showing of a documentary on Yugoslavia, because they felt that many people would want to see it without the temptation of the rival attraction. Instead, they showed some innocuous programme that no one would mind missing. It was a wise capitulation: ninety per cent of the viewers preferred the spies that night.

ZDF has also won enormous audiences with a factual, crime-fighting series called *Aktenzeichen: XY . . . Ungelöst—File on XY Unsolved*. The show is run by an anchorman, Edward Zimmermann, who displays all the poise and polish of Raymond Burr as Perry Mason; the difference is that he is presenting real, unsolved crimes and appealing to the public to help track down the criminals. The programme goes out live ten times a year; each programme is built around three unsolved crimes, which are first grippingly dramatised. Afterwards, Zimmermann discusses the case with the investigating detectives. He asks what vital clues are missing. Who are they looking for? Pictures and descriptions of wanted persons or stolen jewellery are shown. Then Zimmermann tells the TV audience to phone direct to a special desk in the studio or to their local police station if they have any vital information.

The thirty-six million armchair detectives watching the show respond with alacrity. The first twenty-three editions discussed one hundred and fifty-three unsolved crimes; eighty-two were solved through new clues thrown up by viewers; of one hundred and twenty-five suspects whose photographs were shown or who were described, eighty-two were subsequently arrested. The net is spread even outside Germany, for both Austrian and the German-speaking segment of Swiss television carry the show live.

The murderer of a publisher, who was slain with an axe at his weekend cottage in the country, was arrested barely ten hours after one edition had featured the crime. The murderer had stolen the dead man's watch. The police knew the make of the watch and that there were repair marks inside the case that would enable it to be identified. Zimmermann asked anyone who had recently bought that type of watch second-hand to come forward. Barely was the programme over, when several people went to their local police stations with watches purchased since the murder. Sure enough, the stolen watch was turned in by a viewer who recalled buying it in a Düsseldorf pawnshop. Police sped to the shop and learned the watch had been traded in by a known criminal. He was arrested and by lunch-time next day had signed a full confession.

The success of *File on XY Unsolved* has unnerved German criminals, far more than any conventional police dragnet. There is an air of alarm in the underworld every time it comes on. One night the picture of a man wanted for stealing cars and selling them with forged documents was shown. Immediately, a viewer phoned the studio to say the wanted man was at a certain flat in Stuttgart. Police rushed there and found the door wide open and the television set still switched on to *File on XY*. The man had seen his own picture and fled. Later the same night he was caught in Frankfurt with his car brimming with forging equipment. He told the police that he had been sure he would be mentioned on the programme sooner or later. So, every evening it was on, he loaded his car with a suitcase and his forging equipment, topped up with petrol and watched the programme, poised for flight.

Understandably, the ARD network had a hard time against such compulsive viewing, but the situation is not entirely lopsided. Their own criminal proceedings do very well. *Ironside* (known as *Der Chef*) pulls in over sixty per cent of the audience. Paul Temple thrillers by Francis Durbridge do even better. Indeed, Durbridge is almost more successful in Germany than in Britain. WDR Cologne produce a Durbridge serial each year as part of their twenty-five per cent share of ARD drama. Every time they notch up an eighty per cent rating. Each serial is condensed into three hour-long instalments and shown on successive nights. 'During those three nights,' a WDR executive said happily, 'the streets of Germany are empty.'

But ARD's reputation was founded on its news and current-affairs programmes. The main news, *Tagesschau*, at eight o'clock each evening, is frequently watched by more than half the television audience, who regard ARD as the official channel to which one turns automatically, especially in moments of crisis, to be informed of world events. *Tagesschau* is the watershed of an evening's viewing in Germany. Before it come the family entertainment programmes, often imported shows like *Daktari* or *Skippy*, interspersed with blocks of commercials. Afterwards, the children supposedly in bed, come the drama, the documentaries or the current affairs, undisturbed by commercials.

Three current affairs shows, *Panorama*, *Report* and *Monitor*, alternate on Monday evenings immediately after *Tagesschau*. In the public's mind at least, each reflects the political leanings of the station which produces it. *Panorama*, from Hamburg, is regarded as a programme rife with left-wing commentators and producers; *Report*, from Munich, has a more conservative reputation. *Panorama*, in particular, has for years run a gauntlet of criticism for its outspoken views. Editors and commentators, judged to have over-reached themselves, tumble like autumn leaves. '*Panorama*,' a current-affairs producer admitted, 'changes compères as most of us change shirts.'

The political sympathies of German television reporters and commentators are much more apparent than those of their counterparts in Britain. Indeed, the staffing of a station can turn more on political affiliation than ability. The *Intendant*, as the Germans call a director-general of a station, will normally belong to, or certainly be approved by, the most powerful party in his region. In the ranks below, a discreet balance is maintained between the main political parties. 'The whole thing is summed up in the magic word *Proporz*—proportional representation,' a current-affairs producer explained. 'It means the distribution of jobs according to the influence of parties.' *Proporz* applies equally to current-affairs programmes. One Monday night there is the Left-leaning *Panorama,* neatly counter balanced the next Monday by the conservative *Report.* WDR's *Monitor,* which alternates with them, is also regarded as left of centre but is, in turn, offset by the conservative current-affairs output of Sudwest Rundfunk, the ARD station in Baden-Baden. As an editor in Frankfurt put it, 'You can get a nice spectrum—a palette of politics.'

Besides the regular news and current-affairs programmes, both ARD and ZDF carry extensive live colour coverage of important Parliamentary debates. The Federal Government has permitted televised debates since 1964. Although a request has to be made on each occasion, it is a formality. Four colour cameras are permanently installed in the Bundestag. In gentlemanly fashion, ARD and ZDF alternate the coverage; if one carries the full debate live, the other will be content to run an edited summary late in the evening. 'I don't believe you will find such complete TV reporting of Parliamentary affairs anywhere else,' said Franz Wördemann, the political editor at WDR, Cologne, who co-ordinates all ARD reporting from the federal capital of Bonn near by. 'We often televise debates from 10.30 in the morning right through the day and, if it is an important budget or foreign affairs debate, we'll scrap a whole evening's schedule of programmes.'

Some members played to the cameras when Parliamentary coverage first began, while others (especially if their own speech was not shown) complained that equal time was not given to each party. But, nowadays, the politicians have become so accustomed to the cameras that they just get on with the proceedings. The audience ratings may be as high as thirty or forty per cent. Moreover, the televising of debates has helped to make the mass of the German public more aware of their post-war democracy in action.

Equally thorough overseas reporting is also possible because of the wealth of German television. ZDF, for instance, maintains no less than twenty-one correspondents abroad. Both the networks can afford to send current-affairs and documentary teams anywhere to cover wars or famines, earthquakes or elections. In a major crisis one would expect to find German cameramen among the first arrivals of the international press corps along with the Americans, the British and, increasingly, the Japanese.

The German viewer, therefore, never goes short on news or current affairs. Only in Japan, where the public-service corporation NHK provides almost six hours of news and current events daily, is the coverage more thorough. This concern with information has made ARD a particularly serious-minded channel, so that ZDF, coming into the fray later as entertainers, naturally brought in some fresh air with them.

ZDF's light-hearted success has stimulated several ARD programme controllers to demand that their network alter its image to meet the challenge. 'I've been trying to sell the idea to my ARD colleagues that we must revise our style,' Dietrich Schwarzkopf, of NDR Hamburg, told me. 'We should offer the great information programmes—*Tagesschau, Panorama* and so on—nicely surrounded by light entertainment.'

While many other ARD executives and producers reject the suggestion that the network should become a 'channel of joy', there is a determined attempt to develop more popular light entertainment shows. So far, the most successful have been quiz shows, especially 'Kuli's' and '*Einer Wird Gewinnen*' (*Someone Must Win*) from Frankfurt. But the Germans have never evolved comedy shows to match the BBC's *Steptoe and Son* or *Rowan and Martin's Laugh-In.* Indeed theirs is one of the very few services in Europe never to have gained even third prize in the annual Montreux Golden Rose competition for entertainment programmes. Their entry in 1970, however, submitted by WDR, Cologne, was a highly original attempt to create a true colour entertainment show. 'We tried to break out of the conventional variety show,' WDR's entertainment director, Hans Huttenrauch explained. 'We hired the Dutch director, Bob Rooyens, to put together a programme starring Dusty Springfield from England and using every possible electronic trick to make it a dazzling kaleidoscope of colour.' *The Dusty Springfield Show* won a 'highly recommended' at Montreux. 'It was a remarkable use of colour—it showed me what colour television really is about,' one controller told me later. 'It should have won a prize for technical brilliance.' Perhaps this remark is symptomatic of German television; he felt the prize should have been awarded for technical achievement, not because the show was the best in entertainment value.

Despite the ARD–ZDF rivalry, the two networks were not intended to be in competition. ZDF, as the newcomer, is required by law to provide alternative programmes to ARD. Thus, when ARD is screening *What's My Line?* on Tuesdays, ZDF matches it with a documentary or short review; when ZDF has variety on Thursdays, ARD shows a play or film; and Friday night at 9.15 is staked out for an hour's crime on ARD versus a half-hour documentary and half an hour's variety on ZDF. Major events such as international soccer matches, the Olympics, moon-walks and parliamentary debates are divided amicably among them. At the Olympics, ARD covers one day's events live, while ZDF has summaries later; next day it is ZDF's turn for the live broadcasts. Apollo moon-shots have been covered alternately; ARD did all the live televising on Apollo 12, ZDF took Apollo 13, ARD Apollo 14. When Apollo 13 ran into difficulties on the way to the moon and made its dramatic return to earth ZDF had the splashdown exclusively, although ARD were permitted to show it later on the regular news. That crisis caused some hair-tearing across Germany as ARD programme directors argued unsuccessfully with their co-ordinating office in Munich that they, too, should carry the splashdown live and to hell with contrast of programmes for viewers. Normally, however, it is accepted that in the best interests of the viewer he should have an alternative.

The only exception is for current affairs. Each Monday evening, while ARD is putting out *Panorama*, *Report* or *Monitor*, ZDF matches it with a political discussion or 'cultural' documentary. Then, on Wednesdays, when ZDF screens its weekly news magazine, ARD responds with an equally serious programme. Thus the viewer cannot dodge the information programmes by simply switching to entertainment on the rival channel. Two evenings a week he must watch politics or culture for the good of his soul or turn off.

Actually, he has one other choice—the regional third channels of each of the nine ARD stations. No national network exists for the third channels, which began in the mid-sixties and are only on the air for three or four hours each evening. The individual stations sometimes pool third-channel programmes and even operate mini-networks (Hamburg, Berlin and Bremen, for instance, have a common third channel), but basically this channel offers each ARD station a chance to develop its own preferences. Bayerischer Rundfunk in Munich has chosen to emphasise education, particularly adult education. The opposite approach is taken by WDR in Cologne, 'We try to make our third channel a complete service with news, plays, music and documentaries,' said Werner Höfer, the programme director.

Höfer, who is one of the best of West Germany's programme directors, explained: 'We are ambitious, we have an attitude of slight snobbishness. We try to fill the vacuum that is left by the established programmes. Take Saturday night. After *Tagesschau* at 8, most Germans are satisfied with entertainment on ARD or ZDF, but what about the remaining five per cent? That's my market. So we started a magazine called *Spectrum* to make detailed reports on fascinating artistic and scientific developments. We also show the most exclusive highbrow movies you'll find between Hollywood and Vladivostok. We were the first station in the world to show American Underground cinema. Where else can you see Andy Warhol's movies on television?' Enjoying himself, Höfer, a Pickwickian figure in purple-and-white-striped shirt and black tie with white spots, lounged back even further in a black leather chair until he was almost staring at the ceiling. 'Our problem in Germany is "Mother's terror"; it's Mother who decides what the family watches. But, gradually, as more families buy colour television, young people will be able to see programmes of their own choice on the old black-and-white set. We want to stimulate those young viewers, to tell them about the world. We should be a radar station, picking up ideas in the theatre, music, ballet, art and education and feeding them back. More than half our viewers understand England almost perfectly, so we can present plays for them in the original language; we've done plays by Pinter and Wesker. We can do all this even on a small budget. What too few people in television realise is that the best programmes are done with the least money.'

Höfer campaigns for his channel with the passion of a crusader. 'Do you know,' he asked, 'there was a suggestion by ARD that during the summer of 1972, when the Olympics are in Munich, the third programme should *close down*? This is the one time above all others when we should not. We've decided to invite all the countries participating in the Olympics to put one programme of their choice on our channel to show their flag on our screen.'

Höfer's vision of this third channel at WDR is one of the most encouraging signs in German television. The pity of it is that all Höfer's enterprise and energy is going into a regional and not a national network. He was widely tipped in 1969 to become director of television programmes at WDR—thus overseeing their contribution to the main ARD network—but apparently he fell foul of the local political pressures that bedevil West German television. Not only does *Proporz* have to be preserved within the stations, but administrative councils, appointed by the regional Länder, have to approve senior staff. The *Intendant* does not have the right to select his own men. Consequently, anyone who seems too outspoken or whose politics may not please the administrative council has a tough time making headway. Moreover, *Intendants* may be cautious in pressing someone's case too hard, for they themselves are chosen by the regional politicians. 'The election of the *Intendant* by local political bosses has had the bitter result that television stations are too conservative—they take no risks,' complained a senior production executive at WDR. 'We are strangled by the mentality of politicians who know how to run a city museum, but not a television station.'

Many WDR executives and producers tried to push Höfer's case; the Administrative Council, however, declined to listen. Their failure stirred a determination among young television executives, not only at WDR but at other ARD stations and in ZDF, to curb the top-heavy political control of the administrative councils in favour of broader-based groups. The old watchword of *Proporz* is being challenged by the new one of *Mitwirkung*—participation.

'Every group has a right to be represented on television councils,' said Otto Wilfert, one of the most ardent reformers at ZDF, 'but we believe there should be one representative for each group. Up to now, politicians have been the majority on our council. We say, give each political party one representative, and then bring in writers, university lecturers and television producers.'

The campaign has wide support. 'The administrative councils have held television back,' admitted a top programme-planner at ZDF, 'and many young people with fresh ideas have not been able to break through to positions of responsibility.'

The Länder, however, are unlikely to surrender their control without a tough fight. Just as they resisted Adenauer's attempts, a decade ago, to create a federal commercial channel, so they will seek to silence the fashionable cry of *Mitwirkung* in the seventies.

8

France: *Après* de Gaulle

'*La télévision, c'est le gouvernement dans la salle-à-manger,*' a French cabinet minister once remarked during the de Gaulle years. De Gaulle himself certainly tried to carry the spirit of his government into every dining-room in France; as long as he was President the television news at eight o'clock each evening almost invariably began with a report on his activities that day. The cameras followed him everywhere—on his peregrinations through the French countryside and on his tours overseas, his tall, erect figure dominating the scene as he strode through the crowds. In moments of crisis there he was in close-up, raising his arms in supplication to the nation gathered before their sets: '*France, France, aidez-moi, aidez-moi.*' Few politicians have been so compelling on television, and few in Europe have sought to marshal it so completely to their cause. De Gaulle made no secret of its importance in putting over his policies to the French people; he knew the press were largely hostile to him—television, therefore, must be on his side.

The story of French television is bound up with de Gaulle. Throughout his years in power, which coincided with the years when television spread its wings in Europe, he kept L'Office de Radiodiffusion Télévision Français (ORTF) under tight rein, and he even interfered on occasion with other television organisations' plans. Once he refused to allow the French earth station at Pleumeur Bondou to relay to New York by satellite a CBS News programme in which Jean Monnet, the architect of the Common Market, was participating. Monnet had to go to Brussels to make the programme and the signal was then re-routed through the British earth station at Goonhilly Downs.

Only since de Gaulle's fall from power in 1968 has ORTF been able to establish its own identity. The organisation has been completely overhauled by a new director-general, Jean-Jacques de Bresson, and in 1972 will launch a new colour network, giving it three networks in all—one black-and-white and two colour. Then it will boast more television channels than any other public-service broadcasting organisation in the world. It also operates three radio networks. Moreover, ORTF is now the second richest broadcasting organisation in Europe, with an income of over £126 million a year from licence fees of £9 on nearly eleven million TV sets, plus a bonus of almost £40 million a year from advertising. The commercials are held to a mere eight minutes per day—which scarcity makes them highly prized.

France's influence in the world of television is magnified by her championship of her own colour television system, SECAM, and her natural leadership in the growth of television throughout the French-speaking world. De Gaulle's grand design of developing France into a powerful independent nation with her own nuclear capability resulted also in her going it alone on colour television. While everyone else in Western Europe agreed to adopt the German colour system, PAL, the French preferred their own invention. The two systems are not instantly compatible, but special converters have been devised to transfer pictures from one to another. Furthermore, de Gaulle succeeded in persuading the Soviet Union, and consequently all of Eastern Europe, to adopt SECAM. Thus Europe is divided sharply into two colour camps: SECAM to the east and west, PAL in the centre. The French have also exerted great pressure on the Italians and the Spanish, who as yet do not have colour, to persuade them to adopt SECAM. However, these countries have resisted the French overtures and are preparing to join their other European colleagues with PAL. Undaunted, the French are still hoping that Morocco, Algeria and Tunisia, where their influence is strong, will select SECAM when they eventually go over to colour. This in turn might persuade the Arab world to take up the French system. Lebanon has already installed SECAM and, if the North African countries followed suit, the remainder of the Arab world almost inevitably follow (except for Kuwait, which has awkwardly gone for PAL).

The French have found natural programme partners among the '*pays francophone*'—the French-speaking communities of Belgium, Switzerland, Luxembourg, Monaco and French Canada. All six participate regularly, for instance, in a lively quiz, *Le Francophonissime*, which seeks to find the contestant with the best knowledge of the French language. If ORTF buys an American movie or a series like *The Virginian* and dubs it into French, this almost assures its sale in the same version to the smaller Francophone countries who have less money for their own dubbing. The French-language division of Belgian television, RTB, takes most of its drama from ORTF as it cannot afford to mount its own large-scale productions.

The French are equally active in promoting television in their old colonies in Africa and Asia. Just as broadcasting in former British colonies is frequently modelled on the BBC, so ORTF is the example for French territories. For several years a special government department, L'Office de Co-opération Radiophonique (OCRA) helped in the expansion of television in North Africa, the Ivory Coast, Upper Volta and Cambodia. OCRA was merged into ORTF in 1969, but the determination to maintain a sphere of influence remains as strong as ever. The French-language station in Beirut, for instance, gets seven hours of programmes free from ORTF each week, while in such remote outposts as Afars and Issas (formerly French Somaliland) and the island of Réunion in the Indian Ocean. ORTF's overseas division handles the programming. 'These small countries with very little money naturally turn to us,' said

Lucian Renault, associate director of ORTF's foreign department, 'because we share a language and a culture.' The great difference is that the French give programmes away; the British and Americans charge for them.

ORTF's basic role at home and overseas, as laid down in a broadcasting statute approved by de Gaulle in 1964, is 'to satisfy the needs of the public for information, culture, education and entertainment'. This same document also defines ORTF as 'a national institution of the state with an industrial and commercial character': more simply it is a nationalised industry.

The governing body, which determines broad policy, is the Administrative Council, at one time of sixteen members, now twenty-four. All are nominated by the Council of Ministers. It includes twelve representatives of the government, five from ORTF, two from the press (one publisher, one journalist), one representative of the television audience (the president of a group known as Téléspectateurs et Audiéteurs de France) and four other people from public life. The director-general, who is in executive command, is also appointed by the government. During the de Gaulle years, however, ORTF enjoyed little autonomy. Finances were subject to scrutiny and approval by the Ministry of Finance and daily programming was watched closely by the Ministry of Finance and an Inter-Ministerial Committee for Information Liaison. This committee sought in particular to direct news coverage; it met most mornings to decide how to play the day's events. According to some ORTF journalists I talked to, its officers were even on the phone to the control room during broadcasts to insist on last-minute changes.

The manipulation of the news reached its height during the May 1968 disorders. For the first few days of the strikes and student disturbances television news underplayed the troubles and student leaders had no chance to put their case on the screen. But television journalists, increasingly restive at such blatant partiality, finally took the matter in their own hands, defied the management and for several days put out remarkably objective news and comment. Then ORTF's Friday night current-affairs programme, *Panorama,* was suppressed because it proposed to discuss the students' complaints. The journalists and some of the technicians concerned promptly called a strike and demanded freedom to report what was really happening. A committee of ten was formed to press their case. When de Gaulle went on television to call for calm, the committee tried to insist on equal time for opposition leaders. Interviews with these politicians were recorded, but the government would not allow them to be shown. All ORTF's journalists, except about twenty, immediately responded by voting to go on strike. They stayed out for five weeks, while television put out a single emasculated news bulletin a day. In the end the strike collapsed and some sixty-five journalists were sacked at de Gaulle's insistence; other commentators were moved to obscure jobs on the sports' desk. The General, apparently, was outraged: 'Television stabbed me in the back when I was on my knees.' (Anthony Sampson, *The New Europeans*, p. 297.) But the journalists, for all their initial failure to gain reforms, had brought the whole matter of censorship into the open. During the election a few months later to choose de Gaulle's successor as President, Georges Pompidou made reform of ORTF one of the planks of his campaign. He promised that in future all sides could have their say on television.

ORTF today is a very different creature. The Inter-Ministerial Committee for Information Liaison is no more, and all political parties are guaranteed access to the screen. ORTF has taken over most of the responsibilities for its own finances and its bureaucracy has been streamlined in an attempt to give freer rein to creative talent. A new director of programmes has been installed for each channel, with much greater responsibility for dispensing his own budgets and making up schedules. In effect ORTF is striving to make its 13,000 staff think like broadcasters instead of like civil servants. 'What we are really doing,' said Jean-Jacques de Bresson, 'is transforming ORTF from a large administrative department into a proper commercial enterprise with a public-service role.'

A cornerstone of the reforms has been the creation of two quite separate and competitive news divisions; one for the popular black-and-white first channel, which covers all France, and one for the second colour channel, which covers about ninety per cent of the country. The first channel's news director is a small, plump journalist, Pierre Desgraupes, who has a reputation for being moderately left-wing; he has been in broadcasting for many years and made his name on a news magazine programme *Cinq Colonnes à la Une* (*Five Columns on the Front Page*). He was one of the strikers in 1968 and his appointment to take over the news service caused considerable alarm among Gaullists. But Desgraupes is balanced by the news director of Channel 2, Jacqueline Baudrier, a vivacious woman who was a strong supporter of de Gaulle and one of the few journalists not to strike in 1968.

Since January 1st, 1970, it has been Desgraupes against Baudrier in an all-out battle to win audiences to the news on their respective channels. But, more than that, they had to re-establish the reputation of television news in France. 'Television news,' said Desgraupes, 'was suspected of fawning to the government, of being accommodating by omission, distortion and interpretation. I want to make the news credible.'

Competition is regarded as being crucial in re-establishing the credibility of television news. Both channels cover stories separately, each with their own reporters and cameramen. In some overseas bureaux one correspondent works for Desgraupes, the other for Baudrier: a situation which, according to one of them 'is driving us out of our minds. We have to send two reporters on every story and shoot film from different angles, so that it doesn't all look the same.' Madame Baudrier's channel, of course, has the advantage of colour. She has also shown a preference for medical stories; she once opened her news with a long colour report of a liver transplant.

The competition has certainly been a spur to viewing. During the worst days of the credibility gap in 1968 the audience for Channel 1's main evening news was down to thirty-five per cent; while I was in Paris in 1970, when the new system was seven months old, it was up to fifty-seven per cent, and on the second channel, which always has a smaller audience because of its limited coverage and the fact that many Frenchmen have not bought a set that receives both channels, it was up from two to seven per cent. 'Competition is proving a good idea,' said one of Desgraupes' editors. And he added: 'Many politicians now realise that the troubles in 1968 were partly the result of television being silent; people had no forum for their views.'

Nevertheless, there is still considerable scepticism as to how free television really is. Olivier Todd, editor of the Friday night *Panorama*, resigned in June 1970 over cuts in films of French paratroops in Algiers. President Pompidou did not help to restore confidence by stating in the same month: 'Being a journalist on ORTF is not like being a journalist elsewhere. Whether you like it or not, ORTF is the voice of France. You who write the news must always keep in mind that you are not talking for yourself, you are the voice of your country and your government.'

But overall ORTF's news divisions have been rejuvenated and the whole television service is finding a new sense of purpose. Most of the journalists sacked in 1968 have been rehired. ORTF received further encouragement during 1970 from the report of a special commission into the future of broadcasting. The Commission, under a former Minister of Education, Lucien Paye, rejected proposals for a separate commercial television network in France and recommended instead that ORTF be awarded a third channel. The hopes of the strong commercial television lobby, led by Jean Frydman of Télé Monte Carlo, were dashed. The commercial lobby had based their arguments on the British system of ITV in competition with the BBC; ORTF, they argued, needed a similar stimulant. ORTF itself, of course, has had very limited advertising since 1968, but the Paye Commission suggested that advertising time should not be extended significantly and that the cost of the new channel should be largly paid for by higher licence fees.

Yet even without the challenge of a rival commercial network the prospect of a third public-service channel in France from 1972 is intriguing. No other nation, except the Soviet Union, has three channels all belonging to one organisation. Furthermore, the opportunity to start a new channel from scratch, with a clean slate for scheduling, occurs only rarely. The new channel will be directed by Jean-Louis Guillaud, a former head of television news, who is still in his thirties. 'We are not in favour of creating either a new specialised educational or highbrow channel,' he told me, reviewing his plans. 'Nor are we aiming to please some amorphous public taste. We believe there are several potential large audiences defined not by age or where they live, but by their interests. Most men, for instance, prefer sports and information. We want to identify those groups and cater to them. We must put an end to the dogma of unity.'

Finding the right style for a new channel is not easy. 'Why do fewer people read *Paris Match* these days and more *L'Express*?' Guillaud pointed out, 'It's all a matter of style. We have to create our style too. We've already done a survey of our second channel and found there is no clear image of it in the public mind.' In searching for his third-channel image Guillaud is relying particularly on bringing in young people, both from Paris and the provinces. 'Television here is still done by men of the 1950s,' he said. 'This is a chance to create a channel run by, and for, young people.' He hopes that it will pay special attention to social issues. 'So far French television has not concerned itself much with the problems of housing or architecture or pollution. We shall try to do information programmes on all these aspects of our society today.'

ORTF will produce only two-thirds of the programmes for the new channel; the remainder will come from private producers in France together with purchases from overseas. 'Ultimately I think that half of all ORTF's programmes should be made outside. We need to get a much better dialogue going with our film industry and convert them to working more for television.'

Initially, the third channel will put out only three hours of programmes a night—from 7 until 10, which is French prime time. The French go to bed very early (sixty-eight per cent of them by 10.30), so that the television evening is much shorter than in most European countries. The main entertainment for the evening—*la soirée distraitive*, as the French call it—is from 8.30 until 10. By 1975 the new network will cover most of France and its output will be up to four hours each evening. Once national coverage has been achieved it will gradually take over more of the role of the present first channel which, for technical reasons, cannot be converted to colour. The black-and-white network, therefore, will gradually become devoted to educational programmes or old movies.

Until the new channel is born, however, the first channel will hold its strong position; most evenings it has between fifty and sixty per cent of the total possible audience, while the second channel, in colour, musters between twenty and thirty per cent for its more popular programmes. The schedules are designed to complement each other. Thus, on a typical Saturday evening, while Channel 1 offers the latest in a series of Inspector Maigret thrillers, Channel 2 comes up with a documentary on bird migration, followed by ballet from the Paris Opéra. On Sunday afternoon the choice is between football and an interview with the anthropologist, Claude Lévi-Strauss. The following evening the fare is quite serious on both channels: Channel 1 has a two-hour documentary on the role of mayors in French towns, while the rival channel has ballet from the Opéra-Comique and a documentary on the future of sport in urban society. Later in the week *L'Homme de Fer* (*Ironside*) fetches up against a dramatisation of a modern French novel, *Le Thé sous les Cyprès* by Jean-Louis Curtis.

Ironside is one of the few major American series on French television; in prime time in June 1971, for instance, the only others were *The Virginian* and *The Outlaw*. The French normally hold their foreign buying down to thirteen per cent of their output (about the same proportion as the British), of which three quarters comes from the United States and most of the remainder from Britain—both *The Saint* and *The Avengers* have been very successful.

The French are becoming increasingly involved in the growing habit of elaborate co-productions with other European broadcasting organisations. Their most frequent partners are RAI in Italy, TVE in Spain and Bayerischer Rundfunk in Munich. ORTF has backed RAI's major productions, *The Odyssey*, *The Aeneid* and *Leonardo Da Vinci* (to which it contributed a French actor, Philip Leroy, as Leonardo), while it undertook itself the making of an epic based on Dumas' *The Three Musketeers*. It even succeeded for a while in wooing Roberto Rossellini away from RAI to make a film for it on Louis XIV.

The second channel has also evolved a highly successful new format, *Les Dossiers de l'Écran*, every Wednesday evening, in which a film is immediately followed by a long discussion of issues raised by it. After a biography of Louis Pasteur, for instance, they got together a panel of people to talk about the scientist's life and work. A movie about the mysterious disappearance of Commander Crabbe while on underwater exercises near Russian warships in a British harbour, was likewise used as a trigger for a discussion of what really happened to the frogman. A documentary film on the hazards of driving on the Route Nationale 7 to the South of France led to a two-hour debate among doctors, police and motorists on why so many people disregard the dangers of death on the road. While I was visiting Paris a grand debate was staged following a movie about the Tour de France cycle race. Past victors in the race, journalists and doctors all assembled in the studio to discuss the trials and to answer questions phoned in by viewers from all over France. In all the channel devoted two hours and forty minutes that evening to the combined film-debate, from 8.30 until 11.10.

This is, of course, one of the advantages of having complementary instead of competitive channels; one channel can be opened up for coverage of a single topic in depth for most of an evening, while the other presents more varied entertainment. The rapport between the channels is so close that if a new programme is about to start on Channel 2 before the end of a programme on Channel 1, a small 2 appears at the bottom right-hand corner of the screen on Channel 1 to prompt anyone who wishes to switch.

A serious programme on one channel, however, does not necessarily guarantee a popular one on the other. ORTF never forgets the requirement in its statutes about disseminating 'culture'. Documentaries on the lives of great French writers, artists and composers abound. To take just one week during 1971, there were two ballet performances, a concert by l'Orchestre National de l'ORTF, a biography in colour of the poet Eugenio Montale, an hour-long programme on the arts (covering a surrealist exhibition in Bordeaux, a sculpture exhibition in Paris and the Dürer Festival at Nuremburg), a biography of the eighteenth-century composer Rameau and a documentary on Heinrich Schliemann's discovery of the ruins of Troy. In the same week ORTF announced a new season of eight plays to be produced for television by the Comédie Française, including works by Molière, Giraudoux and Feydeau. All good stuff but, as Richard Mayne, a foreign correspondent living in Paris put it, 'Rather stiff and teachy, if not preachy.'

The French also take seriously the question of television and violence, but their policy is to advise the viewer very thoroughly what he is in for and then leave it to his own discretion whether or not he watches. Not only does the weekly programme guide *Télé 7 Jours* indicate the age-group to which a film is most suited—adults only, adults and adolescents or everyone—but throughout a programme considered unsuitable for children a small white rectangle is shown in one corner of the screen. Thus parents tuning in late or without checking are warned at once that the programme may not be appropriate for all the family. ORTF's violence code also insists that if one channel is showing a '*rectangle blanc*' programme, the other must offer something suitable for everyone.

The turmoil through which ORTF has passed during the last few years has made its performance somewhat erratic. As a programme executive remarked: 'We've never had a very methodical approach. In almost every field I think you might say we've done the best and the worst in television.' However, the new autonomy that ORTF has now enjoyed for a year or two and its thorough internal spring-cleaning place it in a position to take a great leap forward in the seventies.

9

Italy: A Passion for History

NEWSPAPER headlines sometimes make Italy seem a country under siege; postmen, dustmen and bus-drivers are on strike, car workers are rioting in Milan and Turin and the people of Reggio Calabria are fighting for their town to be named the provincial capital. A rather different Italy, however, is seen on the two channels of the public-service Radio Televisione Italiana (RAI). The main attractions for the evening may be an excellent dramatisation of Virgil's *Aenid,* depicting the founding of Rome, or a biography of Michelangelo. Italian television delves very willing into the glorious past, but prefers to steer clear of the present.

The trouble is that RAI is beset by political upheavals. Its presidents resign in exasperation, unable to control such a volatile organisation, while executives write furious letters to the newspapers accusing their colleagues of being communists or fascists. When it comes to current events everyone is desperate to make sure his opinion is aired. The main evening news, *Telegiornale*, on RAI's first channel strains to satisfy every shade of the political spectrum. There are no less than six anchormen, each of whom helps to satisfy a political party that its views are adequately represented.

This precarious political balance is preserved throughout RAI's regular staff of almost ten thousand. The director-general is a christian democrat who is neatly balanced by a socialist as a managing director: the two vice-presidents are also allied to these two leading parties. The president of RAI is supposed to preserve neutrality and ensure objectivity, but it has proved difficult to find a suitable co-ordinator. After Professor Aldo Sandulli resigned, early in 1970 (the second president to depart in eighteen months), during the furore aroused by a programme examining the conflict between the Italian constitution and parts of the penal code drawn up during the fascist regime, no successor was forthcoming for over a year.

Many of RAI's difficulties stem from its ambiguous institutional position. Unlike many other broadcasting organisations in Europe, it is not an autonomous corporation. It is owned by a state-owned industrial holding company, IRI, whose portfolio embraces a variety of commercial operations from banks to airlines. IRI, however, has relatively little say in the running of the broadcasting organisation. The real power lies in the hands of a nine-man management committee, composed largely of political nominees. This committee keeps a close watch over programmes likely to cause political controversy, and news items which might embarrass the government of the day never appear at all. Strikes and riots often go unreported and are rarely covered in any detail. Other broadcasting organisations who request coverage of troubles in Italy during the daily conference for the Eurovision news exchange are politely told that no film is available. If they want to report them they must send their own team.

Political considerations, however, have not prevented RAI from making some splendid expeditions to cover the Pope on his travels in Africa, Asia and South America. For these tours RAI spares no expense and mounts a formidable task force, usually led by Vittorio Boni, their director of international relations. Boni and a RAI engineer, Ernst Braun, are recognised throughout Europe as among the finest exponents of the art of arranging television coverage in out-of-the-way places. When Pope Paul went to Uganda, Boni and his team built their own portable earth station, flew it out to Africa and assembled it there in five days so that they could bounce live coverage of the visit, via satellite, direct to Rome.

The Italians have shown equal showmanship in developing the most productive liaison between television and the cinema. RAI makes relatively few of its own feature programmes; instead it contracts them out to the Italian film industry. The film-makers, after initial reservations about possible censorship, have adapted readily. Directors of distinction like Federico Fellini, Vittorio de Sica and Roberto Rossellini are all making programmes for television and being given a remarkably free hand. 'In agreeing with Fellini that he should make five special programmes for us we wanted to stretch the confines of television rather than limit Fellini,' said one of RAI's programme directors.

Consequently, RAI's two black-and-white channels (Italy is the last major European nation not to have colour) have programmes of great originality from time to time that compensate for the conventional staple diet of detective and variety shows. These programmes have even greater impact because of the Italians' restrained viewing habits. Television hours are strictly limited—RAI's main channel is on the air only nine hours a day and the second channel for only two hours each evening, from 9 until 11. The average Italian looks at television for just under two hours a day, normally from about 8.30 in the evening until he goes to bed. Before 8.30 the average is a mere four million viewers out of a potential thirty-seven million adults.

The high-water mark of the evening is *Telegiornale*, the news at 8.30, for which the audience suddenly jumps from four to fourteen million. Television news is of vital importance to Italians, for relatively few of them buy newspapers (daily circulation is only five million). According to Pompeo Abruzzini, RAI's director of audience research, at least ten million people watching the TV news do not see newspapers. Immediately after the news and a short, lively block of commercials known as *Carosello* comes the one major feature programme of the evening. This normally lasts at least an hour.

'Italians will not stay in at nine o'clock for a short programme,' said RAI's director of programmes, 'unless we have a good feature on both channels—they would rather go out for a drink or to the cinema.'

This is where the liaison with the film industry has proved so fruitful. Successful co-productions range from Maigret and Nero Wolfe detective series to a dramatised biography of Socrates, directed by Rossellini. The rapport between television and cinema has arisen partly as a result of legislation which requires the two media to co-operate, but more because television has been able to offer both established directors and newcomers the opportunity to make films that do not have to be a guaranteed commercial success. As a public-service organisation, financed primarily by licence fees of £8 a year on the ten million TV sets in Italy, plus advertising between programmes for five per cent of air time, RAI is in a good position to act as sponsor to film-makers.

The scope of many of these projects has been widened by co-production with other European television organisations, notably France's ORTF, Germany's Bayerischer Rundfunk in Munich (one of the ARD regional stations) and Spain's TVE. 'We have tried to make European rather than exclusively Italian films,' said Vittorio Bonicelli, RAI's linkman with the film industry. Each country chips in about £40,000 for a ninety-minute film; this covers most of the initial expenses, but the film-makers themselves must underwrite part of the cost because they retain the world distribution rights. This formula enables television to put up enough money to attract important film makers; £120,000 or more guaranteed is an attractive proposition.

The most enthusiastic convert to television film-making is Roberto Rossellini. He declares roundly that he has forsaken the cinema in favour of television as the medium of the future. His first major series was a twelve-part epic: *Stories of the Struggle for Survival,* dealing with a dozen crucial events in world history. He followed this with a dramatisation of *The*

Acts of the Apostles. Despite his enthusiasm for television, Rossellini's relations with RAI's bureaucracy have been extremely strained from time to time. Once, he departed for Paris vowing he would never again work in Italy, but after he had made a film on Louis XIV, he was persuaded back to RAI to undertake two ninety-minute colour dramatisations of the lives of Socrates and Caligula.

The prototype of these historical re-creations was *The Odyssey*, filmed in 1968 by Franco Rossi in a joint RAI-Dino de Laurentis production. This seven-hour serial cost £1·5 million and took eight months to shoot. A village was built on a beach in Yugoslavia and three large boats launched to carry Odysseus and his men on their wanderings. Seventeen million Italians eagerly followed the heroic exploits. Encouraged, RAI promptly embarked on a dramatisation of Virgil's *Aeneid* (also directed by Franco Rossi) in six one-hour instalments, together with major series on Michelangelo, Leonardo da Vinci and Benvenuto Cellini.

The historical pageant is almost limitless. RAI's co-production plans for the 1970s include series on the building of the Suez Canal, the discovery and exploration of the Congo and Magellan's voyage round the world. They are equally busy dramatising great novels: Anna Moffo is in *Anna Karenina* and Gina Lollobrigida in *The Charterhouse of Parma*, while the French director, Robert Bresson, has made a ninety-minute film based on Dostoyevsky's *The Devils*.

Although all these programmes are designed for television serials, several of them are later refashioned into films for the cinema. A four-part television serial of *Pinocchio*, for instance, became a two-hour feature film; the *Aeneid* and *Leonardo da Vinci* programmes have also been edited into films.

The close relationship between television and the cinema has bred much discussion on how frequently programmes should be shown on both media. 'It's not enough for a film to have one night's life on television,' said Vittorio Bonicelli at RAI. 'Federico Fellini made a beautiful film for us, *The Clowns*, which we showed at Christmas. This was his own highly personal view of clowns at the circus. You really need to see a film like that two or three times. And now I have a wonderful film by Robert Bresson of Dostoyevsky's novel, *White Nights*. I'm afraid you can't really appreciate it in one night on television. Perhaps it should be shown in an art theatre for six months, so that all those interested could see it there first before it is shown on television. People must be prepared for this film.'

The association with the cinema does not mean that Fellini, de Sica or Antonioni films are on every night. 'What we aim for is ten or a dozen films by such directors each year,' said Bonicelli. 'Fellini will make five films for us over three years.' Italian television has wrung some genuine creativity out of the film industry. 'Our aim is in complete contrast to the Americans',' an Italian director pointed out. 'We give our directors a free hand. The American networks also have programmes made by movie companies, but they must fit an exact commercial formula. They do not give them the chance to be creative.'

Italian television is more inhibited by the politicians and the Catholic Church than by the advertisers. *The Odyssey* or the *Leonardo da Vinci* are safe ground. RAI's problems begin the moment it starts to tackle the contemporary scene. The great debate on divorce reform in Italy in 1970, for instance, caused RAI all kinds of contortions. It has always had close ties with the Vatican and prudently steered clear of delicate topics—once it was reported to have insisted on the word 'divorce' being deleted from a popular song in a television song contest. For a while RAI tried to dodge the divorce debate until one of the promoters of the bill charged them with 'censorship' and 'total lack of objectivity'. RAI then held hasty consultations and, abruptly reversing its policy, came up with ten hours of debate on the divorce proposals.

The divorce Italian broadcasters devoutly pray for is from the politicians. RAI's ten-year licence comes up for renewal at the end of 1972 and many are hoping for some new arrangement that will give broadcasting greater protection from the whims of the government of the day. Business interests would dearly love to capture television for the private sector. Accordingly, they have been in the forefront of a sustained campaign to magnify RAI's weaknesses and discredit its objectivity. Their campaign was helped early in 1970 when one of RAI's vice-presidents, Italo de Feo, wrote in the right-wing newspaper, *Il Tempo*, that the majority of RAI's staff was 'communist, communist-inclined or dissident Catholic'. This accusation was hardly borne out by the facts—RAI has been essentially christian democrat territory for many years—but it was good fuel for 'witch-burning'. However, no Italian television executives that I met felt there was any likelihood of television being handed over to the commercial television lobby. What they do expect is some strengthening of RAI's status. 'We simply must have a complete reorganisation,' said one senior director. 'We must be less political—we are just not serving the best interests of the public at the moment. We are too closely linked with the government in power; what we need is a corporation responsible to parliament.'

Whether RAI will achieve this objective under its new licensing arrangements is by no means certain. 'The politicians here see television as the new power base,' an Italian journalist remarked, 'especially as our newspapers have a very limited circulation. Television reaches all the people every day and the politicians are only too aware of that. It will be hard to stop RAI remaining a political preserve.'

10

Spain: Legacy of the Conquistadors

SPANISH television is a curious cross between European and American, with an extra touch of political control thrown in through the strong arm of General Franco. While Spain is the only European country where the television service, Television Española (TVE), is an integral part of the Ministry of Information and Tourism, it is also the only major country with purely commercial television. TVE is something of a bonanza for the Ministry. The advertising revenue of over £23 million a year goes directly into the Ministry's coffers; they give most of it back to TVE, but use the rest to finance radio, a symphony orchestra and various other activities. Indeed, it is an old joke in Madrid that the television commercials pay for everything the Ministry does.

TVE, anyway, has no independent status of its own, and depends on the whim of the minister of the day. Fortunately for it, the minister for most of the 1960s, Manuel Fraga Iribarne, was a television enthusiast who set his heart on expansion. TVE was rapidly equipped during his regime with some of the most extensive and modern studios in Europe, set amid pine-trees in a park at Prado del Rey, just outside Madrid. Thus fitted out, TVE is swiftly becoming one of the more important programme-producing organisations in Europe. It turns out eighty per cent of its own programmes, several of which have won it international prizes. The delightful *History of Frivolity* won the Golden Rose at Montreux in 1968 for the best light entertainment programme in Europe that year.

The Spanish like to point out with pride that they now rank fifth in Europe, behind West Germany, Britain, France and Italy, in set ownership. In 1971 there were just over five million sets. 'In 1956 we had only three thousand,' said Luis Ezcurra Carrillo, the director of television who has been the prime architect of TVE's growing international reputation, 'and as late as 1962 there were only 300,000. Since then our expansion has been closely tied to the growth of the Spanish economy, and as a commercial network we have created a national market for advertising here.' The sudden upsurge in the late 1960s established Spain as an increasingly important link between television in Europe and South America. 'We are the bridge,' said Ezcurra, 'with the two hundred million Spanish-speaking people there.'

The bridge is created, of course, by the Atlantic satellite which TVE use extensively. In fact they carry more satellite relays than any other television organisation in the world. Quite apart from relaying events such as the Eurovision Song Contest and football matches to South America, they employ the satellite three times every day to transmit their own news programmes live to their regional station in the Canary Islands. Since early 1971 they have become even more involved with the satellite for the news exchange every weekday between Europe and South America. Every afternoon after lunch, TVE hooks into a sound circuit with stations in Brazil, Colombia, Peru and Venezuela for a conference on news stories available on both sides of the Atlantic that day. TVE offers a round-up of the Eurovision news exchange to the South Americans, who respond with details of the film they have available. Prompt at 6.35 every weekday evening the pictures requested at the conference come beaming in from South America via the satellite to TVE in Madrid, who then inject them into the entire Eurovision network. Then, just after seven o'clock, Madrid relays back to South America an edited round-up of the day's Eurovision stories. Argentina, Mexico and Chile also participate in this exchange, if they have important stories to contribute. The evening a new President of Argentina was sworn in in Buenos Aires at 6.30, TVE had full coverage through Madrid relayed to all Europe by 7.

The Spanish are eager to make the most of this legacy of the Conquistadors. Since 1967 a series of annual conventions have been held by leading Spanish and South American television executives to discuss programme exchange and the sharing of satellites. This co-operation was extended in 1971 by the creation of an Iberio-American Television Organisation (IATO), with Spain and Mexico as two of the leading participants, to promote programme exchange in the Spanish-speaking world. Now that South America is shrugging off United States domination of its television, Spain is naturally one alternative source of material.

There is plenty to choose from. Spanish television's two black-and-white channels are on the air for longer each day than any other service in Europe. The first channel begins at lunch-time and continues until midnight (even later at weekends), while the second channel operates from 8.30 in the evening until well after midnight. The Spanish custom of rising and retiring late means that prime time begins at 10 and continues until 11.30. One audience survey conducted by TVE revealed that only half the children under fourteen are in bed and asleep by eleven o'clock and that the remainder are still potential television viewers at that hour. The main features on both channels, therefore, start at ten o'clock. The first channel is aimed primarily at a mass audience, and the second at minority interests. 'Our first channel,' Ezcurra explained, 'is not quite so heavy or boring as some of those in central Europe. We try to have a dynamic, escapist channel. The second channel, however, is not under the same obligation to please the public.' The commercial pressures on the second channel to seek a large audience are reduced by the simple means of not charging a separate price for its advertising. The advertiser buys fifteen, thirty- or sixty-second spots which are automatically shown on both channels for an overall price; he does not have the option of buying one channel or the other. TVE's hand is strengthened in dealing with advertisers by its monopoly. In 1969, for instance, they cut back advertising time by one-third, from an average of nine minutes to six minutes per hour because of complaints from viewers about the frequency of commercials. They avoided any reduction in revenue, however, by simultaneously increasing the price of advertising by a third. The spots (there is no sponsorship) are now among the most expensive outside the United States; in prime time a fifteen-second one costs £1,090. The major advertisers, for once, are not the soap flakes and food manufacturers. The top four on Spanish television during 1970 were all selling drink—Coca-Cola was first and Cola-Cao second, followed by Veterano and Fundador brandies; Omega watches were the fifth largest spender. The commercials are normally shown only on the hour or on the half-hour, so that in a half-hour programme there is no break.

Although the main channel is aimed at a mass audience, it does not consist of non-stop trivia. The Ministry of Information clearly directs that television must provide a public service, so two-thirds of the programmes are billed as information or documentaries. Imported American programmes, once very popular in Spain, are now rare. During 1971 only *Ironside*, dubbed into Castilian Spanish, was on in the peak evening period on the first channel, and *High Chaparral* on the second. Otherwise most of the entertainment is unmistakably Spanish; even the interlude music is guitar. When I tuned in to the most popular late-night talk show, *Estudio Abierto* (Open Discussion), the chat was mostly about bull-fights. But there is a marked preference for re-creating past history rather than looking closely at the scene today. I watched one instalment of a documentary series of forty-seven instalments on Spain in the twentieth century, but the episode I saw was about great bull-fighters before 1920.

Novelas, dramatisations of classical novels, go out every

weekday evening at eight o'clock. When I first saw a *novela* on the programme schedule I thought this would be a Spanish version of the popular *tele-novelas* I had encountered in South America, which tell how a poor but beautiful village girl goes to the big city to work as a maid, is seduced by her employer and ends up driving a sports car and owning a boutique. But the dream of the South American masses is not reflected on Spanish television. Almost all their dramatisations are works by nineteenth-century novelists and playwrights—Tolstoy, Balzac, Dickens, Jane Austen, Henry James, Oscar Wilde and Mark Twain. These are usually in five instalments run on consecutive evenings from Monday to Friday. A few have been dramatised at much greater length: *David Copperfield* went to twenty-five instalments, *Little Dorrit* and *The Three Musketeers* to twenty and *Northanger Abbey* to ten. The productions are often lavish: *The Three Musketeers* called for fifty-six actors and four hundred extras.

This preoccupation with the past is also reflected in thirteen ninety-minute productions resurrecting nineteenth-century Spanish musical comedies known as *zarzuelas*. Each one costs £80,000 to mount (almost American-scale budgeting) and is filmed in colour, although Spanish television is still all black and white. But TVE recoups much of the cost by selling the programme all over Europe and South America. These sales are now earning them nearly £400,000 a year. They are also offsetting costs by joining in European co-production, particularly with ORTF in France and RAI in Italy.

Such epics, often costing more than £100,000, have included a two-and-a-half-hour colour film of Lope de Vega's *Fuenteovejuna*, filmed on location all over Spain, with enormous battle scenes staged in ancient castles. A TVE executive confessed: 'We are going through our Cecil B. de Mille period at the moment.' Not surprisingly, they too are coming up with their own versions of history. When they tackled a dramatisation of the life of Christopher Columbus in co-operation with RAI in Italy, they skirted round the delicate topic of whether

Columbus was Italian or Spanish by birth. 'We didn't mention it at all,' admitted one of the producers. 'Columbus just turned up at the court of Spain without any explanation.' Historical interpretation apart, the battles always make for dramatic television.

So does bull-fighting. Live coverage of a *corrida* provides TVE with one of its most exportable items. During 1971 they set up one spectacular which was beamed by satellite to enthusiasts in South America, the United States (on closed circuit TV, not network) and even Japan and Australia.

The fighting that Spanish television carefully avoids, of course, is in the streets at home. The news programmes regularly show demonstrations or riots in the rest of Europe or America, but never in Spain itself. Nor is any coverage offered on the Eurovision news exchange. Foreign cameramen who arrive to report embarrassing events either do not get a permit to film in Spain or find themselves leaving the scene in a police car for a short stay in jail until the trouble dies down. The obsession with keeping awkward scenes off the screen has even entailed putting out fake crowd noises at a football match, where it was feared that Basque separatist slogans might be chanted: a 'rhubarb rhubarb' tape was kept running and the volume was turned up when it looked likely that a goal would be scored.

Hand in hand with the government the Catholic Church also ensures that TVE does not reflect the permissive society too closely. When I was in Madrid the programme-planners had been watching some screenings of ballet from Denmark. They thought the ballet very fine but had to reject it because several of the dancers were naked. A popular wildlife programme, *Blue Planet*, caused considerable unease among the Catholic Church because its host, Dr Felix Rodriguez de la Fuente, ventured to discuss Darwinism. To reassure everyone, the programme also included an interview with an eminent priest who maintained that evolution in no way denied the existence of God.

Given such restrictions, it is understandable that the energies and abilities of many people in Spanish television have to be directed to producing historical spectaculars set in pre-Franco days. What they all privately hope for is some re-organisation which would free television from the aegis of the Ministry of Information. As one executive said: 'Political control would still be there, but it would be good to find our own personality.'

II

Scandinavia: Resisting the Commercials

I ARRIVED in Helsinki on a dismal, foggy day in late winter; during my stay it never brightened to much more than twilight. So old television standbys like *Peyton Place* and *High Chaparral* in colour were enormously cheering amid all that gloom. Later, in Stockholm, Johan von Utfall, the director of engineering for Swedish television, confirmed my impression: 'Colour television has an extra importance in Scandinavia: most of the year our life is so grey that colour TV is a vital tonic.'

Yet, if television relieves the dreariness of winter, it is almost forgotten the moment the short summer arrives; audiences melt with the snow. Advertising rates on Finnish television—the only network in Scandinavia that allows commercials—are halved during the summer season from mid-June through August. The second channel stops broadcasting completely during those months. Swedish television, which operates the largest and perhaps most thoughtful audience research department in Europe, actually stops its surveys during the summer. In Norway, all the television staff, except those actually putting out the programmes, knock off at 3 p.m. in the afternoon to make the most of the sunshine.

If climate is one formative influence on Scandinavian television, geography is another. The scattered populations of Finland, Norway and Sweden, some of them inside the Arctic Circle, make the provision of complete coverage—which is demanded by the public-service concept of all the broadcasting organisations—inordinately expensive. Only the flat farmland of Denmark is easily served by a mere four transmitters. In Norway, which has less then four million inhabitants, no fewer than forty main transmitters and 1,500 low-power repeater stations are required to cover the thousand miles over mountains and fjords from Oslo to Kirkenes on the Barents Sea (where viewers can also pick up Russian television). 'Many of our transmitters are 5,000 feet up,' Jan Freydenlund of Norwegian television pointed out. 'In winter they are shrouded in ice six feet thick, which makes maintenance a hideous job. Our high technical costs unfortunately mean we have less money for programmes.'

Happily, these adversities, coupled with the inevitably tiny budgets available to four nations with only twenty-two million people between them, have been a spur to some of the most original thinking on television in the world. These small broadcasting organisations have one great advantage: if someone has a bright idea, it stands a good chance of being implemented; it will not be lost amid clouds of corporate thinking.

Excepting Finland, where advertising revenue accounts for forty per cent of television's income, the Scandinavian broadcasting organisations are dependent on licence fees, which are among the highest in Europe. Sweden, with nearly 2½ million TV sets, has enough revenue from a licence charge of £14·50 —a year to sustain two channels which will be putting out a total of a hundred hours of programmes a week by the mid-1970s. The Norwegians and Danes, however, with only 800,000 and 1·2 million sets respectively, are hard-pressed. They operate only one channel each for less than forty hours a week. The Danes are proposing a second channel, but this will mean pushing up their licence from £12·65 a year to over £20, which would be the highest in the world. The Norwegians, who charge a licence fee of £12, supplement their revenue by a ten per cent tax on the sale of sets; even so their annual income is less than £7·5 million (compared with the BBC's £100 million).

During the 1960s the sharp rise in the sales of television sets at least assured each organisation of an increased budget every year. Now that almost every home has a set (the Swedes, for example, have thirty sets per hundred of their population, the highest proportion in Europe and exceeded only in the United States), the only way of increasing income is either to raise the licence fee or to permit advertising. The Swedes, Danes and Norwegians are all stoutly resisting advertising. 'We can give people three radio programmes and two television channels for the same price as one daily newspaper costs them per year,' argued Laurits Bindslov, director of Danish television. 'We don't need commercials.'

There is an understanding that any one of the three countries will consult the others before introducing advertising; for, once one gives way, the others must follow because of overlaps in viewing areas. Sweden is the pace-setter since her programmes can be seen in nearly half of all Norwegian and Danish homes. Indeed, the Norwegians and Danes study the Swedes' programme schedules and tailor their own output accordingly. If Sweden accepted advertising, Norwegian and Danish firms could dodge the ban in their own countries by booking spots in Sweden.

Even with limited advertising, however, the television organisations would still rely on buying many of their programmes cheaply overseas. The Norwegians are charged as little as £65 for a half-hour American programme; even the richer Swedes pay only £170. All the Scandinavians depend on importing up to fifty per cent of their programmes, although they have largely avoided the cheapest American screen-fodder. The exception is Mainos-TV, the commercial company owned by Finnish industry, banks, advertising agencies and insurance companies, which provides the programmes for part of each evening on both of the Finnish Broadcasting Company's channels. Mainos-TV originates forty-nine per cent of its own programmes but otherwise buys almost exclusively American serials; in 1969 ninety-four per cent of their serials time was filled with American programmes—the remaining six per cent were French. The Finnish Broadcasting Company itself purchases about half its foreign programmes from the United States and a third from Britain.

The other Scandinavian countries rely heavily on British material. The Swedes buy sixty per cent of all their foreign programmes from the BBC and Independent Television, and select the rest open-mindedly from other countries.

'There is a reaction here against American series,' Olof Rydbeck director-general of Swedish Broadcasting Corporation until the end of 1970, told me. 'We've made it our policy to seek truly international fare.' Consequently, Swedish television offers a broad variety—ballet from Russia, a thirteen-part crime series, *The Sinful People of Prague*, from Czechoslovakia (this before the Russian invasion in 1968), children's films and documentaries from Japan and a Polish series, *Captain Kloss*, about a World War II resistance fighter, which gained thirty-five per cent of the viewing audience in the late evening on Channel 1.

The international outlook is echoed in news coverage. Swedish television maintains twelve full-time correspondents overseas. 'Sweden's welfare depends on trade and foreign contacts,' Olof Rydbeck said. 'I have made it a deliberate policy to break away from the habit of considering any story here more important than events overseas. Parochialism lingers on in television in many countries, but not, I hope, in Sweden. One of our most important tasks is to increase our contact with, and knowledge of, the world around us.'

This open-mindedness has led also to an attempt to create within the Swedish Broadcasting Company two competing television channels, each with a clear identity of its own. The concept of competition began with the start of the second channel, TV2, at the end of 1969. Although both TV1 and TV2 share the same technical facilities and a joint news department, they are otherwise given far-reaching independence. Each channel is presided over by a director who can make his own decisions on how to spend his annual budget and shape his programmes according to his own design. 'We believe this will give greater stimulus to programme producers and a wider freedom of choice to the public,' Rydbeck said. 'Writers and artists will not be dependent on the verdict of one monolithic organisation; if the director of TV1 does not like their ideas, perhaps the director of TV2 will.'

Two men of very different background were selected as the first directors of TV1 and TV2 to encourage diversity. 'For TV1, which was the existing channel, we chose Hakan Unsgaard, from within our own organisation,' Olof Rydbeck explained, 'but for TV2 we wanted someone from outside who would not be stamped with our traditions. We selected Orjan Wallquist, the editor of a socialist weekly magazine.' Producers and other staff were also divided between the two channels; TV1 tended to get the older, more conservative producers, TV2 the young, radical ones.

Not surprisingly, TV2 quickly established itself as a channel concerned with serious social problems, which pleased some Swedish socialists, but not the viewing audience at large. Many criticised it for being too radical, for upsetting the political and social balance, which is a cornerstone of public-service broadcasting in Europe. In the first few months the new channel barely won ten per cent of the audience, although three British programmes bought from the BBC—*The Six Wives of Henry VIII, Softly, Softly* and *Lulu and the Young Generation*—gained much higher ratings.

As a further stimulant to competition, the rigid format of departments for education, current affairs, drama and light entertainment within each channel has been cast aside. Hakan Unsgaard, director of TV1, explained: 'I felt my producers would prefer flexibility for many types of programme. So, instead of departments with their own fixed budget, we have established project groups, each with producer, director and script writer. We've broken the year down into five periods of ten weeks, in each of which a project group may work on a different subject. So a producer who has specialised in current affairs in the past may find himself a project leader in children's television for ten weeks, before spending another period making a documentary on wild life.'

The current affairs group does not have quite such frequent fluctuations of staff, because continuity is needed in building up contacts with politicians at home and abroad, but Unsgaard reckons to change even his current affairs chief every six months.

Once a project group has been assigned a programme and the budget agreed, it is then free to proceed as the project leader chooses. A senior executive may request a special showing of a finished programme if it is on a particularly controversial topic, but the aim is to leave producers maximum freedom. 'We've got to go to the frontiers of taste and opinion,' said Unsgaard, 'and every year we push that frontier a little further forward—we never go back. The real differences we have with our producers are about how far forward we push the frontier at a given moment.'

The hazards of pushing the frontiers too far too fast were demonstrated in Finland. Until 1965 Finnish television had developed slowly and cautiously. 'Television here was passive—all memories of the past,' Dr Kaarle Nordenstreng, the Finnish Broadcasting Company's young director of research explained. 'There were codes of what not to do—don't report strikes, no slang, nothing on sex, no experimental programmes. All this was changed by the appointment in 1965 of a new director-general, Eino S. Repo. Repo was the liberator. He gave everyone their head. It was like working on another planet.'

Programmes on sex education were shown; documentaries challenged many traditional aspects of Finnish society; the insurance companies were attacked in one devastating report, pollution by the state chemical industry was criticised in another; television drama dropped cosy comedies in favour of dramatised documentaries attacking private ownership and the uneven distribution of property in Finland.

Many young producers felt that they had moved into the 'Golden Age of Television'. The average viewer, politician and newspaper editor did not share their enthusiasm. The press was almost completely united in its condemnation of Repo's 'liberating' policy and the future of broadcasting became a major election issue by 1969. When the conservatives gained strength at the election, the reaction came quickly. Repo was replaced by Erkki Raatikainen, the secretary of the Social-Democratic party. Another politican, Pekka Silvola, secretary of the Agrarian party, was made programme director for television. Repo himself was shuffled to the sidelines as director of radio. 'We have been politicised,' complained one bitter supporter of the Repo regime.

The status of the Finnish Broadcasting Company made this counter-revolution an easy manoeuvre. The state owns ninety-two per cent of the stock in the company and normally only gives it a broadcasting licence for one or two years at a stretch. Parliament appoints all the members of the board of governors, and invariably nominates politicians.

Erkki Raatikainen, the new director-general, was quite frank about his role in bringing a new—or as some would say old—look to Finnish television. 'I'm the Husak,' he told me—comparing himself to the premier who replaced Dubcek in Czechoslovakia, 'I have to normalise television. We've been too international, some of our programmes have been too advanced. The ordinary viewer has been puzzled. Now we are going to do more down-to-earth programmes on home affairs.'

The Finnish experience is a clear warning of the reaction that can be caused if a television service changes too quickly, particularly if in doing so it drops any claim to a balanced presentation of the views of the nation.

Danish television has also been under pressure, particularly from the producers of its cultural and youth programmes, to push left-wing ideas, but has so far succeeded in holding moderate balance. One producer, however, who refused to stop promoting left-wing views, was fired. 'We can ask questions about the framework of society,' said Laurits Bindslov, the director of Danish television, 'but we must give the broad spectrum of people's feelings.'

Danish television still conducts, on its one channel, the limited television service that vanished in many countries in the 1950s. On weekdays the programmes are from 7.30 in the evening until 10.30, and Saturdays and Sundays there are afternoon programmes. But the total is only thirty-eight hours a week, including three hours of repeats on weekday afternoons for those who may have missed programmes the previous evening through working on a late shift (a very considerate policy adopted in several Scandinavian countries). The Danish approach to television is that it is something to be viewed after dinner in the evening, just as one might go to a theatre or concert, it is not conceived as visual muzak. 'My family and I would never watch television while we eat,' a Danish television producer told me. 'Danish families like to have their evening meal in peace and then, perhaps, see what is on.'

Norwegians receive even shorter television rations—thirty-three hours a week, of which three and a half hours are repeats. Cultural and information programmes far outweigh entertainment, which rates as little as twenty-five per cent of transmission time. 'We are inclined to be heavy on the information side,' said Jan Frydenlund, deputy director of television programmes, 'and many of our programmes are like visual radio shows.'

Despite this conservative tendency, the Norwegians have come up with one of the most original television shows anywhere—*Idebanken, The Bank of Ideas*. It was conceived by a strapping Norwegian journalist and television commentator, Erik Bye. 'I got tired of using television as a means of killing people's time,' Bye told me. 'I wanted to put it to a practical use. Some countries have found television very effective as a way of collecting money for charity; so I decided we wouldn't ask people for money, we'd ask them for brain power, we'd set up a Bank of Ideas. We are a small country, we can reach all our people through television, so why not pick their brains to solve our problems?'

The first problem *Idebanken* tackled, when it began in 1967, was how to improve the conditions of the fishermen working in Norway's fleet of 36,000 fishing-boats; no two boats were alike, most lacked proper toilet facilities or comfortable quarters for the crew. Bye discussed the topic with a panel of fishing experts, then asked viewers for ideas on how to mass-produce, cheaply, a more comfortable fishing boat. One Norwegian shipbuilder responded with plans for a modern boat; other ideas from viewers were incorporated. The new boats, whose progress was carefully filmed for the programme, cost twenty-five per cent less to build than custom-built boats, and combined excellent galleys, sleeping quarters and toilets for the crews. Six of the new boats were in service by 1970. 'They are the most advanced and thoroughly tested in Norway,' Bye reported proudly.

From this encouraging start, *Idebanken* went on to tackle everything from helping rural craftsmen to sell their products in the cities to advising on how to keep schools going in the depopulated areas of Norway. 'Many farmers make excellent wood carvings,' said Bye, 'but they have no idea how to market them. We helped them meet the right people. One old chap who was making marvellous grandfather clocks got in touch with a professional buyer through our programme and he's now selling them all over the world.'

Idebanken's very success, however, became a problem. The resources and staff to back up the ideas it unleashed were too small to cope. When Bye did a programme on how to make simple eel-traps, they were swamped with 8,000 requests for more details. *Idebanken*'s advice on how to keep schools going in remote areas drew the charge that the programme was meddling in politics. Reluctantly, therefore, the programme was called off after two years. 'We came under very heavy fire,' Bye admitted, 'although we were not trying to play politics. I'm now trying to revive the programme with a separate organisation to follow up the ideas that we stimulate. We must still make every possible use of television as a tool to get things done.'

The difficulties of maintaining technical excellence and high-quality programmes in the Scandinavian countries may well lead to the creation, within a decade, of the world's first supranational television network. Norway, Sweden, Finland and Denmark, together with Iceland, already work closely together in an organisation called Nordvision, through which they exchange programmes free of charge. The main exchange is in news and sports programmes, but the nucleus of co-operation is there for an eventual Nordvision channel serving 22 million people (just as Denmark, Norway and Sweden share an airline, SAS). Laurits Bindslov believes that such a third channel, probably using a satellite to beam its programmes throughout Scandinavia and to Iceland, could play an important role in breaking down parochialism. 'I believe a third channel could bring the debate on the future of Europe into Scandinavia,' he said. 'We should invite a great European personality to be its director, so that it is not just a local channel, but a truly European one.'

12

The Netherlands: Fair Shares for All

NO one can compete with the Dutch when it comes to giving all-comers a chance to have their say on television. Where else do the League of Humanists, the Ancient Order of Freemasons, Moral Re-Armament of the Society for Sexual Reform have programme time set aside for them to propound their views? The Dutch Society for Sexual Reform, for instance, is entitled to twenty minutes every eight weeks. 'We believe,' a spokesman for the society told me, 'that we should employ our programme time to spread information regarding sex and human relations.' Accordingly, their programmes discuss homosexuality, abortions, pornography, contraception, sex education and modern marriage. Broadcasting is theoretically open to every pressure group, whether social, political or religious, within the country. The Dutch proudly point out to visitors that their television system is the most democratic anywhere.

You begin to suspect something unusual the moment you arrive in the little town of Hilversum, twenty miles east of Amsterdam, where Dutch television makes its home. Instead of operating from some impersonal, steel and concrete monolith with miles of corridors, the Dutch broadcasters work from a score of elegant white-painted villas scattered among the elm lined avenues of Hilversum. Well-trimmed lawns and carefully tended flower-beds surround each villa, creating an environment quite different from the frenetic atmosphere of other headquarters. You stroll around to call on the Catholic broadcasters, or the socialist broadcasters, each in their own villa.

In the Netherlands any organisation which has more than 15,000 members (who must all have purchased a television licence) is entitled to apply to the minister of culture, recreation and social work for time on the country's three radio and two television networks. Initially, a budding organisation will be allowed one hour of programme time a week for a two-year trial period. During this probation, the organisation, through its programmes and other activities, seeks to raise membership to 100,000. If successful, it then qualifies as a 'C' category company entitled to two and a half hours on TV each week (plus a radio allocation); but if it fails to win the magic 100,000, its right to make programmes lapses. Later on, if its membership keeps rising, at 250,000 it graduates to 'B' status with five hours on TV a week, and finally, at 400,000, to 'A' category, rating eight hours a week.

During 1971 four associations were rated 'A'. The largest was AVRO (General Society for Radio Broadcasting), which is actually the least politically or religiously orientated of all the groups. 'AVRO,' a Dutch broadcaster explained, 'is the silent majority's programme company; it is conservative, pro-establishment, for the *status-quo*.' Much more committed, however, are NCRV (Netherlands Christian Radio Society) representing the Reformed Protestants, KRO (Catholic Radio Society) and the socialist VARA (Workers' Radio Amateur Society). There were no 'B' companies, but two 'C' class—the Liberal Protestants' VPRO and a newcomer TROS. TROS began life as a pirate television station operating from an old war-time fort off the coast in 1964, but two years later achieved land-based respectability, with the required number of members. It is conservative, but has no special political affiliation and is generally regarded as a second platform for 'the silent majority'. Another newcomer, the Evangelical Broadcasting System (EO), notched up 15,000 members in 1970 and is struggling to achieve its

100,000 by 1972. EO is a society of orthodox Protestants concerned to raise the moral tone of programmes in this permissive age.

Besides these seven associations, twenty-seven other political, religious and social minority interests which claim that their views are not adequately represented are allowed occasional programmes of their own. The Society for Sexual Reform, the League of Humanists and Moral Re-Armament (a meagre half an hour a year) all qualify. The twelve political parties represented in the Dutch parliament are entitled to ten minutes each four times a year.

Every group granted time receives a proportional slice of the income from the television licence fee of seventy-five guilders (£8·75) a year and from advertising, which is permitted in four short blocks immediately before and after the news broadcasts at 7 and 8 each evening. The principle of fair shares for all communicators is applied even further by diverting forty per cent of the revenue from TV commercials to newspapers and magazines, who share it among themselves according to circulation. This extraordinary act of generosity was decided upon when commercials first began in 1967. The press complained loudly that they would suffer from the loss of revenue and that some publications might go broke. The government mediated and awarded them a slice of TV advertising revenue to soften the blow.

The assorted programme-makers all co-operate with the Netherlands Broadcasting Foundation (NOS), which provides studios and technical facilities and co-ordinates the programme schedules. NOS also takes care of news and sports coverage, together with special events like Apollo moon-shots. Although NOS cannot dictate policy to any of the programme associations, it is authorised to show children's and educational programmes if it feels these subjects are not adequately covered. For instance, it put out the BBC's *Civilisation* series under the guise of an educational programme. Overall NOS produces a third of the seventy hours a week on the two colour channels;

the seven programme associations and the variegated minorities fill two-thirds.

'I know it all sounds most complicated,' admitted Gerhardus van Beek of NOS, 'but you must realise that in the Netherlands we have always had a "pillarised" view of society—the roof held up by an assortment of pillars. Everyone belongs to some political party or Church which represents one of those pillars. So people find it natural to follow this through in broadcasting; two million of the three million people who have television licences in the Netherlands belong to one of the seven programme societies. It's all very democratic. And if your views aren't represented, you just start your own society. As for NOS—think of us as a printing plant which prints a variety of newspapers and magazines each week, reflecting many shades of opinion.'

Despite their special affiliations the programme companies tread delicately in propounding their own creed. And all have to rely on buying many overseas programmes, for the total television kitty of only £14 million a year provides slim programme-making budgets.

Bonanza, The Andy Williams Show and *The Debbie Reynolds Show* all appear on KRO's broadly based schedule. NCRV prefers a diet of brisk British thrillers such as *Scarlet Pimpernel* and *Softly, Softly*. Both broadcast church services and religious discussions on Sundays, but they are cautious not to appear overburdened with religious programmes. Indeed, they are much less militant platforms for their faith than they were in the days of radio before World War II. Then, KRO was strongly pro-Catholic, NCRV fiercely Protestant; nowadays a Protestant minister may be invited to join a discussion on KRO, although the chairman will always be a Catholic.

Beliefs are more strongly displayed in the programmes of the two main political groups, the socialists' VARA and the Liberal Protestants' VPRO. During its eight hours of programme time each week VARA is constantly concerned with social and political issues. They have established a reputation for hard-hitting documentaries on problem groups like unmarried mothers, divorced women and homosexuals. 'We always make programmes on downbeat topics, while AVRO or TROS like upbeat ones,' one of their producers explained. 'We'll do unemployment, while they make a programme on the biggest and best new factory in Holland.'

Not surprisingly, VARA has close relations with Granada in Britain. Lord Bernstein's philosophy dovetails neatly with VARA's. 'Many Granada programmes are naturals for us,' VARA's overseas programme buyer told me. 'We've been running *Coronation Street* for years. Now we are taking their *Family at War*.'

VARA's programme schedule occasionally looks like a British one translated into Dutch. They have run *The Forsyte Saga, Cathy, Come Home* and early *Z Cars*, together with their own productions of Harold Pinter and Alun Owen plays. Whether it is despite or because of its socialist conscience, VARA is remarkably successful at notching up good ratings. Normally only AVRO, with a diet including *Peyton Place* and *Tom Jones*, gets more programmes in the Dutch Top Ten.

The Liberal Protestants' VPRO, which has two and a half hours each week, concentrates more on message than audience. 'VPRO is the least concerned with audience ratings of all the companies,' a Dutch TV critic explained, 'in fact any VPRO producer whose show gets high ratings is likely to be fired.' Nevertheless, VPRO display some cunning in getting the word across. I watched their programmes one evening. To begin with, the announcer mentioned that during the evening one of the leading Dutch comediennes would be on, but he neglected to mention the precise time. So, instead of switching to the other channel for a while you had to watch all the VPRO offerings to be sure to catch her. These began with an earnest discussion about the problems of unemployment, prompted by the announcement that day of the closure of a large Dutch factory. Eventually, those who stayed with it, were rewarded with a highly professional half-hour colour show with the comedienne, and the evening closed with a programme on old age. VPRO constantly teeters on the brink of losing its qualification to broadcast, for it barely musters the 100,000 members required for its 'C' category. Indeed, in 1970, it was found to have only 93,000 but was generously given a year's grace to win back the extra 7,000. Apparently, its future is secure. All kinds of people rally round and join if they think VPRO is in danger.

The scheduling of this jumble of programme associations is handled by NOS. Some evenings they divide the time among two or three groups, but Monday, Tuesday and Thursday evenings are fixed; Monday night teams the political VARA on one network with the religious NCRV on the other; Tuesdays are set aside for KRO and AVRO—again basically a religious and political balance (if one regards AVRO as being conservative); Thursdays are shared by TROS and VPRO. This Thursday combination often works in TROS' favour, because VPRO, as we have remarked, are not preoccupied with ratings. With a minority watching VPRO on one channel, TROS piles up viewers on the other. This enables TROS to achieve the highest ratings of all the main programme groups—thirty-seven per cent of viewers watch its Thursday night shows; VPRO gains a mere nine per cent. AVRO is the second most popular association, averaging a thirty-four per cent audience; VARA chases it hard with thirty-two per cent.

Audience research has revealed special viewer loyalty to VPRO and NCRV, but the majority of viewers are not concerned with which association happens to be presenting programmes. And these days many of the highest-rated shows are not presented by the programme companies at all but by NOS, because they handle all the great international sports events. NOS had thirty-three of the top hundred programmes in 1969, almost all of them sports.

Half the secret of a successful programme company seems to be in producing a colourful TV guide. By law only the seven recognised broadcasting groups can publish full details of the

TV and radio schedules, so to find out what's on you must subscribe to one of the seven programme guides published weekly. Most Dutch families qualify as members of an association simply by purchasing its guide. The association with the gayest magazine clearly has the advantage, because it will attract the uncommitted. The most lavish weekly is AVRO's *Televizier*, which is crammed with colour pictures of TV stars. It sells over 800,000 copies, giving AVRO almost twice as many members as any other programme association. This lesson has not been lost on the former pirate group, TROS, which puts out a handy *Reader's Digest* style guide called *Kompas*. If I lived in the Netherlands, I would probably buy *Kompas* because of its convenient size and professional flair and thus swell TROS' membership.

Each association claims that in good democratic fashion it respects the wishes of its members and puts out the programmes they want; theoretically the ideal relationship between broadcaster and audience. How well it all works in practice is debatable. Members certainly gush with ideas, but the professionals often politely dismiss them as impractical, too costly or not good television. AVRO holds an annual conference which its 800,000 members can apply to attend. 'There's lots to eat and drink and the chairman and programme executives make nice speeches,' said a rather cynical rival executive. 'All the members clap, say, "We are the best association," and go back home.'

VARA invites its members to Hilversum twice a year and listens with a sympathetic ear. Following suggestions at one meeting, they started a consumer programme discussing 'best buys'. On another occasion their members overuled VARA's plans to drop an attractive lady announcer. No society can afford to be too cavalier with its members; after all, they have the ultimate weapon: vanishing membership spells vanishing programme time.

The only weakness in all this display of democracy is that television in the Netherlands often seems slightly incoherent, because no one group of planners is sitting down to work out a comprehensive evening's or week's viewing. Since each association is left to its own devices and is at liberty to screen what it chooses (guided only by a generalisation in the broadcasting act that its programmes must 'inform, educate and entertain') certain areas may be neglected. Children's programmes, for instance, for the children, as yet, have no pressure group of their own. Because of this, NOS is now stepping in to provide better children's coverage.

Indeed, the role of NOS, not only as a central co-ordinating and technical organisation, is likely to increase as television costs rise each year and co-productions with other countries become more common. Their success in gaining so many places in the Dutch Top Ten with moon-walks and sports coverage is putting them in a privileged position. But it would be a pity if NOS became all-powerful, for the Dutch broadcasting system at the moment stands out as a refreshing oasis of originality. Luckily, NOS are quite aware of this. 'I am sure we must take on a more definite role,' one of their board of directors said, 'but we cherish our democratic television here and we don't mean to give it up.'

THE COMMUNIST WORLD

13

The Soviet Union: The Blue Screen

THE first clue to the nature of Soviet television is the cover of the weekly TV and radio guide. No sign there of the blondes or western heroes who so frequently smile from the covers of television weeklies elsewhere. Instead, there is usually some sombre portrait of a scientist, engineer or academician whose achievements will be profiled on what the Russians have christened 'the Blue Screen'. When that much-travelled serial *The Forsyte Saga* opened on Moscow television in 1971, it was discussed only in a discreet article inside. The cover and top billing that week went to 'one of the best workers in the famous plant of plants, Ural Mash, who will appear in the first of three broadcasts on our country's leading heavy-machinery-building enterprises'. The cover just prior to that featured the director of the Metallurgical Institute of the U.S.S.R. Academy of Sciences, who was appearing in a series, *The Lenin University of Millions*, about the history of the Communist Party in the Soviet Union.

While American television is primarily in the business of selling goods, Russian television's concern is promoting socialist achievement. Its priority is educating people in the ways of Marxist–Leninism and stimulating their pride in the new state they have created. Films, music, plays and sport abound on television, but the theme of Soviet achievement comes through all the time. Even the sports commentators are highly nationalistic. No one was ever more partisan in commenting on football or ice-hockey internationals—the Soviet players are all doing a grand job, their opponents are clearly having a bad day. The integrity of the referee, if he is not from the Soviet Union, may frequently be questioned. Sentiments are entirely in keeping with the basic programme policy, which is shaped in best Leninist tradition 'to maintain a basic patriotic spirit . . . so that every inhabitant feels himself to be a citizen of the great Soviet Union . . . If an individual feels himself to be a citizen of the country, he feels solidarity with the country's politics.'

Lenin himself was always enthusiastic about the possibilities of mass communication as a tool of the revolution. Indeed, the Soviet Union regards the first radio broadcast ever made there as having been Lenin's announcement from the cruiser *Aurora* in October 1917 that the communists had won the Revolution. Although Lenin never lived to know television, no doubt he would have embraced it as the perfect propaganda machine. For the Soviet Union, after all, is an immense country of many peoples, speaking some sixty different languages. Television would have given him the chance, as it does the Soviet leaders now, to be seen by all from Leningrad to Vladivostok and beyond all in the same moment—assuming, that is, that some of them stayed up fairly late at night. One of the biggest problems of organising television in the Soviet Union is its ten time zones; early evening in Moscow is early morning in Vladivostock.

But the size of their country has not daunted the Russians from attempting to bring the blue screen into the homes of all their 240 million people. Today there are over thirty million television sets in the Soviet Union—more than in any other single nation except the United States. Well over three-quarters of all the homes can watch at least one channel, while in nearly fifty cities there is both a national channel from Moscow and a regional channel. Leningrad has three channels, Moscow itself boasts four. The Russians are not content to rest at that. The main national programme from Moscow will blanket the entire Soviet Union early in the 1970s, including the remotest and most sparsely populated regions. In addition, regional television centres with five channels are being built at Tashkent and Frunze in the south and at Vilnius near the Polish border. The ultimate aim is to have five channels available to every Soviet citizen.

Already their television dwarfs the development in most other countries. Thirty-five thousand people are employed in broadcasting, while the new television centre completed in the Moscow suburb of Ostankino in 1970 is as abundantly equipped as any in Europe, the United States or Japan. Each of the twenty-one studios has between six and eight colour cameras (the norm in the west is three or four), plus two videotape recorders. There is an additional videotape centre with no less than sixty-four recorders—compare this with NHK in Tokyo, whose facilities are universally admired, who have only thirty-six. One Western technical expert, who has studied television centres throughout the world, told me he found the Moscow establishment the most elaborate of them all. And dominating the Ostankino skyline is a lanky 1,700-foot-high television tower. The tower, which has a restaurant appropriately named the Seventh Heaven near the summit, is reputed to be the tallest building in the world. From a distance it looks like an outsize multi-stage rocket all set for launching.

Regular colour television began in 1967, the same year that most countries of Western Europe launched their colour programmes. For the Russians to be able to see the Red Flag in 'living colour' was, of course, a suitable way to make the fiftieth anniversary of the October Revolution. Their colour system is the French SECAM, which de Gaulle successfully persuaded both the Soviet Union and the communist countries of Eastern Europe to adopt (although so far only East Germans among the satellites actually have colour). In the Soviet Union the changeover to colour has been relatively slow. In 1971 about twenty hours out of one hundred and sixty hours a week on Moscow television were in colour. One drawback, as in most countries, has been the cost of colour sets. They sell for over

£400 in Moscow, and so can be afforded only by tourist hotels or workers' clubs. The difficulty and cost of constructing a complete television system for so immense a land—it is 4,500 miles from Moscow to Vladivostok—meant that the Russians could never really contemplate establishing a conventional land-based microwave network for the entire Soviet Union.

Regular television programming began in Moscow as far back as December 1939. It broke off during the war, but resumed again shortly afterwards in December 1945. During the Stalin era expansion was slow. Because of the distances television developed on a regional basis, with the first stations in the capital cities of each of the fourteen republics of the Soviet Union. Mini-networks spread out within each republic. In all about 130 local stations were built, many of them making a good proportion of their own programmes, often in the regional language. Cities like Leningrad, Kiev, Minsk, Tallinn and Riga, in the west of the Soviet Union, were also slowly linked by landline to Moscow.

The first Sputnik, however, in 1957 not only marked the opening of the space age, but heralded a great leap forward for Soviet television. The Russians soon became the first nation anywhere (Canada will be the second) to use communications satellites as an integral part of their domestic television network. The first 'Molniya' communications satellite was launched in 1965. Within two years an initial network of twenty-four 'Orbita' earth stations were built up, mostly to the east of the Urals. The Orbita stations, close to such cities as Novosibirsk, Alma-Ata, Vladivostok and Magadan, pick up the pictures beamed to the satellite from Moscow and feed them into local networks. The initial batch of Orbita stations, which brought twenty million people within the range of television for the first time, were inaugurated as part of the celebrations for the fiftieth anniversary of the Revolution in 1967. The network has since been extended with another three stations, bringing into the fold remote cities like Anadyr on the Bering Straits, opposite Alaska.

Unlike the Intelsat satellites, poised at fixed positions over the Equator, the Molniya satellite goes loping round the earth in an oval orbit (it cannot be 'fixed' over the Equator as the television pictures bounced back would then miss most of northern Siberia). Thus Molniya does not provide cover throughout the twenty-four hours; instead it comes swinging in over Siberia twice a day. It is in range for about six hours at a time to relay the pictures from central television in Moscow. Each Orbita earth station tracks the satellite automatically as it passes by, catching the television pictures in huge dish aerials thirty-six feet across. To cope with the harshness of Siberian winters, the Orbita stations are all designed to withstand temperatures of minus fifty degrees centigrade and wind speeds of up to twelve miles per second. The Moscow and Vladivostok Orbita stations can send and receive pictures; the others can only receive.

The satellite network has also been expanded to embrace Mongolian Television in Ulan Bator, where an earth station opened in 1970. Mongolian television, incidentally, has a single channel on the air for about three hours a day, serving a few thousand sets. The Russians have talked of extending the Molniya club to the communist countries of Eastern Europe and even to Cuba. And when President Pompidou of France visited Moscow in 1970 the French earth station at Pleumeur Bodou on the coast of Brittany temporarily switched from its regular place in the Intelsat system and trained its antennae instead on the Molniya satellite to relay live pictures of the visit.

Obviously the Russians would like their Molniya system to be accepted eventually as a world-wide alternative to the Intelsat network for inter-continental television relays. Eino Repo, the Finnish president in 1970 of OIRT (the communist bloc's equivalent of the European Broadcasting Union) told me: 'Within the next five years the Russians will be offering a fully alternative system. It will be just as practical—and a shorter distance—for pictures from Japan to France to be relayed via Molniya over Russia as via Intelsat's Indian Ocean satellite.' Whether non-communist nations will actually leap at the chance of sending their pictures via a communist satellite, when they already have their own, is another matter.

Within the Soviet Union the state has organised television on two levels; at the top is 'central' television operating out of Moscow and then regional administrations for each of the fourteen republics. Central television is administered by the state Radio and Television Committee, whose seventeen members are appointed directly by the Council of Ministers. The chairman, who is the equivalent of the director-general or president of a broadcasting organisation in the West, is usually an important political figure. The post frequently seems to go to former ambassadors. Beneath him are four vice-chairmen—one each for radio, television, external broadcasting and engineering. Regional television follows much the same pattern, with the local Radio and Television Committee being nominated by the administration of each republic. All television is financed out of the state and regional budgets; there is no annual licence fee for owning a set.

But Moscow is the pacemaker. Of the four channels, each has its own distinct role. The first channel is the flagship. It is on the air for eleven hours every day, from nine o'clock in the morning until midnight, with a four-hour break in the afternoon. Most of the programmes it originates are seen throughout the Soviet Union—although not simultaneously because of the time zones. This is the general-interest channel that carries all the big news and sports events, plays and films. During the day, however, much of the time is given over to programmes on industry or farming. At Tuesday lunch-time, for instance, there is a farming programme that may show livestock breeding in Moldavia or the achievements of a new tea-harvesting machine in the fields of Georgia. Another daytime programme *Science in the Sunny Republic* reports from the Institute of Deserts in the republic of Turkmeni, near the Caspian Sea, about improvements in cotton growing in difficult climates.

Then an early evening show goes to a factory in the Urals to interview the local party committee secretary and the construction bureau leader about how they are achieving their planned targets and on the need for scientific and industrial progress in their factory. All kinds of workers come in for a special pat on the back. On 'Food-industry workers' day' or 'Fishermens' day' special documentaries review the progress of the industry and explain five-year-plan targets. The chairman of a regional fishery co-operative explains how his collective is exceeding their planned cod and herring target for the season. And on Sunday evenings in 'prime time' there is a concert for the workers of the sea, in which choirs from fishermens' collectives join national artists in a musical soirée.

The emphasis on self improvement is constant. Saturday lunch-time there is a series *Looking After Your Eyesight*. This is followed by a programme on Mongolian art. In the evening a documentary commemorates the fiftieth anniversary of the Mongolian People's Revolution, pointing out that 'with the 1960s the Mongolian People's Republic entered the final stage of building socialism. In the last five years alone GNP has increased by 160 per cent.' The North Vietnamese get their recognition too in a 'diploma' performance by Vietnamese students who are studying at the Moscow Circus and Stage College.

The main channel, many of whose programmes are distributed over the satellite network, is backed up in Moscow by the second channel concentrating primarily on the capital scene. This is really Moscow's own 'regional' channel, covering events of the day, local sports and including plenty of live coverage of concerts and ballet. The third channel, which is only on the air for three or four hours in the evening, is purely educational. On a typical Thursday evening in July 1971, for instance, its schedule began with an engineering lecture and then a German lesson. The rest of the evening included what were billed as 'popular scientific films'; the first was about various 'elixirs' of plant growth, the next explained the technique of super-imposing pictures in film and television, while the evening rounded off with a study of the intricacies of ice-skating.

Moscow's fourth channel is highbrow. It carries a heavy concentration of concerts, opera, folk-singing and talks by writers and scientists plus lessons in that favourite Russian pastime, chess. The programmes do not begin until 7.30 in the evening and normally last until 10.30. One evening may embrace a performance of Dvorak's Ninth Symphony, a documentary on gardening and a concert from the All Union Festival of Youth Songs, and the opera *Anna Snegina*, based on a lyrical poem about country life in Russia between the February and October Revolutions of 1917.

All this serious fare does not mean entertainment is neglected. *Pravda* and other publications often rebuke housewives for spending too much time watching variety shows. There is extended colour coverage of circuses and spectacular ice shows, sometimes going on for two or three hours at a time. A highly successful quiz, *KVN*, has two teams challenging each other to do impromptu skits based on the news. Old war movies (Russian made) abound, but the latest films are also shown immediately on television. One advantage of the communist system is that films do not have to make the cinema circuit for years until they are finally hived off to television. The newest productions can turn up on the blue screen and then go into cinemas later. Sport, of course, is covered very thoroughly. Indeed, the only regular programmes that the Russian viewer sees from outside the communist world are international soccer matches and ice hockey. In turn the ice-hockey on Russian television is the one event which draws plenty of viewers from outside the Soviet Union in Finland, where the regional station of Tallinn can be picked up.

However, a discreet survey of audience reaction to television in a Moscow suburb, which was published in the Soviet press in 1967, revealed considerable dissatisfaction with the amount of entertainment. Furthermore, it showed that many Russians wanted more travel films, as they felt cut off from the outside world. 'Above all people want less persuasion and more entertainment and there is a shrewd suspicion that it is being kept from them.' One person quizzed on the survey said: 'They are sly, those people in television. If there is a lecture on one channel, you can be pretty sure there's a round table discussion on the other.' (*The Times*, London, May 10th, 1967.)

Actually, the choice is not quite as severe as that. Most evenings between 8 and 10 entertainment can be found on at least one channel. The choice in Moscow, for instance, at eight o'clock one Tuesday in July 1971 was—U.S.S.R. soccer championships on Channel 1, a profile of a worker in a vacuum cleaner factory on Channel 2, a German lesson on Channel 3 and a new film, *Bracelet* 2, on Channel 4.

The programmes chosen for relay over the 'Orbita' satellite network are a rather mixed bunch. In a single day they may include a programme for amateur photographers, a children's story, a recital by David Oistrakh, football, a talk by an award winner of the Lenin Youth Organisation and a play about life on a collective farm. The satellite channel normally transmits up to twelve hours a day, with the majority of the programmes now being in colour. News goes over the satellite network at least twice every day.

News is frequent on all channels, except the educational one. The first Moscow channel has five broadcasts a day. Several of the news readers are women but, whether male or female, their style tends to be stiff and formal. The stories are often just bulletins from the Soviet news agency, *Tass*. If the Central Committee of the Communist Party makes any important pronouncement it will be read out in full, with long lists of the names of everyone attending the meeting.

The Soviet interpretation of what is and is not news differs markedly from the West's. A factory that exceeds its tractor output target is news; a plane crash is not. Human interest has low priority. Sometimes the news readers will say 'and now we go direct to Tashkent' as if some major story is breaking there.

However, up come pictures of a tractor sowing the first of the spring wheat that day. As one Western correspondent remarked, after viewing the news on television daily for four years in Moscow, 'there is no sense of occasion'.

When the three Soviet cosmonauts were killed by a cabin leak on re-entry in June 1971, it was six hours before Moscow television broke the story. Such dilatoriness in giving the latest space news has sometimes caused quite unnecessary speculation within the Soviet Union that something has gone wrong when, in fact, all is well. Although the Russians are now slightly more forthcoming with their television pictures of space flights, the Russian viewer has yet to be told in advance of a launching and see a live lift-off. But he has become thoroughly familiar with the regular chief reporter on space, Yuri Fokin, the amiable Moscow counterpart of Walter Cronkite. Undoubtedly, the Americans' openness with their space programme has forced some relaxation on the Russians. However, it is important to remember that the average Russian viewer has no idea of the lavish coverage afforded American space flights. He sees only short, thirty-second clips of film of American flights tucked away in the news. His own country's reticence, therefore, is not as obvious as it is to regular television viewers in the West. On the other hand, the hero's welcome accorded the Soviet cosmonauts on their return is always given massive coverage. The first Russian television I watched was in 1961 when all Moscow turned out to greet Yuri Gagarin on his return from man's first space flight; the Russians relayed the pictures through to Helsinki and then into the Eurovision network for all of Western Europe.

While home news on Russian television plays up Soviet triumphs, the troubles of capitalist countries are gloated over in some detail. Strikes, Vietnam War protests, riots in Northern Ireland are all shown to underline bourgeois decadence or repression of the workers. Soviet television not only has its own foreign correspondents but subscribes (and contributes) to Visnews, the international news film agency. A full daily round-up of world news film is thus available. News and comment are closely intermingled. It is always the 'aggressive Americans' in Vietnam. Russian television executives visiting Western Europe are sometimes staggered to find that news and comment there are usually kept apart. One leading television news editor, after visiting the BBC in London, finally conceded to his British host after watching the news for several nights, 'You really do keep comment out!'

Both news and current affairs programmes steer well clear, however, of any kind of controversy about the Soviet Union. The watchword is always '*bezkonflictnost*'—avoiding conflicting viewpoints. Laudatory detail has it over dissenting comment. Even in 'discussions' everyone reads carefully from prepared scripts.

This inflexibility naturally cramps television's style. Everyone is so wary not to step out of line that the results can hardly be sparkling. One Western observer of Russian television over several years summed it up: 'Slowness and lack of spontaneity are among the most marked weaknesses and spring from the fact that producers cannot make independent decisions about programme content.' (Kyril Tidmarsh, *The Times*, London, May 10th, 1967.)

Once any decision is taken at the top it is followed obediently. When radio and television were duly ordered by the Central Committee of the Communist Party to celebrate both the fiftieth anniversary of the Revolution in 1967 and the centenary of Lenin's birth in 1970 they went at it obsessively. For the Revolution's anniversary they prepared a documentary on each of the fifty years. Despite the detail possible in fifty programmes, embarrassing events and people like Trotsky were passed over without mention. A Russian television executive visiting London during the anniversary year remarked how difficult they had found it dredging up enough material for fifty programmes. He also said how interesting he found a British programme on the Revolution compared to the turgid ones at home.

For Lenin's centenary they went at it even harder. The tone was set by the deputy chief editor of Central Television, N. Ivankovitch: 'Television journalists are well aware of the honourable and responsible task entrusted to them by the Central Committee of the Communist Party of the Soviet Union, to provide complete and all round possibilities of satisfying the vivid interests of millions of television viewers in the Lenin theme. The most experienced and talented script-writers and editors, producers and tele-operators, political reviewers and artists are enthusiastically preparing television programmes devoted to the Lenin Jubilee.' (OIRT Journal, No. 4, 1969.)

This devotion resulted in thirty documentaries on places Lenin visited, including most of his childhood haunts, the headquarters of the October Revolution, Red Square and his study in the Kremlin. Channel 1 backed this up with a series *Your Leninist Library* designed 'to help the broad masses of working people to acquire a better and more comprehensive knowledge of Lenin's most important works'. Another series, naturally, was *They Met Lenin*, with memories trotted out by old acquaintances everywhere from Moscow to Helsinki and London. The children had *Stories about Lenin* and *Children of the October Revolution—The Grandchildren of Ilich*. That was merely the start. There were series on *Leninism—The Flag of our Epoch*, surveying the world-wide impact of socialism, *Lenin and the Party* about the development of the communist party, *Leninist Trials* and *We are Reporting to Ilich*—on his lieutenants during the revolutionary flight.

Amidst this deluge, Russian television has found little time for programmes from outside the communist bloc. Unlike the countries of Eastern Europe, where American, British and French films and television series are common, the Soviet Union has rarely taken anything from the West except news and sport. During the 1960s intermittent exchanges took place. The precedent was set in 1961 when Yuri Gagarin's return to Moscow after his space flight and the May Day parade were relayed live to Western Europe; in return the Russians showed the Queen at the Trooping the Colour in London that summer. Similar exchanges have taken place since—the Russians prefer swops to outright buying. They also initially agreed to participate in June 1967 in the multi-national *Our World* programme, which linked together by satellite the television services of five continents for a two-hour live look at the world. At the last moment, however, they quietly withdrew because of the tensions created during the Six-Day War just prior to the programme. But since then there have been signs of a more general thaw. The real breakthrough came in the summer of 1969 when Dennis Scuse, the general manager of BBC Television Enterprises, succeeded in selling the Russians the twenty-six-part *Forsyte Saga*, for a reported price of £10,000. This is the first—and only—drama serial sold to the Soviet Union from outside the communist bloc. (In the celebration *that* called for, Scuse and four Russians downed between them one bottle of Armenian brandy, a bottle of vodka, a bottle of champagne and a bottle of Vat 69.)

The Forsytes are an understandable choice for the Russians. Galsworthy has always been one of those authors, along with Charles Dickens, who is highly regarded in the Soviet Union. Many of his books have been approved by the censors for translation. Quite what the Russians made of the serial is another matter. After a two-year wait to put it out, the Saga started in July 1971 simply with a narrator speaking in Russian over the English voices. According to Western correspondents reviewing it in Moscow, the mixture was almost unintelligible. Naturally the Forsytes' picture of the class structure in Britain provided the Russians with a little useful ammunition. An article introducing the series in the weekly television magazine explained that 'the Forsyte family were the nucleus of bourgeois society, represented in England at the end of the last century and the first quarter of the present. Well-known features remain today.'

The Forsyte sale showed that the Soviet Union is very slowly becoming a more open market. A newly created Foreign

Exchange Studio, offshoot of Central television in Moscow, spent a reported £140,000 on foreign programmes in 1969. Thames Television in London sold the Russians *Now that the Buffalo's Gone*, a documentary narrated by Marlon Brando on the vanishing North American Indian. France's ORTF joined with Moscow television to re-create *The Battle of Moscow* from World War II. And from the United States CBS Enterprises exchanged *The Secret of Michaelangelo* and *Casals at at 88* for a prize-winning television film of the Bolshoi Ballet in *Romeo and Juliet* and a play *Blind Rain* from the regional television centre at Kiev. NBC sold *Profile of America, Homeland U.S.A.* and *The Vanishing 400*, a documentary on the changing character of high society in the New York and Washington establishment. The emphasis, clearly, is on culture or programmes—like the Thames documentary on the Indians—that do not show the non-communist world at its best. As yet, however, there is no sale for *Bonanza*, the biggest television hit in most other communist countries.

Perhaps *Bonanza* hardly fits the style of Soviet television. Gun-toting westerns were certainly not in the mind of the 23rd Congress of the Communist party which directed television, along with the other media, 'to mould a Marxist–Leninist outlook and promote the political and cultural development of all the Soviet people'.

14

Eastern Europe: Cowboys and Commissars

An old Humphrey Bogart movie on Saturday night, Peter Sellers capering about in *Only Two Can Play* on the midweek evening, Rupert Davies puffing hard on his pipe as *Maigret*. Television in London perhaps? Sydney? Rio de Janiero? No, East Germany. And the biggest fan club anywhere for *Bonanza*? In Poland. In the first two months of 1971 NBC supplied over five thousand photographs of the Cartwright brothers to *Bonanza* addicts there, compared with a modest two thousand in the United States. And the third largest batch of 750 went to Rumania, where the local cattle ranchers frequently write to the Cartwrights, care of NBC Burbank, for their advice on stock breeding.

Television in Eastern Europe does get bogged down sometimes in sermons on increasing tractor output but, compared with the Soviet Union, most of the satellite countries fit in a surprisingly high proportion of light entertainment, most of it from the non-communist world. Take just one week in Poland in May 1971; the films shown on the two channels of Polish television were from France, Italy, Britain, the United States and even Brazil. Saturday night there was a Joel McCrae western.

The art of the scheduling game appears to be to preserve a modest balance of programmes between East and West; naturally there must be slightly more programmes from communist countries than from non-communist. East German television, for example, selects two-thirds of its imported programmes from socialist states, one-third from capitalist. At any sign of pressure from the Soviet Union that a country is not toeing the communist line sternly enough, the Western (and particularly American) programmes are withdrawn overnight. Folklore or worker's discussions suddenly become the fashion. Rumania dropped *The Untouchables* rather sharply in the early summer of 1971 at the first rumblings of a political shake-up. Czechoslovakia also became abruptly closed to most Western programmes after the Russian clamp-down in 1968. Quite apart from selecting their programmes from all over the world, the Czechs had previously built up a fine reputation for the annual Prague Television Festival, which attracted a high class of entry from television services everywhere. The festival has continued since 1968 but, according to regular visitors, is a shadow of its former self.

Nowadays television throughout most of Eastern Europe is as commonplace as in the West. There are sixteen million sets, or one among every six people. Only Rumania trails significantly behind with one for thirteen. The undisputed leader is East Germany which, with four and a half million sets or one for every four people, is on a par with penetration in West Germany, Britain and Japan. Television in East Germany, in fact, has achieved the highest standard of technical and programming skills found anywhere in the communist world. Television producers in West Germany have to concede that productions of plays by Brecht or dramatisations of Thomas Mann's novels by East Germany's Deutscher Fernsehfunk are better than their own. As a drama producer in West Berlin explained: 'Although some of their plays stick too much to socialist realism, their attention to style results in first-rate productions.'

The East Germans, of course, are in direct competition with West German television just over the border. Every home in East Berlin and most throughout East Germany can watch television from the West. The rivalry has secured full government support, therefore, for Deutscher Fernsehfunk. They must keep pace. The East Germans, for instance, began colour television in 1969 some three years before any of their communist neighbours, but only a year or so after the West Germans started their switch into colour. And Deutscher Fernsehfunk's second channel is on every night of the week, while elsewhere in Eastern Europe there is still either only one channel or a second channel that functions just three or four evenings a week.

State control of television is absolute in all the communist satellites. Usually their organisation is similar to the Soviet Union's, with a State Radio and Television Committee appointed by the Council of Ministers. In East Germany there have been separate committees for radio and television since 1969. Normally, there is also a Broadcasting Council made up of representatives of the Council of Ministers, trade unions and workers in drama, journalism and other activities associated with broadcasting. Unlike the Soviet Union, however, television in Eastern Europe relies chiefly on annual licence fees for its income, rather than on a direct state grant. The fee is modest: in Poland and Czechoslovakia it is about £5 a year, in Hungary £8. Everyone supplements their income with a very limited amount of advertising; normally two or three blocks of five minutes between programmes in the early evening. The commercials, however, are too infrequent to make much real difference to budgets. In Czechoslovakia, for instance, they account for well under twenty per cent of television's income. Little hard selling goes on. The advertisements are really informing the public about a new radio, refrigerator or tractor, rather than pressing them to buy. The advertiser, after all, must not appear to be trying to make a profit but simply to serve the public need.

The overall character of a country's programmes reflects its degree of adherence—or lack of it—to the Moscow line. In Poland it seems to be a question of how much Western material they can get away with. Deutscher Fernsehfunk, on the other hand, despite those old Bogart movies, followed Walter Ulbricht's loyalty to Moscow. So there are documentaries like *Unknown Citizens* delving into the lives of the working people to reveal 'the poetry of a normal socialist day'. And the East Germans describe the two-thousand-mile long coaxial cable that links their television with that of the Soviet Union as 'a line of friendship'. Like the Soviet Union they have not yet succumbed to buying American entertainment series (as opposed to old movies). They are always playing up socialist achievement and are wary of buying programmes from any of their less hard-line communist neighbours if they are at all controversial. They were most reluctant to take programmes from the Czechs, for instance, during the two or three years prior to 1968, when Czech television was the most independent-minded of any communist nation. Since the Russians cracked down in Prague in August 1968, however, the East Germans have been busy making co-productions with them.

The expertise and wealth of television in East Germany also makes Deutscher Fernsehfunk much less dependent on importing programmes than most communist television services. Their main channel is on the air for ten hours every day; the second channel for four hours each evening, with most of the programmes in colour at the weekends. The first channel begins at 9.30 on weekday mornings and 8 on Saturday, but the mornings are taken up mainly with repeats of important programmes from the previous evening for the benefit of those working then—a practice common in television in all communist countries. (Whether many from the night-shift actually watched is doubtful; audience research indicates that most are asleep and only old age pensioners tune in.) In the evenings both channels carry an even blend of entertainment, sport, news and current affairs. Since the introduction of their second channel in the autumn of 1969, Deutscher Fernsehfunk have tried to give their viewers a reasonable choice. A dramatisation of Balzac's *Père Goriot* on Channel 1 is matched with sport on Channel 2, or a film contrasts with the Philippines National

Ballet. The exception is for news and current affairs. The main evening news is at 7.30 on both channels. Current-affairs programmes (as in West Germany) are usually matched against a serious documentary or cultural programme. Both sides of the border refuse to put light entertainment against current affairs; the viewer must watch the serious stuff or turn off.

The East Germans also share the West German passion for thrillers. Quite apart from importing the BBC's highly successful *Maigret*, *Airline Detective* and *Sherlock Holmes* series, they have produced plenty of what they call 'politically engaged criminal films'. One such three-part drama, *The Lady of Genoa,* unveiled a plot to steal an old master painting in West Germany. Along with the criminal fun and games, the play also knocked the unscrupulousness of the art market there. The crooks in the thrillers often turn out to be Western diplomats or millionaries from such right-wing dictatorships as Portugal.

The more serious drama is frequently drawn from the classics. A serialisation of Charles Dickens' *Nicholas Nickelby*, colour productions of *King Lear* and Shaw's *Androcles and the Lion* and a mammoth three-and-a-half-hour dramatisation of Dostoyevsky's *The Brothers Karamazov* spread over two evenings were the highlights, for instance, in the spring of 1971. Plays actually written for television, however, tend to take a more stereotyped, socialist line. One much publicised production, *Irena*, was about an 'encounter' between an East German mechanic and a Russian girl, Irena, who met while working on a building site. 'This encounter,' the producer explained, 'serves as an example of the unceasing promotion of friendship existing between the citizens of the German Democratic Republic and Soviet citizens.'

The theme of Soviet achievement pops up again and again. Deutscher Fernsehfunk made a documentary series *I Serve the Soviet Union*, and the four-part *Shield and Sword* on the Soviet Army during and after World War II. Regular documentaries during 1970 were devoted to travels through Siberia to see construction work there. A Saturday-morning series of lectures on 'socialist economy' contrasted its benefits with the ruthlessness of capitalism in the United States.

When the East Germans started their second channel in 1969 they emphasised that its aim was 'to educate highly cultured personalities with all-round interests and a firm class standpoint. It will help to satisfy better the growing intellectual-cultural demands of the working people.' They hoped that 'in the sphere of dramatic art efforts will be concentrated on productions promoting the role of German television in the formation of socialist state consciousness and in the creation of our socialist national culture.'

Polish television, in contrast, underplays socialism. The prospectus for their second channel, which opened in October 1970, stressed that the new channel 'will include encyclopaedic data as well as themes fostering the cutural and intellectual standards of our society. Scientific and technical broadcasts will play an important part.' No mention, however, was made of socialism.

Although Polish television lacks the resources of its East German neighbours—it had to get by with very rundown old studios and poor equipment until a new TV centre opened in 1970—its schedules are a rather remarkable medley of television from East and West. Along with *Bonanza* from the United States, the Poles have become devoted to *The Saint, The Baron* and *Randall and Hopkirk Deceased,* all purchased from British commercial television. The chief editor of television news in Warsaw suddenly dropped everything in the midst of a conversation with one British visitor in the summer of 1971 to say, 'Time for *Randall and Hopkirk Deceased*, we mustn't miss that.' As for *The Forsyte Saga*, 'That,' a Polish broadcaster told me, 'was rather like an earthquake.' The Poles ran each episode twice a week; the first time through with Polish narration over the English soundtrack, the second night simply the full English-language version. 'No one in Poland would answer their telephone while that was on,' said the broadcaster.

The difficulty, apparently, is maintaining an equal balance with programmes from the Soviet Union and other communist countries. There are no gripping drama series to be had from Moscow. The makeweights, therefore, tend to be Russian documentaries and educational programmes. Set against them, the choice from the capitalist world often seems remarkably refreshing. During May 1971, for example, the fledgling second channel put on both a Japanese and French evening, with all the programmes drawn from television services in Tokyo and Paris. Another night they had Ken Russell's television film of the life of Delius. The main drawback is the lack of foreign exchange, which inhibits the Poles from buying more programmes from the West. They are allowed a very limited quota, so their purchases have to be very selective. In the summer of 1971 they were carefully saving up their allocation to buy from Britain the rights to a new BBC drama series of six plays on Casanova, written by Dennis Potter.

The Poles' own popular series focus almost exclusively on World War II. The most widely shown wartime saga has been the adventures of a resistance hero *Captain Kloss*. The good captain, posing as an officer in the German Army, fights his way out of all sorts of traps every week. The series has been a hit throughout Eastern Europe; even in Sweden it won high ratings late on a Saturday night. *Four Men in a Tank and a Dog* scores with a humorous account of the exploits of a tank crew and their Alsatian, while *The Girls of Nowolipki Street* recounted what befell four girls, Frania, Kwiryna, Bronka and Amelka on that Warsaw street during the hostilities. 'We have a great nostalgia for that period,' a Polish actor told me; 'we slept somewhere different every night, never knowing what would happen the next day. Nothing exciting has happened since then.'

But it isn't all war games. Polish television has been able to draw on a lively theatrical and film tradition. Although they lack the resources to mount many large-scale productions themselves, their output during May 1971, for example, included Eugene O'Neill's *Long Day's Journey into Night,* a dramatisation of Hemingway's *The Old Man and the Sea* and Mozart's opera *Don Giovanni.*

The most ambitious project, however, is a Television Technical College developed jointly by the Ministry of Education, Polish television and UNESCO's Department of Mass Communications. Faced with a serious shortage of well-qualified technicians and engineers, the Poles have started to use television systematically to improve their technical education for adults. This technical university of the air puts out physics, maths and chemistry lessons in the late afternoon just after everyone gets home from the factory. This enables workers, who never had the benefit of a formal university education, to expand their understanding of technology. During the first year of the experiment, some 60,000 sent in for booklets to go with the television courses.

The Poles' toughest fight has been to keep their television service going with very antiquated equipment. Whatever the sparkle of some programmes, they have acquired a reputation for an erratic technical performance and constant unpunctuality. The director of programmes even took the leading page in the weekly TV guide in May 1971 to apologise to viewers for the 'lack of punctuality' and the frequent lack of co-ordination between programmes advertised and what actually went out. The trouble was, he explained, that people often started work on a programme *after* the time for its screening had been published, so if they hit any snags it simply was not ready when promised. 'And,' he complained, 'our equipment is far from satisfactory. Current investments can at best only smooth over the consequences of neglect for many years.' The problem, apparently, is that no one dreamed television would expand so fast, and a fateful decision was made ten years ago that existing cutting rooms and laboratories could cope with all television's requirements for the foreseeable future.

These hazards, however, have not prevented Polish television from taking a much more enterprising line in the last year or two, particularly since Giereck replaced Gomulka as party leader. The most noticeable innovation has been a programme called *Citizens' Forum*. This is a live hour and a half in which viewers can pitch questions at ministers and leading members of the Communist Party. The first two Forums in 1971 tackled housing and agriculture. Although questions may be sent in advance, there are sixteen telephone lines (one for each province of Poland) open to the studio for supplementary questions as the programme proceeds. Three outside broadcast units are also stationed in towns and villages to televise questions live. The programme, which has been created at the suggestion of the communist leadership, not the television service, is an attempt to improve communications with the people. Many of the questions, apparently, are not known in advance. According to Polish-speaking Western broadcasters who have seen it, the questions are often very tough. Ministers have sometimes been quite taken aback and, lacking good briefing, have stumbled in dodging the issue. Politicians in communist countries are much more accustomed to speaking from prepared scripts. Up till now they have not had to get used to the rough and tumble of the live television interview that is part of every politician's life in the West. Consequently they often fumble.

No doubt they will shortly have to learn. The *Forum* idea is spreading rapidly in Eastern Europe. Hungary had it a couple of years before Poland. The pioneer, however, was Czechoslovakia. There the programme was a vital part of the new air of independence that flowered on television briefly during the Czech 'spring' of 1968. Indeed, television really showed the way to the new style of socialism that evolved in Prague that year. The renaissance was due largely to a lively and intelligent man, Jiri Pelikan, who was director of Television in Czechoslovakia from 1963 to that fateful August of 1968, when the Russians invaded. Pelikan now lives in exile in Rome, while Czech television has shrunk back into a new dark age. Several writers and commentators of that period are in prison.

While the flexibility lasted, however, Czech television was an example of what can be achieved in a communist society. Not only did the international reputation of the service increase as some lively programmes began to win prizes at television festivals everywhere, but the Prague Television Festival itself, with Pelikan as a genial host, became a notable event.

I asked the exiled Jiri Pelikan what he had set out to do. 'My conception of television,' he said, 'is that it is a powerful means of democratisation. In a Greek democracy the leaders could address everyone assembled in the main square. We cannot get that intimacy now, but television does enable the leaders to speak to everyone in their home. So to start with, television can make everyone much better informed. But it can also democratise the culture of a country. Previously only an élite went to the National Theatre, the opera or the ballet in Prague; now television can make their productions accessible to the people.'

The cornerstone of his policy was to try to persuade politicians to open up on television, to subject them to questions and interviews, instead of letting them read prepared statements. A regular hour-and-a-half live *Forum* was started in which ministers and leading experts on travel, housing, defence or wages were confronted with viewers in the studio to debate the issue. The programme, therefore, went one stage further than the Polish *Forum* because it actually included discussion instead of politicians simply fielding questions. Such frankness appalled President Novotny, who complained that television was going too far and discrediting government policies. But the public response was enormous. The sight of people challenging politicians on issues like commuter trains and buses was a breath of fresh air. Each programme produced a vast mailbag, which was reviewed in a half-hour sequel the next week. What also came out was that several ministers were totally ignorant of subjects which they were supposed to control. Without a civil servant to prompt them they simply floundered. 'It was a great scandal,' said Pelikan. 'Here were ministers revealed on television as being quite incapable of government.'

While ministers had to be more candid on the screen, television news also became more objective. The censorship was eased, until early in 1968 Alexander Dubcek told Pelikan that television news could exercise its own judgement in deciding what to report and how to say it. The candour of the news was, of course, one factor that most incensed the Russians. But, for a few months before they stepped in to control it, its credibility with the Czech public soared.

Pelikan also sought to raise the standard of drama on television as part of his determination to bring good theatre to the masses. He insisted that his television cameras went out and about to many of the eighty theatres in Czechoslovakia. A competition was started among the theatres for the best production suitable for television. But above all he sought to persuade Czech writers to contribute. Previously, playwrights had been very nervous of trying their hand at a TV play because of censorship. This tended to be tougher on television (as a mass audience saw it) than in the theatre (with a few hundred audience). After 1966, however, censorship eased considerably. Pelikan considers that between then and 1968 he conjured up twenty good plays especially for television. He also launched a very successful crime series *Sinful City of Prague*. One episode, *Lady Macbeth from the Suburbs*, won several international prizes.

He attempted also to persuade the Soviet Union to let him show some of the best drama productions put out by their own regional television stations. The trouble was, he found that the Russians always wanted to let him have plays or documentaries about Lenin instead. 'I told them that was quite unacceptable to our viewers,' he said. 'I wanted good plays from Estonia.' The Russians paid no attention.

But Pelikan did succeed in increasing the activities of Intervision—the communist counterpart of Eurovision. Intervision is an offshoot of OIRT (Organisation Internationale Radiodiffusion et Télévision), the broadcasting union of the communist world. Actually, OIRT is a direct descendant of the pre-war International Broadcasting Union to which most broadcasting organisations throughout the world belonged. In the tense period of East–West relations in the late 1940s the communist countries tried to use this Union (by then renamed Organisation Internationale Radiodiffusion)—OIR, purely for propaganda purposes. So the Western countries, at British initiative, formed their own European Broadcasting Union, took over the old OIR administrative centre at Geneva and the technical centre in Brussels, while the rump of OIR itself moved to Prague. When television came along OIR added the T for Television. Then in 1960 OIRT, seeing the growing success of Eurovision, set up its own version, Intervision, co-ordinated from Prague. Although Intervision is sometimes rather pompously described as 'international television in the service of Marxism–Leninism', it is essentially a clearing house for programme exchange just like Eurovision. The original members were Czechoslovakia, Hungary, East Germany and Poland; the Soviet Union, Bulgaria and Rumania joined the club later. Finland is also a member of OIRT and Intervision, as well as being an active member of the EBU and Eurovision. The maverick Yugoslavia, of course, has thrown in her lot with the EBU.

The prime job of Intervision has been to co-ordinate the exchange of news and sport within the communist bloc. Sport accounts for more than forty per cent of Intervision transmissions, news for over twenty per cent. A news exchange, similar to the Eurovision pattern, started in 1964. Initially the exchange was once a week, but it was gradually built up to a daily exchange by May of 1970. Every morning each Intervision member must telex to Prague by 10.15 an outline of the stories on which they can offer film that day. The Intervision Programme Co-ordination Centre in Prague then distributes a complete story list, again by telex. During the afternoon there is a final story conference over the permanent Intervision sound circuit to confirm running time of each clip of film and details of its contents. The actual exchange, with all the television services linked together on a vision circuit, begins at 4.25.

The daily story-list emphasises the communist bloc's distinctive understanding of what makes news. Consider its make up for November 3rd, 1970. The Soviet Union offered film of five items; a session of the Supreme Soviet to ratify a new Soviet–Finnish treaty; preparations in Moscow for a military parade; the arrival in Moscow of an Italian parliamentary delegation; an international geological exhibition in Moscow; and what was described as the reunion of a Soviet soldier and a Czechoslovak teacher, who first became acquainted twenty-five years before—at the end of the war. The reunion was clearly an exercise to underline good Soviet–Czech relations—a theme also reflected in Czechoslovakia's own story suggestions that day. They had film of a 'festive meeting and performance in a Prague theatre, marking the anniversary of the October Revolution' and the opening of the 'month of Czechoslovak–Soviet friendship'. Their suggestions concluded with the unveiling of a Lenin memorial in Prague. East Germany proposed 'decorations and promotions of new officers and generals attended by Walter Ulbricht', the return from Hungary of the vice-chairman of the Council of Ministers. Poland came up with the visit to Warsaw of the West German Foreign Minister, Walter Scheel.

The Intervision countries usually exchange about eight stories a day; the total in 1969 was 2,432 stories. A special review of the kind of story on the exchange made in June 1970, revealed that of the 224 items, 109 were 'social-political', 46 cultural, 61 science, technology and economy and 8 sport.

The Intervision exchange is, of course, also linked to the Eurovision news exchange. The full Intervision list is telexed from Prague to Geneva, so that Western countries can pick up any items. Similarly, Intervision gets the Eurovision list. The Intervision headquarters in Prague also listens to the Eurovision story conference on a sound circuit but, at the insistence of the West Germans, is not allowed to participate in actual discussion.

Broadcasting liaison between East and West is now much easier than it was in the frosty period immediately after the forming of the European Broadcasting Union and OIR's departure for Prague. The real thaw began, appropriately enough, in a Finnish sauna bath.

A special EBU–OIRT summit meeting was arranged in 1963 in Helsinki, which was obviously a suitable meeting place, as the Finnish broadcasting organisation belonged to both bodies. The presidents and vice-presidents both of the EBU and OIRT attended. When the conference began relations between the two sides were simply very correct and business-like. After a while, however, a group of four leading broadcasters from East and West, including Sir Hugh Greene, director-general of the BBC, Olof Rydbeck of Sweden and Sikorski of Poland left their staffs to get on with the detailed discussions and accepted an invitation to use a private sauna in Helsinki to which the Finnish cabinet repairs when it is deadlocked. As Sir Hugh Greene recalls it: 'We went into the sauna at 270° Fahrenheit several times. Those sessions transformed our relationship into one of warm and lasting friendship.' Television relations between East and West have been better ever since.

Although Eurovision and Intervision now work together daily, tension crops up again from time to time. The toughest test was the invasion of Czechoslovakia in 1968. Intervision took a great deal of film during the next few months that had been shot by cameramen from western agencies and was offered on the Eurovision exchange. Ostensibly the film was for the news, but it is widely believed that it was used primarily to help security forces identify demonstrators. During the same crisis the Russians also offered to the West film purporting to be their side of the invasion. In fact it showed military manoeuvres earlier in the year—the leafless trees revealed the fraud.

Intervision is also reluctant to pay for coverage of American moon-shots. They argue that pictures of Americans landing on the moon are good propaganda and should be free. Eurovision, which handles the satellite relays to Europe on such occasions, does not agree and insists on a share of the satellite charges. Actually, most communist countries show only clips of the moon landing in their news bulletins; only Poland, for example, went for extensive live coverage of the first manned landing on the moon in 1969.

The news is naturally the most tightly controlled aspect of all television in Eastern Europe. News and comment intertwine. The Egyptians never open fire across the Suez Canal; it is always 'the imperialist, aggressive Israelis'. Reports from the West usually come late in the bulletins. Even the surprise announcement of President Nixon's visit to Peking in July 1971 came near the end of the news.

However, in several of the communist countries it is difficult for television to suppress stories completely. Not only do many people listen to Radio Free Europe, The Voice of America, West German radio and the East and Central European Services of the BBC, but television from the West penetrates into millions of homes. Over the last decade a spirited confrontation has been maintained between television at East and West.

15

Television Jumps the Wall

FROM the top floor of the fourteen-storey television centre of Sender Freies Berlin (Radio Free Berlin) on Masurenallee in West Berlin there is a fine panoramic view out over the entire city. At that height the grey wall topped by spikes and barbed wire that divides it so unnaturally in half is hardly visible. For a moment it seems one city again. The television producer pointing out the landmarks echoes the sentiment. 'Down there you see all of Berlin. We are here to serve the whole city and I make my programmes for *all* of Germany.' For television, in fact, the Berlin Wall does not exist. Where people, newspapers, magazines and books cannot pass freely, television flits daily with impunity.

Every home in East Berlin and for eighty miles all around in East Germany can watch the programmes of Sender Freies Berlin just as easily as the two channels of East Germany's own network. And vice versa; West Berliners have the same chance to see television from the East.

Television has made not only the Berlin Wall but the Iron Curtain everywhere within the range of its transmitters, totally transparent. Right up beyond the Arctic Circle, Norwegians in Kirkenes and Russians in Murmansk can watch each other's programmes. In Helsinki the Finns turn to Russian television coming in from Tallinn across the Gulf of Finland to watch the ice-hockey games, while the people of Tallinn are avid fans of *High Chaparral* and *Bonanza* from Finland. Further south,

Austria is ringed by the communist bloc so that television from Vienna radiates easily to Czechoslovakia, Hungary and Yugoslavia. Indeed, the Austrians are in the curious position (like the broadcasters in West Berlin) of having more viewers for their television in surrounding nations than within their own domain. The seven million Austrian viewers are quite outnumbered by the four million Czechs, three million Hungarians and three million Yugoslavs who can regularly watch two channels of the Austrian network ORF. As a leading Austrian television commentator, Hugo Portisch, put it: 'We are rather like an aircraft carrier penetrating into foreign waters.'

The communists, of course, hasten to point out that this is very much a two-way traffic. 'Millions of people, especially in West Germany, West Berlin, and also in Denmark and Southern Sweden are able to receive the transmissions of the Deutscher Fernsehfunk,' the official guide to East German television explains. 'Thus, many television viewers are able to receive truthful accounts of the peaceful economic and cultural socialist construction of our republic.'

The most spirited battle to present each side's version of the truth in this television wall game is between the divided halves of Berlin. Elsewhere the electronic eavesdropping from one country to another is primarily to enjoy the normal programmes put out for the local viewers, especially sports or special events not shown in the communist world. Every Easter, for example, many Catholics in Eastern Europe turn to Western television to see the Pope's annual blessing in St Peter's Square in Rome. Communist television does not carry programmes about religion.

In Berlin, however, television is actively concerned with scoring points off the other side; programmes are tailored with full awareness that they may be viewed by millions in another regime. 'We are an outpost, a lighthouse,' said a news editor at Sender Freies Berlin (SFB), 'and we believe that three-quarters of the homes in the East look at us regularly.' The station is one of nine comprising the West German ARD network.

The majority of the programmes it beams out over the Wall are those of the full ARD network, so that East Germans can watch identical television most of the time not only to West Berliners but to all West Germans. SFB itself contributes eight per cent of the programmes of the ARD network. This share of the programming is calculated basically on the 750,000 television licences in West Berlin. Strictly speaking, these would only entitle the station to a five per cent programme contribution. However, in recognition of the city's unique political and geographical position, giving it access to another 4·5 million sets in East Germany, it is allowed eight per cent, plus a cash bonus of £2·5 million a year from the other ARD stations to help underwrite its operations.

SFB makes the most of what it sees as its responsibility to its East German viewers. Every year, for instance, the station produces eight or ten plays for the full network. 'Our aim is always to produce plays about the problems around us in Berlin today,' Dr Erich Proebster, SFB's drama director told me. 'We aren't interested in classical or historical plays—we leave those to the other ARD stations.'

During 1970 four out of SFB's eight plays were actually set in Berlin. *Kinderehen* (Child Weddings) focused on the problems created by so many West Berliners marrying much younger than is customary elsewhere in Germany. *Tatort Berlin* was a thriller based on the unique dilemma facing a criminal on the run in West Berlin. He is trapped in the city, as if on an island, for East Germany is all around. The play included a scene in which gangsters, bent on murdering their leader, tempted him close to the Wall. A shot rang out from the East Berlin side and the gangster fell dead. The authorities took it for another escapee shot coming over the Wall; in fact the gangsters had set it up with a gunman in East Berlin. Along with these plays the West Berliners also broadcast a colour production of a dramatised version of Alexander Solzhenitsyn's novel, *Cancer Ward*, knowing full well that it is banned throughout Eastern Europe.

The desire to needle the East Germans authorities even influences the planning of SFB's schools programmes. 'We are a window on the free world,' said Paul Wallnisch, the director of schools television. 'Our programmes are aimed partly at the children and teachers in East Germany. We realise they cannot watch officially in the schools, so we screen them in the late afternoon between 4 and 4.30 when they can watch at home. We have shown, for example, a series of twelve lectures on politics and economics designed to teach children here in West Berlin about their country, and for those in the East to see how capitalism really works. We also put on plenty of travel films in the geography lessons, because children in the East cannot travel easily to see for themselves what other countries are like.'

When the building of the Berlin Wall in August 1961 so abruptly cut off East Berliners from half their city, SFB responded at once with a special transmission of three and a half hours of programmes every morning to help them keep in touch. This early session, aimed entirely at the East, is supported by both the German networks, ARD and ZDF. The actual broadcast is handled by the Berlin station which culls the output of both networks, and adds some original material of its own. The main television news magazines *Panorama*, *Report*, *Monitor* and *ZDF Magazine* are all repeated on this morning round-up, which also includes fresh news bulletins and a daily review of the international press. Twice a week, on Wednesdays and Saturdays, SFB compiles a local magazine show on the latest news and gossip from West Berlin. To ensure that every possible home in East Germany can watch this morning session, it is also relayed by transmitters of other ARD stations in Hamburg, Frankfurt and Munich, who are nearer the border to achieve blanket coverage.

The East Germans are naturally fully aware that millions of their people watch this 'propaganda'. At one time viewing of West German television was illegal, but nowadays the authorities do little to check it. They have tried marketing sets that receive only their channels, but most families find a friendly electrician who can usually adapt the set to receive the West. The law does say that it is illegal to pass on information gained from foreign television, but this is interpreted to mean it is all right to watch in the privacy of your home, though unlawful to invite a friend in to view with you.

The director-general of Deutscher Fernsehfunk in East Berlin keeps a special colour set in his office tuned to Sender Freies Berlin, so that he is alert to what they are showing and can decide, if necessary, how to respond. Providing, of course, that he knows what line to follow. During the Russian intervention in Czechoslovakia in 1968 he could see SFB alive with almost non-stop reports and film of Russian tanks moving into Prague but, lacking orders from Moscow, could not report the crisis at all on his own network. East German television made no mention of the invasion for twenty-four hours, so viewers got all the news from SFB over the Wall.

Normally, however, the East Germans try to get their own back every Monday evening in a half-hour programme, *Der Schwarze Kanal—The Black Channel. Black Channel*, say the East Germans, 'deals with the transmissions of the revanchist West German television.' The host, ever since the programme began in 1960, has been Karl-Eduard von Schnitzler, an adroit East–West sniper. After avidly watching the news magazines on West German television, von Schnitzler culls from them material that he either denounces as propaganda or uses to demonstrate the iniquities of the capitalist system. For good measure the programme is repeated twice in the daytime later in the week. When *Black Channel* first started the West Germans countered for a while with their own disclaimer of von Schnitzler called *Red Uptake*, but eventually decided that he was not worth answering; the less said about his programmes, they felt, the better.

Plays and documentaries on East German television also seek to attack Western decadence. One favourite target has been Axel Springer, the powerful West German publisher. In a dramatised documentary *I—Axel Cäsar Springer* the East

Germans explained that 'the basic reactionary developmental tendencies in West Germany since 1945 are reflected in the life of Springer, in the rise of this publisher to be a dangerous manipulator of opinions and a leading personality in the psychological war.' They also pulled off a rather neat coup in 1968 by getting a long interview in West Germany with Dr Walter Becher, spokesman and self-styled 'President in Exile' for the Sudetenland Germans, whose homeland is now part of Czechoslovakia. Dr Becher, apparently, was under the impression that he was talking to *West* German television reporters, because they said simply they were from German television. The remarks he made, thinking they were for West German consumption, naturally provided ideal propaganda for East German television intent upon showing aggressive policies in the West.

How many West Berliners regularly watch East German television is not known. Most people I asked in West Berlin simply dismissed it as 'very few' and hurried on to talk of something else. But they will agree that the East German television's 'Little Sandman', who bids the children good night and scatters dream dust for them each evening at seven o'clock, is much more sympathetic to most tots than his West Berlin rival. 'The trouble is he comes during an advertising period here,' a West Berlin producer complained, 'and in the West we don't spend money on programmes during the advertising periods.' So most Berlin children are sent happily to bed each evening by a communist lullaby.

But those commercials opposite the sandman also make their impact in the East. Many viewers there watch the commercials avidly to keep abreast of the latest consumer goods and gadgets, which they ask friends and relatives to bring over during the rare occasions when visiting across the Wall is permitted. And when a West Germany brewery started advertising its beer on television, the sales of a brewery in East Berlin, which has the same name, soared by forty per cent.

Beyond the beer sales, the real significance of this constant exposure to West German television has been to make the use of the medium in East Germany the most professional to be found anywhere in communist countries. Even the weekly television guide is lavishly produced, with many colour photographs. It is laid out almost identically to the most popular TV magazines over the border. Programmes are often close copies of their Western counterparts. The news—*Aktuelle Kamera*—which comes on at 7.30 each evening has the same crisp style as *Tagesschau* which starts half an hour later on the West German ARD network. While television in several communist countries is technically poor, with 'snowy' screens and frequent breakdowns, the East German service is acknowledged, both in East and West, as technically first-class. They enjoy not only the biggest budget in Eastern Europe but have studios at Berlin-Aldershof that are the envy of several Western European nations. And, along with the Soviet Union, they are the only communist countries to have switched to colour. Their colour channel opened in October 1969 and two years later was putting out more hours of colour each week than even the Soviet Union. Like the Russians they have adopted the French SECAM colour system, which effectively segregates them from West Germany with PAL colour. The disparity of colour systems, of course, is a hurdle in the television viewing over the Wall; a SECAM set will not show PAL colour. The eavesdropping, therefore, will have to be done on old black-and-white sets.

Although SFB in West Berlin no longer bothers to respond to von Schnitzler's *Black Channel*, two other ARD stations in Hamburg and Cologne maintain a special team, Ost-West Redaktion, who make sixteen programmes a year on life in East Germany. Their task is somewhat hampered by the fact that the East Germans will not allow West German television reporters and cameramen in. Film, therefore, has to be obtained in a roundabout way. Usually the Ost-West team just monitor television in the East and film items that interest them direct from the screen. Occasionally there is more subterfuge. When a Danish TV crew were permitted to make a film on life in East Germany on the implicit understanding that they would not then sell it to the West Germans, the Ost-West men just filmed the Danish programme off the screen and used it anyway.

The West Germans have no qualms at such open picture stealings. 'Occasionally the East German broadcaster's lawyer writes and accuses us of piracy,' admitted an Ost-West editor in Hamburg, 'but we just write back and say "You do the same thing."'

While West and East German television snipe at one another over the Wall and pirate each other's pictures, the Austrians in Vienna normally have a more formal relationship with their neighbouring communist television services. Vienna is the official co-ordinating centre hooking together Eurovision with the Intervision network centred on Prague. Every morning, for instance, the list of news stories from Eastern Europe on which the Intervision countries can offer film that day is relayed down from Prague through the Eurovision co-ordinator at ORF in Vienna to Eurovision headquarters in Geneva. Then in late afternoon ORF videotapes the Intervision film over the circuit from Prague and feeds it to all Eurovision members. Similarly, news and sports from the West are routed through Vienna to Prague and into the Intervision network stretching from East Berlin to Vladivostok.

This regular liaison between Vienna and Prague, which began in September 1965, enabled news editors and technicians in both cities to establish a good working relationship, which paid an unexpected dividend in August 1968. The Russian invasion of Czechoslovakia that month to snuff out the Czech 'spring' suddenly transformed their daily link into the last precious lifeline of Czech freedom.

The pictures of Russian tanks rolling into Prague during those summer days of August 1968 must rank as one of the most moving events yet recorded in television's short history. This was the first invasion ever to be seen as it happened in living-rooms around the world. That remarkable coverage was achieved through the cool co-operation of a handful of Czech and Austrian producers and engineers. Long before the Russians moved in there was an informal understanding between the two sides that in an emergency, if normal circuits were cut out, ORF would only have to direct its antennae to certain prearranged locations in Czechoslovakia to pick up pictures from mobile transmitters. 'All we had to do when the invasion started was to push the button,' said an Austrian engineer. 'We knew where the secret Czech transmitters would be from hour to hour.'

Dodging down the side roads with their mobile transmitting flotilla, the Czechs stayed one jump ahead of the invaders, while their cameramen, covering the scene in Prague and other cities, raced with their film to constantly changing rendezvous. Their call sign was 'Free Television Station of Prague'. The Austrians, having locked on to the clandestine signals, kept on monitoring them, even after one or two mobile units went off the air abruptly with a quick warning from a technician: 'We have to give up now, goodbye.' On one occasion the Czechs actually left the camera on in a small town studio after their departure, so that the Russians moved in and took over the studio without realising they were on television.

As the Russians gradually eliminated transmitter after transmitter, Czech and Austrian cameramen kept the film coming by driving to the border and smuggling their film through the checkpoint. In seven days in August 1968 Austrian television relayed, through the Eurovision network and by satellite to the United States and Japan, almost ten hours coverage of the invasion. And those same pictures, of course, were seen by millions in Czechoslovakia, Hungary and East Germany, who had only to tune to their Western station to see the whole invasion. As Horst Jancik, the Eurovision co-ordinator in Vienna, said: 'We screened every cough we could get from Czechoslovakia. I don't know if it helped the Czechs, but it was something we had to do.'

That week all eyes were on Czechoslovakia. Normally, however, it is the Czech and the Hungarians who gain a wider view of the world by watching Austrian television's two channels. Many Yugoslavs also look in but, since their own television service is closely allied to the Eurovision network of Western Europe anyway—and carries many American and British series —the appeal of the alternative Austrian channels is much less. For the others, however, ORF, Vienna, is a precious glimpse of the West. In Czechoslovakia, Prague itself is on the fringe of reception, but the large cities of Bratislava and Brno enjoy good pictures. In Bratislava so many aerials tuned to Vienna have proliferated on the rooftops that they are known locally as 'the Vienna woods'. The Austrian signal even radiates, in good conditions, as far as Budapest. 'We are high on the eastern end of the Alps, on the roof of Central Europe,' Alfons Dalma, the chief editor of ORF said in Vienna, 'so our pictures are carried great distances. Reception is possible even 150 miles beyond our borders. It's quite startling to be stopped on the streets in Prague or Budapest by strangers who say, "You're Dalma. Thank you for your programmes." We are a major source of news for these people.'

Since many of these viewers over the Iron Curtain speak some German, they have little difficulty in following programmes and they learn the schedules by purchasing the Austrian communist daily paper, which is permitted to circulate in Eastern Europe.

What they see is a cross-section of the best and worst of Western television, ranging from concerts by the Vienna Philharmonic to the local *What's My Line* and *Lassie*. The Austrians, unlike the West Berliners, are not constantly trying to trim their programmes to the tastes of their external viewers; this is Austrian television for the Austrians. Actually, since Austria is a small nation ORF has to rely on importing forty per cent of its programmes. They work closely with the second German network, ZDF, with whom they mounted sixty co-productions in 1971. Some shows, like the popular German crime detection series *File on Case XY Unsolved,* go out simultaneously in West Germany and Austria. These mingle with American and British imports—*The Man from Uncle, Daktari, The Virginian* and *The Avengers.*

'We are the showcase for the Western world,' said the television commentator Hugo Portisch. 'We notice time and again that Poles, Bulgarians or Russians, who cannot see Western television, are far more surprised by the capitalist scene when they come to Vienna, than the Czechs or Hungarians, who can. The visual impact of watching the ordinary day by day television of another country is enormous—much more than listening, for example, to the Voice of America Radio, which everyone knows is propaganda. The real advantage here is that the Czechs and the Hungarians see the programmes we make for our own people. They see all the arguments in our current affairs programmes and documentaries.'

Of course Austrian television's position as a shop window does earn it some special favours in the West. When I was in Vienna, Hugo Portisch and Sepp Riff, one of the best-known cameramen in Austria, had just returned from the United States where they had made a documentary, *Missiles for Peace*, about the American missile defence systems. The documentary was to be shown to coincide with the SALT disarmament talks in Vienna. The Austrian team had obtained special White House permission to film inside the Minutemen rocket silos in the United States—the first foreigners ever permitted to shoot there. The Americans doubtless felt that the documentary was an excellent way of showing millions in Eastern Europe their side of the arms race.

Over the border, the Czech and Hungarian authorities regard these Austrian incursions with mixed feelings. For several years the Czechs were officially forbidden to watch Austrian television but everyone did anyway. 'The problem was that a good aerial was necessary,' a Czech broadcaster told me. 'If you went to your local TV repairman he would say, "I cannot put it up for you because the state forbids it and I work for the state." Then he might add, "But I stop working for the state at five o'clock and if you like I'll do it for you afterwards." ' The formal prohibition was finally withdrawn in early 1968 as part of the Czech 'spring'.

How much Austrian television influenced that 'spring' is hard to say. Some Austrian television commentators believe that daily viewing of their channels helped to stimulate a more refreshing climate in Prague. Certainly Jiri Pelikan, the lively director-general of Czech television from 1963 to 1968, who contributed so much to the liberalising of television there, occasionally invoked the ease with which Austrian television could be seen in Czechoslovakia as a bargaining counter in winning some of his battles. One of his difficulties, Pelikan told me afterwards, was getting the necessary foreign exchange from the government so that he could buy from Eurovision coverage of important soccer matches in Western Europe. The Minister in charge of broadcasting was always reluctant to allocate the hard currency. 'Right,' Pelikan would threaten, 'I shall announce to our audience that we cannot show the game as we are not given the foreign exchange. You know that every Czech will then watch it on Austrian television. You are making football a political issue.' Faced with this mild blackmail the minister often relented.

Any impact, however, was short-lived. Pelikan, as has been said, was replaced after the Russian intervention and now lives in exile in Rome. Several distinguished television writers and commentators are in prison. The Russians, in reimposing their will on the Czechs in 1968, made it quite clear that 'priority is to be given to control over the mass media, which must serve the cause of socialism. It is agreed that the mass media shall discontinue anti-socialist pronouncements.' So Czech television is back in a new dark age. The news, which was so frank for a few months in 1968, is now once again a stiff statement of the official party line. What has not been curbed is the Austrian television signal still going through to the 'Vienna woods' on Czech rooftops. Those tall aerials are a reminder of how transparent the Iron Curtain has remained.

THE ARAB WORLD AND ISRAEL

16

The Search for Arab Unity

On a summer night in Beirut a little astute fiddling with the tuning of a television set conjures up the programmes of no less than five nations, spanning between them the whole confused spectrum of Middle East politics. Quite apart from Beirut's own three channels, it is possible to get Syrian television from Damascus, Jordan television from Amman. Egyptian television from Cairo and, of course, Israeli television from Tel Aviv. This mosaic out of the Arabian night is made possible by a phenomenon known as 'tunnelling' or 'ducting' which occurs at that end of the Mediterranean in the summer. The television signal, instead of radiating out into space as usual, is trapped by certain atmospheric conditions so that it 'tunnels' along close to the earth over great distances. The Cairo signal, for instance, comes in quite strong to Beirut almost five hundred miles away. The frontier hopping thus achieved has enhanced television's role as a propaganda weapon, not only within the Arab world itself but in the Arab–Israeli conflict. Both in Jordan and Israel, television programming is dominated by the desire to outwit the rival station over the border. The Jordanians study Israel's schedule before making up their programme patterns; the Israelis in turn try to get their own back by putting on popular programmes in Arabic to conflict with the news on Jordan television. Paradoxically, both sides have relied heavily on American advisers in establishing their television services.

No one makes any secret of the fact that television is there primarily as a propaganda weapon. 'Jordan television was set up purely as a political tool,' admitted one of the Americans closely involved in the establishment of the Amman station. 'The idea was to win a large audience both in Jordan and Israel with popular programmes and then slip the propaganda in between—the sugar-coated pill.' The station even came equipped with a special helicopter landing pad, so that King Hussein could always arrive in an emergency and be seen instantly over the air. In Cairo Egyptian broadcasters were equally frank. 'In Arab nations television is the sure way to rule people,' said one of the directors of the United Arab Republic's television service. 'This is how the people get to know and love their leader. Everywhere I go in the Arab world I tell the rulers to "learn how to be loved by your people through that marvellous machine".' 'Nasser himself,' he went on to point out, 'was not really known by our people until we had television. Before that they had only *heard* him (he tweaked his ear) on radio, but after 1960 everyone *saw* him.' The television coverage was meticulously prepared. Cameramen had precise, written instructions on how to film the President if he was making a speech. 'We showed him full face, concentrating on his eyes,' one of the men who drafted the rules told me. 'If he mopped his brow or coughed that was cut out. Everything was done to give him dignity.'

The lesson has not been lost on other Arab leaders. As television has spread throughout the Arab world, from Morocco, on the shores of the Atlantic, to tiny sheikdoms like Qatar and Abu Dhabi on the Arabian Gulf, it has been carefully installed under the wing of the Ministry of Information (the one exception is Lebanon, which has private commercial stations). In countries like Iraq, television has become a regular political weapon to demonstrate the realities of power. The Iraq leader, General Kassem, was actually shot in the television station in Bagdad in 1963 and the cameras turned on his body and those of his colleagues. Since then the director-general of Iraq television has made something of a speciality of conducting 'spy confessions' on the screen—a macabre *This is Your Life*, in which hapless prisoners confess their misdeeds. In the autumn of 1970, after fourteen Iranian soldiers were caught in Iraq during a border clash, they were paraded before the cameras to confess their guilt as the television commentator intoned, 'Inevitable death awaits all those who seek to enter Iraq illegally.'

Syria and the Sudan have used the same technique to drive home to the viewing public the success of a political coup. After the military take-over in the Sudan, in the summer of 1969, extra television sets were distributed to group viewing-centres so that the public could watch live coverage of a 'people's tribunal' set up to impeach the rulers of the previous regime.

Television is not always so grim. From day to day there is the conventional round of Western and Arabic popular programmes. In Cairo you can take your choice of *The Virginian*, the *Adams Family*, *The Avengers* and *The Fugitive*, all with Arabic subtitles (dubbing is too expensive); in Amman *Perry Mason*, *The Saint*, *Marcus Welby, M.D.* and *Ben Casey* are all active. But most Arab nations—and Israel, whose television must be considered in the same context—are placing increasing emphasis on television as an educational tool not just for schools, but for improving agriculture, health and hygiene. A prospectus for Sudan television even envisages 'programmes transmitted for social change, such as the abolition of harmful social traditions, superstition, sorcery and the combating of tribal and minority squabbles'.

'In an under-developed country we must make the maximum use of television in all forms of education,' said Sad Ladib, the director of programmes for U.A.R. television. 'We propose, during the next two or three years, to turn our second channel over completely to education for schools during the day and for adults in the evening.'

The Egyptians have long been the pace-setters for television in the Arab world. President Nasser realised the potential value of the medium in moulding the Egyptians into a strong, united nation in the late 1950s and, in one of the first agreements signed with the United States after John Foster Dulles refused to provide funds for the Aswan Dam, approved the Radio Corporation of America (RCA) installing a television network in Egypt. So while the Russians helped with the Aswan Dam, the Americans provided television. Since the work went ahead at the time of Egypt's abortive union with Syria, RCA also installed television in Damascus as part of the same deal.

The Egyptian installation was on a grand scale. The facilities are quite unequalled anywhere in the Arab world today; indeed, few other nations anywhere have quite so much apparatus. Eleven television studios are housed in a vast, circular building crowned by a 28-storey tower-block on the banks of the Nile. The largest studio is the size of a full-scale theatre and is equipped with a revolving stage and five cameras; even the most sophisticated television stations in Britain, West Germany and Japan don't have anything much bigger. No less than 2,500 programme staff and 1,000 engineers are required to run this establishment—rather more people, as far as I can make out, than are employed in broadcasting by all the other Arab nations put together. Almost half the staff are women, who seem to be treated equally with men on the television scene: they direct programmes, read the news and even do the sports reporting. I watched a half-hour sports review in which a woman interviewer happily questioned footballers and basketball players. And a half-hour weekly programme on architecture, painting and sculpture has been written and directed for many years by the wife of one of the chief television news editors.

Ambitiously, the Egyptians started almost from the beginning with three television channels, putting out programmes for a total of twenty-four hours every day. The first channel, covering virtually the whole country, concentrated on popular entertainment, news and sports. The second channel, reaching Cairo and the Nile Delta (in fact the majority of the set-owning population) carried minority programmes and imported serials, while the third channel, just for Cairo, was given over entirely to foreign programmes—mainly British and American—with news in English and French. The third channel, aimed at the diplomatic community, European expatriates and tourists, was clearly something of a luxury but, as long as President Nasser lived, it was kept on. The broadcasters I talked with all said they felt it was too much of an indulgence for a relatively poor country and that it was imposed on them 'from above'. Shortly after President Nasser died in 1970 the third channel stopped broadcasting; but it restarted in October 1971.

The two channels for the Egyptians themselves now operate for seven hours each a day, with some sixty per cent of the programmes locally produced. Imported entertainment programmes have always come primarily from Britain and America, but Egypt's increasing involvement with the Soviet Union has naturally been reflected in more programmes from communist countries. During my stay in Cairo, you could take your choice of a Bulgarian series about a resistance hero, a Czech documentary on industrial safety (a very solid programme) and Hungarian ballet. Although the Egyptians are proud of producing a high proportion of their own programmes, they choose to put on a wide selection of imported shows. 'Cairo has always been a cosmopolitan city,' said Sad Ladib. 'We believe in taking programmes from all over the world.'

There is no reliable audience research to demonstrate whether home-grown or foreign programmes are the most popular, but the Egyptians can draw on the best pool of talent for the whole Arab world. Small television stations starting out in Kuwait, Saudi Arabia and the Sudan have had virtually no tradition of acting or variety entertainment to build on. Cairo, however, has always been the artistic and film capital of the Arab world and television has benefited accordingly. 'We are the Hollywood of the Middle East,' said an Egyptian producer proudly.

Along with variety shows featuring the best Arab entertainers, Egyptian television has created everything from detective serials to soap operas. The most popular when I was there was about the foibles of an ageing Cairo schoolteacher and his family, who had an endless succession of visits from their relatives living in remote villages of the Nile Delta. These productions are ideal, not only for home consumption, but for television stations in other Arab countries, and Egyptian entertainment can be seen nightly on screens from Rabat to Khartoum and Algiers to Aden. Egypt's ability to supply programmes is especially important for nations like Syria which, for political reasons, decline to take the normal package shows from Britain or America.

The Egyptians, understandably, are delighted at this state of affairs and use it to propagate their views widely. They are skilled at playing off one nation against another. If Kuwait, for instance, declines to take one of their programmes, then they offer it free to Iraq television for its station at Basra, which can be received clearly by everyone with a set in Kuwait. If it proves popular, the Kuwaitis come along after a while and agree to run the show, as they are not anxious for their own viewers to make a habit of watching Iraq television. Nevertheless, several Arab nations, especially Saudi Arabia and the small sheikhdoms down the Arabian Gulf, are notably reluctant to take too many Egyptian programmes because of the inevitable indoctrination slipped into them. Saudi Arabia refuses categorically to take any Egyptian productions.

But, propaganda aside, the Egyptians are trying to use television to best effect in overcoming problems of illiteracy and disease in their own country. Their television service, to its great credit, has developed schools, health and agriculture programmes on its own initiative often in the face of indifferent or complete lack of co-operation from the responsible ministries. Although schools have sometimes refused to help in discussing curriculums, the broadcasters have gone ahead anyway in putting out two hours of secondary-school-level language, physics and mathematics programmes daily. In 1968, U.A.R. television embarked on a special project to overcome illiteracy by organising some three hundred viewing groups nationwide to watch a nine-month reading course. The experiment had mixed success, because of the administrative problems involved and lack of set maintenance, but at least the attempt was made. Now, in the seventies, senior Egyptian broadcasters are determined to build on this past experience in gradually shifting their second channel entirely to education.

The difficulty, however, is that after more than a decade television in Egypt is still not a truly mass medium. Despite the early encouragement given it by Nasser and attempts to establish community viewing-centres, television is essentially for the middle and upper-class—who are probably literate anyway. There are only 600,000 sets for a nation of 34 million people; for the majority a television set is still too expensive. Moreover, only one-third of the villages have electricity, so that television is often almost unknown outside the towns. 'Television here isn't really serving the people,' said Hamdy Kandil, one of Egypt's best-known television commentators and managing director of the Arab States Broadcasting Union. 'The peasant doesn't see it.'

But that is not to decry Cairo's position as the most influential television centre in the Arab world. No other Arab nation can match either its programme output or its relative wealth; U.A.R. television has a budget of around £4 million a year, sustained by an annual licence fee of £6·25 and a limited number of commercials which yield about £400,000 a year. Most other Arab countries have to get by with less than half a million pounds a year from all sources.

The sole challenge to Cairo comes from Lebanon, where Beirut has developed as a rival production centre for Pan-Arabic programmes. Lebanon has the only purely commercial television in the region, which has been established and run with considerable help from outside. There are two stations: Compagnie Libanaise de Télévision (CLT), which has extensive French backing, and Télé-Orient, which is partly owned and managed by the London based Thomson Television International (TTI). CLT operates two channels, one broadcasting in French, English and Arabic, the other exclusively in French. And it works hard to maintain the French influence in Lebanon. Indeed, the French-language channel is almost an arm of France's own ORTF; it receives seven hours of programmes free from ORTF each week, and no commercials are permitted to interrupt them. CLT's other channel shares many of its programmes with Télé-Orient, under an arrangement of joint networking and combined advertising sales, which came about when the two companies decided there simply was not enough advertising in Lebanon to sustain two fully competing stations. The total commercial revenue available for all three channels is a mere £1 million a year, and all sales are co-ordinated through a single company, Advision. This co-operation, however, has not prevented Télé-Orient from developing a highly profitable sideline of its own in syndicating Arabic programmes to many countries. Télé-Orient's success arises partly because Beirut is a cosmopolitan city that naturally attracts entertainers to its casino and night clubs, but more because, unlike the U.A.R., its programmes are not trying to put over a political line. As a commercial station, Télé-Orient is concerned with popular entertainment for mass audiences; the resulting programmes are welcomed by other Arab television stations that are always wary of the message infiltrated by the Egyptians. 'We are a-political,' said Harold Jamieson, Télé-Orient's General Manager, 'and we've succeeded in selling our programmes to every Arab country. This year (1971) we'll earn about £250,000 through sales.'

Télé-Orient's programmes are carefully conceived to avoid giving any offence in Arab countries, particularly Saudi Arabia, which adopt a high moral tone towards sex or violence. The Saudi Arabians have taken to television very slowly. When their stations in Riyadh and Jeddah were first set up by NBC International, they were most reluctant for women to appear on the screen—even wearing a veil. But, as the country had absolutely no acting or entertainment tradition to fall back on for programmes, it had to import them. That has meant slowly adopting a more tolerant attitude to women. They can now be seen without the veil, but they must be very correctly dressed at all times—mini-skirts, for instance, are forbidden. Adultery is frowned on, as is stealing or any kind of violence, unless the culprit is seen to be punished.

Télé-Orient has taken all this into account and, consequently, has become a major source of programmes for Saudi Arabian television. The most widely distributed are variety shows featuring the top Arab singers like Sabah, but Télé-Orient tackles anything from situation comedies to a series on the lives of the great Arab philosophers. Operating from one very cramped studio, into which they somehow squeeze half a dozen sets at once, they can turn out a half-hour drama in a day at a cost of about £600. These productions may not be very polished or sophisticated but they rate far higher with the local audience than imported programmes. Télé-Orient, for example, put a comedy show in Arabic against *Bonanza* (with Arabic sub-titles) on CLT on Monday evenings and get more than double the audience.

Since they pay their way by advertising, both the Beirut stations concentrate heavily on popular programmes and, apart from CLT's specialist French channel, have little time for education or minority programmes. Although they are the only television outlets in the Middle East not under the direct control of the local Ministry of Information, they tread warily to avoid upsetting the Lebanese government. From time to time direct censorship is imposed, but normally the stations censor themselves.

Beirut's location enables its programmes to be seen regularly —even without that summer-ducting phenomenon—in Syria, Jordan and Israel. The sales promotion for the stations even boasts the fact that advertisers can be sure of reaching 135,000 homes in 'Palestine'. But the Lebanese stations have never been involved in the intense rivalry that exists between the stations in Jordan and Israel.

Jordan's television station, just outside Amman, which was completed at a cost of half a million pounds in 1968, is regarded as one of the best equipped in the Arab world. The studio facilities were designed to enable the Jordanians to make plenty of local programmes both for viewers in Jordan itself and in Israel. Originally, the Jordanians had invited the BBC to help them in the organisation of the station and training of staff, but the British lost to Radio Television International (RTV), a New York-based organisation that has long specialised in advising on the establishment of radio and television in developing countries.

The Jordanians and their American advisers hoped that the station would be an important propaganda weapon, but events have somehow blunted its thrust. To begin with, during the Six-Day War a fine new television mast and transmitter that the Jordanians were about to instal in Jerusalem fell into Israeli hands. Happily for the Israelis, the plans on how to erect it were packed in the captured crates of equipment and, in no time at all, the Israelis had it all assembled and hooked into their own television service.

After the war, the delicate situation in Jordan between King Hussein and the Palestinian guerrillas also made the station tread carefully. It played safe wih *Here's Lucy*, *Ben Casey*, *The Fugitive* and *Perry Mason* rather than deal in controversial local shows.

However, they did make a remarkably realistic twenty-six-part drama series about the guerrillas. Several of the actors were truly members of the *fedayeen* and everyone, quite naturally, used live ammunition. Indeed it was often hard to discern whether skirmishes were for television or for training. One morning an American adviser driving out of Amman to the television station suddenly came upon a guerrilla roadblock; putting his foot down, he drove through it and fled at full speed. The guerrillas came tearing after him in a Land-Rover, gesticulating wildly. They caught up with him as he got to the television station and surrounded his car. It turned out to be the 'actors' trying to stop him on the road because they needed a special microphone he was carrying. The only trouble with the series was that, by the time it was finished, King Hussein had begun his drive against the guerrillas' challenge to his authority and the programme could not be shown. Other Arab countries also showed remarkable reluctance to buy it.

The high level of American series sustaining Jordan television had one intriguing side effect on Israeli television. Many Israeli viewers began to tune in to Amman to catch the latest American shows. Israeli television, which began originally as a purely educational service and only eased reluctantly into general programmes, had to respond with more popular programmes.

The Israelis, in fact, have had quite a time trying to dodge programmes from Arab countries. Apart from the strong Jordan signal, the ducting in summer means that Egyptian television can be received in Tel Aviv. In an attempt to avoid these foreign incursions the Israelis decided in 1970 to switch over to UHF television (Jordan, Egypt and Lebanon are VHF). At the same time, however, they try hard to seduce large Arab audiences with their own programming. Since 1969, they have put out two hours of popular shows in Arabic early each evening aimed not only for Arabs still living in Israel but at refugees who fled from the west bank of the River Jordan in 1967, and at Jordanians themselves. From time to time they even resort to showing old Egyptian films to woo the Arab audience.

Israeli television itself, however, has had a somewhat chequered career. The whole notion of television was firmly rejected until the mid-1960s; Ben Gurion was implacably opposed to it as long as he was Prime Minister, since he felt that Israel had to give priority to more important tasks. Finally, an Instructional Television Centre under the Ministry of Education began daytime programming in 1966. The attraction of entertainment, however, that could be picked up from Jordan, Lebanon, Egypt and even Cyprus eventually forced Israel to respond with some popular programmes. The Israel Broadcasting Authority started general programming in the summer of 1969 and extended this to a daily service later that year. There was great argument for a while on whether television could broadcast on the eve of the Sabbath. The government tried to prevent it, but an enterprising private citizen took the issue to the Supreme Court, which ruled in favour of television on the Sabbath Eve. The national network is now given over to the Instructional Television Centre from 8 in the morning until 6 in the evening and to the Israel Broadcasting Authority from then until 11 at night. But progress has been erratic. One director of television departed in the summer of 1970 and his successor lasted barely eight months. At the same time, a proposal to introduce commercials to help out the service's miniscule budget was vetoed at the very last minute by the Israeli Prime Minister, Mrs Golda Meir, on the grounds that advertising on TV would 'foster conspicuous consumption'. 'Our television,' conceded an Israeli journalist, 'is constantly in a rather precarious state.'

The development of television in Israel has, nevertheless, caused great debate in all the Arab countries. The Arab League considered the possibility of jamming the Israeli signal, but ruled it out as technically impractical. They decided, instead, that all Arab countries should help Jordan with contributions of free programmes. Most Arab countries, however, chose to ignore developments in Israel in their own programming. The one exception is Kuwait, which regularly puts out a report on the Israeli scene: *Know Your Enemy*.

Kuwait television is one of the most advanced in the Middle East, for the simple reason that the country is so small it can be blanketed with one transmitter, while the profits accruing from oil comfortably sustain the high costs. Moreover, the majority of the population can afford a set; Kuwait has almost 100,000 television sets—one for every five people, compared to one for

very fifty people in Egypt, or one in every three hundred in
he Sudan. Originally, Kuwait got television through the
magination of the local RCA salesman and without the official
pproval of the ruling sheikhs. The RCA man was anxious to
ell TV sets; there was no TV, so he just went ahead and
tarted his own station, using imported programmes. Later the
overnment took over. Soon two modern studios were built
nd by 1970 Kuwait was putting out seven hours of TV a day
vith more than half the programmes locally produced. Kuwait
vas also the first Arab country to instal an earth station, en-
bling it to pick up live pictures, from the Indian Ocean satel-
ite, of moon-walks and sports events. Most other Arab nations
till have to wait to receive film a day or two later. Plans were
oing ahead in 1971 on a £14 million project to give Kuwait
hree colour-television channels—one with popular pro-
rammes, one cultural and the third educational. Every school
n Kuwait is being equipped with a special room for audio-
isual teaching, complete with television set and cassette player.

Kuwait television has also branched out in the Arabian Gulf
n managing the station at Dubai, the little sheikhdom in the
Trucial States, which is one of the world's great gold and
vatch-smuggling centres. To match Kuwait and Dubai, the
ther sheikhdoms along the Gulf have also installed television.
Previously, the only station along the Gulf had been run by
n American oil company at Dhahran for its employees and
everal sheikhs had installed enormous antennae to pluck
Bonanza, like a mirage out of the desert air. Abu Dhabi
nd Qatar had their own television by 1971, while Muscat and
Oman, finally emerging from centuries of feudal rule after a
oup in 1970, was busy negotiating for a station. With virtually
o local talent to draw on initially (Qatar only has a population
of 80,000), these stations inevitably run almost solely imported
programmes from America, Cairo and Beirut. There is a
narked preference for Beirut's Arabic output along the Gulf,
because the station managers fear the disguised propaganda in
the most innocent seeming Egyptian shows.

The Egyptians, of course, are not alone in seeking to use television to promote their cause. The Americans, the French, the British and the Japanese are always anxious to provide both technical and programme advisers to fledgling television stations in any developing country of Asia or Africa. Having a hand in television is a very good way of maintaining a sphere of influence. Embassies of many nations are always delighted to dole out free 'tourist' and other films to television stations that cannot afford to buy all their programmes on the open market. The French are particularly adroit at this; they seek to maintain a sphere of influence in television in all their former colonies. We have noted already ORTF's assistance to the French-language channel in Beirut; equal ties are established along the North African coast with Morocco, Algeria and Tunisia. These countries all take a high proportion of their imported programmes from France. Educational television in Tunisia, for instance, has been co-ordinated and paid for by the French. And a special division within ORTF devotes itself to studying their requirements. They judiciously select programmes to match the spirit of the regime. 'If we have a pro-monarchy programme we try to sell it to Morocco,' said ORTF's liaison man with North Africa, 'if it's anti-monarchy we try Algeria.'

These North African countries also have close links with the European Broadcasting Union and are consequently much more integrated into the European television scene than most of the Arab world. Morocco is hooked into the Eurovision network across the straits of Gibraltar, Algeria is linked via Majorca and Barcelona, while Tunisia is connected through Sicily. This enables them not only to take all Eurovision programmes live but to participate, if they wish, in the Eurovision news exchange. Tunisia, for instance, joins the European story conference every morning and takes almost all the news items offered. These three Arab countries also tried a limited live programme exchange between themselves for a month at the end of 1970.

The real breakthrough, however, will be to link these North African countries, at the western end of the Mediterranean, with Libya, Egypt and beyond. For potentially, if individual political differences can be overcome, there is a natural network to be developed embracing all 120 million Arab-speaking people from the Atlantic to the Arabian Gulf. Indeed, along with the Spanish-speaking countries of South America, the Arab world represents an ideal basis for interchange of programmes between nations with a common language and culture.

This is one of the targets of the Arab States Broadcasting Union (ASBU), which was established in Cairo in 1969. Within two years, all the major Arab nations, except Morocco and Tunisia, had joined this newest of the broadcasting unions. Although European broadcasters are inclined to view the union as a purely political association to further the Arab cause, it undoubtedly makes considerable broadcasting sense. Previously, the Arab countries of North Africa had close associations with the EBU, while Egypt and some other Arab nations of Asia belonged—and still do—to the Asian Broadcasting Union. Yet in practical terms the Egyptians, for example, have little common interest with broadcasters in Japan, New Zealand or the Philippines, who also subscribe to the ABU. An Arab States Broadcasting Union, therefore, is a logical development. The main distinction between the new ASBU and the EBU—or the ABU—is that the ASBU is clearly an intergovernmental organisation, while the others pride themselves on being associations of broadcasters. The ASBU makes no secret of its political links. 'We are created within the framework of the Arab League,' said Hamdy Kandil, the managing director of the ASBU in Cairo. 'Of course we are under the influence of governments—but you show me broadcasters who are not in some way. We are a natural union sharing a common culture and language.' The Union states that one of its main tasks is 'making known the nature, aims and aspirations of the Arab nation and carrying out the objectives of the League of

Arab States Charter'. But together with this political goal, the Union proposes not only to encourage the interchange of programmes between Arab countries but to co-ordinate all their requirements in the same way that the EBU handles its members' needs at major news or sporting events. The ASBU plan to open an office in Beirut for the joint purchasing and marketing of programmes and hope to establish an Arab Television News Agency. Their most ambitious project, looking ahead five or six years to the late 1970s, is for a communications satellite for the Arab nations that could be used primarily for educational television. A preliminary report, prepared by UNESCO and the International Telecommunications Union in 1971, stated that complete television coverage of several Arab nations, notably the Sudan, Saudi Arabia and Algeria would be prohibitively expensive by conventional microwave networks; an Arab satellite could do the job.

But the real necessity before any firm satellite plans are made is for all the Arab countries to agree on a strong commitment for educational television. At the moment, as the UNESCO–ITU report pointed out, existing television facilities are being under-used for educational television. Only when they are used to capacity, and all the Arab countries agree to accept common educational programmes, can a satellite really be worth while. The Egyptians, naturally, are great campaigners for the satellite and the ASBU for, as major producers of television programmes, they stand to gain most. But for that very reason, the essential agreement may be hard to achieve. As Télé-Orient in Beirut has shown so clearly, what most Arab nations really want to pick up from anyone else is nice, innocuous entertainment; they prefer to do the propaganda themselves.

ASIA

17

Wasteland into Fertile

A FEW miles out into the country beyond New Delhi our driver spun the jeep off the road down a narrow dirt track. For a while we bumped along past fields ghostly in the full moon and then, by a low pile of haystacks, turned into a walled farmyard. Half a dozen black Indian buffalo were dozing in one corner. We parked by them and stepped out across the dusty compound towards a group of perhaps twenty men sitting or squatting on the ground before a twenty-three-inch TV set, in a small open porch in front of the farmhouse. The men were wrapped in blankets to ward off the chill of the December evening. One of them took occasional satisfying pulls at the long stem of a hookah, another was busy writing notes in an exercise book. The men belonged to the teleclub of the village of Chattarpur and they were all engrossed in the 'prime-time' show—*Krishi Darshan*—a half-hour agriculture lesson. The programme, which goes out from 7.30 to 8 three nights a week, demonstrates the scientific techniques of farming and encourages farmers to make the best use of fertilisers and insecticides. Almost every farmer in Chattarpur turns up to watch. Tonight the programme began with a short film about a woman who was running her own poultry farm near Delhi, then it went on to explain the latest bank credit facilities available for farmers and finally turned to the spraying of sugar-cane with insecticides. Everyone watched with deep fascination.

'We relate these agricultural programmes exactly to the

farming calendar,' said the television producer from All India Radio, who had guided me to the village. 'If it's sugar-cane planting time, then our programme shows exactly how it should be planted and protected from diseases.'

The village headman, in whose farmyard this community TV watching took place, told me how much the programmes really helped the farmers in the village. 'It has changed all our farming,' he said, 'I used to plant one crop a year, now I find I can take three crops a year off my land. We no longer plant our wheat three or four inches deep, television has shown us to plant it only one inch into the soil. We had heard these things on the radio, but that was only sounds, on television we see exactly the best way to plough or to spray insecticides.'

For these farmers in Chattarpur and in eighty other villages near New Delhi that also have teleclubs, television, for once, is not a wasteland, but a medium that can help transform waste into fertile land. Although television in India is still in its infancy, its potential for educating a nation, not only to read and write but in agricultural skills, social welfare and family planning is already being explored.

By day All India Radio's television service puts out two hours of schools programmes, which are seen by twenty thousand children in four hundred schools around New Delhi; in the evening most of its three hours of programmes from 6.30 until 9.30 are devoted to education or information, with the occasional lightweight English film. These initial experiments, limited to the New Delhi area, have been painfully slow; there has been little expansion in almost ten years, but India's Prime Minister, Indira Gandhi, is finally beginning to encourage television as one possible way of helping to solve the country's massive problems of illiteracy and poverty. Before becoming Prime Minister she was Minister of Information, where her portfolio included All India Radio. The first-hand experience gained there convinced her that television must be developed. Progress is still tentative. Until 1971, All India Radio's television service reached only a twenty-mile radius around the capital of New Delhi. There were a mere twenty thousand privately owned television sets plus a few hundred others at village teleclubs and in schools—in a nation of six hundred million people. More recently stations have opened at Bombay and Shrinagar, while others are planned for Madras, Calcutta and Lucknow. Yet it will be a couple of decades before television in India becomes the mass medium it is in Europe, America and Japan. The simple cost of the television set is still at least two months' salary for many upper-middle-class people; for the millions of India's poor it is more than their income for a year.

The possible short cut to television as a method of mass education in India is a satellite, beaming pictures directly down to five thousand community receivers scattered in villages throughout the sub-continent. The project is a joint venture between the Indian Atomic Energy Authority and NASA, in the United States, under which NASA will launch two Application Technology Satellites (ATS) during the early seventies, each equipped with a VHF–FM transmitter capable of relaying one television and two radio channels. The Indians will provide all the programmes, transmitting them up to the satellites from a ground station the Atomic Energy Authority is building at Ahmedabad; the satellites will bounce the pictures back to the community receivers scattered in villages throughout India.

This experiment, which was initiated by Dr Vikram Sarabai, the director of India's Atomic Energy Authority, will be a crucial test on how effective satellites can be, not only in India but throughout the developing countries, both in educating villagers when no integrated schools system exists and also for building a national identity.

'We hope that by providing both entertainment and education of a high standard on television, we can produce a genuine improvement in rural life,' Dr Sarabai explained, 'and that way we may reduce the attraction of migration to our overcrowded cities. The potentials are truly staggering for improving India's agriculture, wiping out illiteracy and uniting isolated villages.'

This satellite project could switch on television in Asia. With the very notable exception of Japan, it does not yet exist there as a mass medium; there are probably more people who have never seen it than those who have. Even when television does become a mass medium, it is likely to fulfil an educational rather than an entertainment role throughout most of Asia. In India, Malaysia, Singapore and Iran this is already the priority.

Singapore has what is widely regarded as one of the best educational television systems in the world, with a high degree of co-ordination between the television teachers and the schools. Programmes are specifically tailored to meet weak points in the conventional syllabus. And in Iran the government actually bought out, in 1969, the existing commercial television network, which had been run for several years by the family holding the local Pepsi-Cola bottling concession; they are now extending the coverage to provide primarily an educational service throughout Iran.

Asian television is not, of course, entirely harnessed to the alphabet or the plough. In Bangkok you can watch *Bonanza*, *Mission Impossible* or *Peyton Place* with live dubbing into Thai as the story unfolds (or turn down the sound on TV and hear the English soundtrack on FM radio); in Hong Kong *The Man from Uncle, The Flying Nun* and *Marcus Welby, M.D.* are all speaking fluent Cantonese on the Chinese channels. *The Lucy Show* seems to be on all the time whether you are in Singapore, Karachi or Manila; *Ironside* travels just as widely, around what the trade in the Far East calls 'the Sampan Circuit'.

The prices paid around the Sampan Circuit for these programmes often hardly justifies their distribution. Malaysia, Singapore, South Korea and Taiwan, for instance, pay only £20–£30 for a half-hour episode. Yet every country that I visited in Asia was at pains to explain at once how much less they relied on package programmes nowadays; instead they are all pressing ahead with local programming, despite shoe-string budgets. In Pakistan the normal expenditure on a local half-hour programme is about £60 to cover all costs of writers, actors and incidental expenses. To save a little money they never have television there on Mondays. And throughout most of Asia television is still limited to four or five evening hours.

Coverage rarely extends outside the main centres of population; microwave links creating nationwide audiences do not exist (always excepting Japan). The real problem, of course, is money. Governments cannot afford to finance television services themselves; there are too few sets to make any worthwhile revenue from licence fees. The only alternative, therefore, is commercial television. Sir Charles Moses, secretary-general of the Asian Broadcasting Union explains: 'Television in most Asian countries can only be financed by advertising, but that does not mean a free-for-all. I think the best combination is a public broadcasting organisation earning money from a limited number of commercials. You must control the ads—don't let them control you.'

Whatever the precise formula, no government in Asia these days is likely to let television develop independently; all of them are anxious to keep it strictly under their own control. In India it is part of the Ministry of Information. In Pakistan, where television began in 1964, the government has a fifty-one per cent stake in the commercial Pakistan Television Corporation. The secretary of the Ministry of Information is chairman of the board of directors, while the managing director, the finance director and the director of programme administration are all government appointees. Until 1970, when Pakistan was under the direct rule of a President nominated by the army, television simply avoided any political coverage at all. This policy was relaxed only during the elections in 1970 to allow each of the fifteen political parties equal time.

In Thailand the public relations department of the Ministry of Information runs one commercial station and supervises the programme of another, while the army has two channels of its own.

The Thai Army's television station, HSTV, is unique. The

chief of the programming department, Tawon Chueyprasit, is a fully fledged colonel of the Signals Corps, who spends his mornings on more conventional army assignments and the afternoon supervising television. Resplendent in his olive-green army uniform with three gold stars on the shoulder, the colonel explained that the army originally went into television because they felt their signal corps should be fully conversant with this new medium of communications; they also thought it might be useful for training soldiers. Moreover, on manoeuvres or in battle, television could give commanders a view of action right up at the front. They quickly discovered, however, that the expense of running TV was far more than the army could afford. 'So,' said the colonel cheerfully, 'we became a commercial station.' HSTV now operates one black-and-white and one colour channel in Bangkok showing *The Andy Williams Show*, *Bonanza* and *The Saint* along with several rather charming local soap operas. Their most popular show is *Pipop Mujjurag*, about the 'King of the Hill' to which all Thai souls go when they die. The news department is run, very appropriately, by army intelligence. Just to keep up its army image HSTV still tucks in one military programme a month, normally explaining how to combat the communist guerrillas who are infiltrating Thailand. As the colonel said, 'Everything is aimed against communist insurgence.' The whole operation, apparently, is remarkably profitable so that the signals corps is one of the most popular branches of the army to join. The true profits are a well-kept military secret but, according to one officer-turned-programme-executive, they have been as high as £250,000 a year. 'But perhaps,' he said, 'you had better not write too much about the profit.'

In Hong Kong the control of television by the British authorities is more subtle. The worry is not so much programme content, as limiting the viewers. The policy is that the programmes should *not* be seen by people in communist China just a few miles away. The delicate diplomacy of keeping this toehold on the Chinese mainland apparently dictates that the

Chinese should have no grounds for complaining that their population are being bombarded with Western propaganda. There isn't any written rule about this,' said a Hong Kong broadcaster, 'the government just arranges things so that our television is sealed off from China.' For ten years all television in Hong Kong was closed-circuit cable.

The British company, Rediffusion, started a closed-circuit English-language commercial channel in 1957, which has developed into the world's largest cable system. Rediffusion added a Chinese channel in 1963 and by 1971 more than 110,000 Hong Kong homes were hooked directly into their cables. This closed-circuit network ensured no viewers over the border in China but, in 1967, the Hong Kong authorities relaxed enough to allow the establishment of a conventional commercial television station, TVB, with English and Chinese channels; the English channel is christened Pearl, the Chinese is Jade. Although all the directors of TVB are local businessmen, NBC and Time-Life from the United States and Anglia and Thames from Britain hold shares in the station. Its transmitters, however, are very carefully positioned to give good coverage to Hong Kong itself and also limited reception in the Portuguese colony of Macao just across the Pearl River, but preclude reception within mainland China. Programmes are subject to censorship in case they might give offence to China; but the censors are normally reasonably benevolent. A forthright Yorkshire Television documentary on the twenty-year struggle for China was passed without query. Local political issues are ignored by television, a decision based on the theory that Hong Kong as a British Crown Colony has no party politics. Coverage of Church services is expressly banned in case they appear to be 'advertising' Western religion, thus giving offence to the 3·5 million Chinese in the colony.

Just across the border in China itself, television is still recovering from the cultural revolution, which shut it down completely for many months. Not that it was a very going concern even before the Red Guards came along in 1967.

Although the Central People's Television Broadcasting Station opened in Peking in 1958, growth was slow. The very size of China makes network television an expensive business, so it has developed city by city on a regional basis. The only link-up before the cultural revolution was between Peking and the nearby port of Tientsin. Elsewhere in Nanking, Wuhan, Shanghai and Canton the programming relied on local production or 'bicycled' film from one city to another. Chairman Mao could not—and still cannot—expound his thoughts to the assembled nation at once.

Their television studios were very primitive and reminded one visiting British broadcaster of 'an English church hall'. Their equipment was a jumble of Russian, East German and British cameras and lenses. And no real attempt was made to 'present' programmes. The techniques of 'mixing' pictures from several cameras in a studio was not used. Instead someone would step before one camera, announce, say, an acrobatic or juggling act, step back out of view and the artists would then move into the picture to perform.

Shortly before the cultural revolution, however, Chinese television was becoming a little more enterprising. In 1965 they signed up with Visnews, the international news film agency in London, both to take their service and to provide them with news pictures out of China. Their leading broadcasters were showing keen interest to learn more about the uses of television. The Red Guards stopped that abruptly. Television closed down throughout China, several leading broadcasters disappeared and some have not been heard of since.

The revival was slow. Since the cultural revolution had made all art and culture suspect, no one was sure what could be put out. The simplest and safest tactic was to show nothing. Even in 1970, by which time television was back on the air for three or four evenings a week, much of the time was taken up just showing captions of the thoughts of Chairman Mao on the screen. A British broadcaster, who visited Peking in October 1970, counted up that eighteen minutes out of a total twenty-six minutes of the main evening news bulletin one night were rolling captions of Mao's thoughts with background music of 'The East is Red'.

The uncertainty as to what was permissible meant that the handful of programmes known to be officially approved were repeated again and again. The schedule, therefore, differed little. The staple fare most evenings after the news at seven o'clock was yet another screening of one of the five 'Peking operas' approved by Mao's wife. The operas, *Taking Tiger Mountain by Strategy, White-Haired Girl* and *The Red Lantern*, together with a ballet *The Red Detachment of Women* all glorify the communist guerrilla campaigns against the old Chinese regime and the Japanese. *The Red Lantern* tells how communist railway workers sabotaged Japanese troop trains. The operas were all shown in live performances direct from theatres. Since many theatrical groups put them on, the repetition at least had the benefit of a different cast each night.

As television regained confidence, however, the choice of programes widened. The great May Day parade in 1971, for example, was shown for five hours, with relatively elaborate coverage from five outside broadcast cameras. The pictures were then relayed direct to other cities by landline—where it existed—or by videotape to cities throughout the country. The international ping-pong tournament in Peking, that marked the beginning of the relaxation in China's relations with the outside world, was also shown live. A much-heralded documentary *Red Flag Canal* reported on the building of an irrigation canal through treacherous mountain country in Honan province. Even on the evening news, Mao's thoughts gave way to world news, as Peking agreed to start taking agency news film again.

But television is clearly far from being a mass medium in China. In all some fifty cities are now reported to have television stations. Even Lhasa in Tibet is due to open a station shortly. But millions in China are still outside the television's range. The easiest way to cover the whole country would undoubtedly be a domestic communications satellite, relaying pictures to community antennae.

Television's role, however, is likely to be very different from the way we know it. Sets are not owned privately; they are all in factory canteens, hotels and other communal centres. Thus everyone can be assembled together to watch an educational programme or some speech by Mao calling for greater industrial or agricultural production: an ideal captive audience. And, as television grows up in China, it is likely to be harnessed even more than in the Soviet Union to both educational and political indoctrination.

By contrast the most casual government direction of television in Asia is in the Philippines, where commercial channels have proliferated and most are losing a fortune. Manila has seven television channels all competing for a mere £4 million potential advertising revenue. Profits, however, are less important than the prestige they bring to the wealthy Philippine families who own them; a television station here, as in South America, is a status symbol. Thus the most successful station, ABS-CBN with two channels, is part of the Lopez family empire which embraces newspapers, radio stations, insurance and even the Manila electric light company. The Elizalde family, whose fortune is based on rum, steel and newspapers, owns Channel 11; the Soriano family added Channel 13 to their ownership of San Miguel beer, the Coca-Cola concession and various engineering enterprises. 'The result,' said Almeida Lopez, the general manager of ABS-CBN, 'is a disaster.'

The stations are so busy fighting each other for ratings that no one has time to consider a more rational growth of television throughout the Philippines. Television is concentrated almost entirely in Manila; 320,000 of the 400,000 sets in the Philippines are in the city and its suburbs. There are a handful of regional and relay stations, but no comprehensive national plan to extend the networks in an orderly way throughout the islands. We are so busy competing here in Manila,' said

Almeida Lopez, 'that there's no time or money to think of expansion.'

Moreover, their costs are constantly rising because viewers in the Philippines, as in every other country these days, are clamouring for locally produced shows. All top fifteen programmes in the Philippines ratings are local, mostly live variety programmes or talk shows. ABS-CBN, who have all the top ten programmes, run eighty per cent live shows on their Channel 2. What they lack in polish is often made up for in enthusiasm and sheer local topicality.

In the early evening ABS-CBN run a two-hour programme called *Patrol* which is really just a public noticeboard for the city of Manila. All kinds of local titbits turn up. Insurance agents are advised that their exams have been postponed. Boy scouts are told when and where to report for a jamboree. Payment is offered for 500 cc of a rare type of blood urgently required to help a fourteen-year-old boy suffering from bone cancer; anyone who can offer a transfusion is asked to phone the studio immediately. Even photographs and descriptions of several children missing from home in the slums of Manila are given. *Patrol* calls itself 'the public service programme that makes a city move' and it outranks the imported *Bonanza* in the ratings.

Rather surprisingly, amidst all the commercial frenzy, the Philippines also has the beginnings of one of the better educational television systems in the Far East. The development comes through the Centre for Educational Television, a non-profit-making educational foundation, which has backing from the Ford Foundation and the World Bank. The centre is run by a lanky Jesuit priest, Father Leo Larkin, who explained, 'We have an emergency in education. Thousands of children have to be turned away from schools every year because of an acute shortage of teachers. We cannot train enough new teachers overnight, so what do we do with the sheer numbers who must be educated *now*? I am convinced that television at its best can make all the difference in a nation like the Philippines between quality education and none at all.'

The priority is in elementary and secondary schools. Larkin hopes that his centre can develop eight completely new courses for these schools each year and, by repeating programmes over several years, build up a total library of fifty different courses covering a major part of the school syllabus. Initially, the centre broadcast programmes to schools in Manila by its own small transmitter, but Larkin has persuaded Andres Soriano, owner of commercial Channel 13, to allow his network to be used for the schools programmes during the day. This spreads the coverage to most of Luzon province around Manila and to four other cities where Channel 13 has affiliates. Over one hundred schools watch the programmes regularly. Yet even this still leaves eighty per cent of the Philippines' school population outside the range of television. There a stumbling block to further expansion is not just the absence of TV stations—but simple lack of electricity. Until electrification is extended to rural areas, television cannot follow. 'I get so frustrated when I see how little coverage we actually have,' said Father Larkin sadly.

For all its limitations, the Philippines experiment is setting an important precedent for television in Asia. Father Larkin finds that half his mail is requests from other Asian countries to come and advise them on how to start their own educational television. While he is always ready to help, he believes that, in the long run, it is much better for each country to devise its own educational television system tailored to the particular deficiencies of its schools. 'Frankly every single developing country ought to have its own centre for educational television,' he said, 'where the local educators could come and learn the theory of educational television and get some practical experience; then they can help their country develop its own network. I find we never get down to the nitty-gritty unless people think it out for themselves.'

The inter-change of ideas between Asian broadcasters is now being increasingly co-ordinated by the Asian Broadcasting

Union, which was created in 1964 after several years of sustained campaigning by the Japanese. The ABU has a sprawling parish extending half round the world; it accepts a very broad definition of 'Asia', so that its membership includes nations as far apart as Egypt and Samoa, South Korea and Australia. The broadcasting experience of these nations ranges from the sophistication of Japan to India and Indonesia, which are just starting to come to terms with television, and to Afghanistan and Ceylon where it has not yet arrived. Initially, one of the problems of starting an Asian Broadcasting Union was this enormous diversity among its broadcasters; the Japanese were so far ahead that they were bound to dominate. Ultimately the Australian Broadcasting Commission was persuaded to join the proposed union, thus bringing into the fold a nation where television was also relatively advanced. 'The participation of Australia and later of New Zealand filled in the gap between Japan and the smaller countries,' said Ichiro Matsui, the ABU's honorary deputy secretary general in Tokyo. The ABU thus established its headquarters in Tokyo, but the secretary-general's office is in Sydney where Sir Charles Moses, the former general manager of the Australian Broadcasting Commission, is the secretary-general.

The real challenge facing the ABU is to aid the developing nations within its domain in improving their broadcasting skills, without falling foul of the politicians who are increasingly dabbling in communications. Their first major achievement has been to organise, with UNESCO, a regional training school for Asian broadcasters which will open in Kuala Lumpur, Malaysia, in 1972. They have also persuaded their members to take advantage of Japan's expert understanding of satellite communication by setting up a co-ordinating centre at NHK, Japan's public-service broadcasting corporation, in Tokyo for all satellite relays for Asia. Eventually, the ABU would like to have its own satellite to help bridge the vast distances not only between its members but within their own countries. 'We need one here for Australia if we are ever to serve the outback,' said Sir Charles Moses in Sydney, 'bu that's nothing to the problems facing India, Malaysia or Indonesia. You realise Indonesia is made up of three thousand islands scattered over three thousand miles of ocean?—you're never going to cover a country like that without a satellite. Satellites and the future of broadcasting in Asia go hand in hand.'

18

Japan:
The Golden Samurai

PRECISELY at six o'clock every weekday morning, as the sun rises behind Mount Fuji, more than nine million Japanese bound out of bed and switch on their television sets to catch the opening programmes of the day. Two hundred thousand of them settle down to watch a choice of English conversation lessons offered by the educational channel of NHK, Japan's public-service broadcasting corporation, plus a commercial station; a quarter-million more are immediately engrossed in a computer lecture on another commercial network, while nearly nine million energetically follow a brisk calisthenics course on NHK's general channel. Thus enlightened or refreshed, they become part of a thirty-one-million audience—almost one-third of the entire Japanese nation—who watch NHK's first major news bulletin of the day at 7 a.m.

As this early-morning appetite for television suggests, the Japanese are among the world's most compulsive viewers. The majority of them spend almost half of all their leisure time before the box. Although television was introduced into Japan relatively late—the first programmes were in 1953—they have exploited it with their customary diligence, introducing several innovations that no one else has yet thought of.

Today, in wealth and number of sets (twenty-three million, including five million colour), Japanese television is second only to the United States. They began regular colour programmes as far back as 1960—long before anyone in Europe—

and their harnessing of computer technology to television is the envy of broadcasters everywhere. In concocting a formula combining public-service and commercial television, they have sought to extract every possible advantage from the medium. NHK, the public-service corporation, runs the world's most comprehensive educational channel for eighteen hours a day, seven days a week, as well as an all-colour, general network for eighteen hours daily; even the commercial stations pitch in with self-improving programmes.

The diet is not as serious-minded all the time. On my first evening in Tokyo I watched a programme called *Play girls*, on a commercial channel run by the Japan Science Foundation, displaying a bevy of three gorgeous girl private eyes who knifed, shot and stripped their way through an hour-long crime series; in the course of outwitting the crooks one of them posed nude for artists in a club, while another took a revealing shower. The Japan Science Foundation's television licence actually specifies that sixty per cent of their programmes should be 'of scientific educational' content; *Play girls*, therefore, is a little light relief among all those computer lectures.

The term 'educational', however, has an extraordinarily wide interpretation on Japanese television. Another of Tokyo's commercial stations is National Educational Television (NET). Its licence duly requires it to carry fifty per cent educational programmes, thirty per cent cultural and a mere twenty per cent of entertainment; NET's interpretation of 'educational' is, as one of their programme executives put it rather charmingly, 'very subtle'. He pulled out a programme chart in which all the educational programmes were crayoned in in yellow; they included, besides normal morning schools programmes, coverage of a golf tournament and even an hour's professional wrestling. Was that really education? 'Of course. It helps people understand wrestling.'

Most evenings during the peak hours of 7 to 10 p.m., which the Japanese call 'golden time,' NET keeps up its 'educational' quota with samurai dramas. These samurai series, set in feudal

Japan and showing roving young war-lords touting out the baddies, are the westerns of Japanese TV. They have the same essential recipe as any western, except that guns are replaced by splendid curved swords and no one seems to own a horse. The swords are much more dramatic than guns on TV because there can be swashbuckling duels, full of grunts and groans, before the sword is plunged into the victim's writhing body. Moreover, the design of the Japanese house, with sliding walls instead of doors, makes for spectacular confrontations; just as the innocent is about to be disembowelled, the wall flies back and in leaps the samurai to the rescue. Whether such antics are educational is highly debatable. To the suggestion that, by the same token, *Bonanza* or *The Virginian* must also be labelled educational, NET responds by agreeing politely that indeed they are. 'After all,' said an executive, 'the story of a sheriff in the West is teaching Americans about their history; our samurai programmes tell the Japanese about their heritage.' He added, 'Perhaps you might say it is a typical Japanese solution.'

Actually, the solution has much to do with the economics of running a commercial television station; advertisers do not queue up to buy time on a Chinese lesson, but they will pay £600 for a thirty-second spot on an 'educational' samurai show. NET's definition of 'education' has earned it the nickname of National Erotic Television among Japan's more caustic TV critics.

Japan's prosperity has enabled its television to produce eighty-five per cent of its own programmes. Every single programme in the top twenty is Japanese. American programmes were widely shown during the early years, but nowadays the Japanese are highly selective in their overseas buying. They can afford to be. NHK earns more money from licence fees—£104 million a year—than any other public-service television organisation in the world, out of which it finances the two television channels and three radio networks. The commercial networks compete for a television advertising cake of £250 million a year—the largest anywhere outside the United States.

Tokyo has five commercial stations, of which four 'key' stations have programming networks throughout Japan, operating up to twenty hours every day, with all golden-time programmes in colour. The majority of Japanese, therefore, have a choice of six channels; in Tokyo it is seven. Actual ownership of commercial stations is strictly controlled; no individual or company is allowed to be a major shareholder in more than one station. But this restriction has not prevented the development of networks for programming purposes, controlled by the four major commercial stations in Tokyo; Tokyo Broadcasting System (TBS), Nippon Television Network (NTV), Fuji and National Educational Television (NET). The Japan Science Foundation's Channel 12 in Tokyo has no affiliates.

The frequency of the commercials is not officially controlled, but the stations claim to adhere to a voluntary limit of ten per cent of total broadcast hours given over to advertising, with up to ten minutes per hour during 'golden time'. However, with Japanese flair, they have developed simultaneous programmes and advertising; the message is superimposed over the continuing programme with no commercial break. So just as the samurai drama reaches its climax, a caption flashes up FLY JAPAN AIRLINES, BUY SAKURA COLOR FILM, or DRINK HONEY WINE, before the struggling swordsmen on the screens. Sponsors normally have three of these plugs in each half-hour. At news time the sponsor's name is superimposed over the breast pocket of the news reader as he gives the headlines. The blending of ads with programmes may well seem the nadir of commercial television, yet in some ways it is much less distracting than an actual commercial break at the crucial moment in a film or play, especially as the ad is never more than a three, or four-word caption. It is not more worrying than a subtitle in a foreign movie.

A surprising number of the full commercials are in English or use English phrases; potato crisps are 'Super Duper', one sports car is the 'now' car, another is a 'Hip Up' coupe. A Lux soap commercial begins 'Yes, Lux from England' over the pictures of a guardsman marching up and down. The strident drumming home of the message in so many American commercials is absent; instead a commercial for a washing machine shows a Japanese housewife getting on with her delicate flower arrangement while the machine does the work. And the Japanese do not appear to be plagued by those perpetual headaches, stomach upsets and ghastly colds for which remedies are so constantly promoted on American television. Instead, they listen to Mozart through the fine tones of the latest hi-fi equipment advertised by Sony or Hitachi.

When Japanese commercial television began in 1955 three of the major newspaper groups, Mainichi, Asahi and Yomiuri, invested in TBS but, as commercial TV expanded, the newspaper groups reshuffled their holdings, leaving Mainichi linked with TBS, Yomiuri with NTV and Asahi with NET (the U.S. ABC network also have a five per cent stake in NET). The fourth major newspaper group, Sankei, has always been tied with Fuji. The prosperity of television, however, is increasingly making the stations the most prominent partners in these deals. Sankei newspapers, for example, are now a subsidiary of Fuji-TV.

These four commercial stations in Tokyo are responsible either for making or purchasing from local production companies most of the programmes for their networks; their affiliated stations in other cities mainly produce their own local news and regional magazines. The exception is the city of Osaka which, like Tokyo, has four 'key' stations. Each is affiliated with a Tokyo station, but they originate many more programmes for their local viewers and contribute two or three hours each week to the commercial networks. Since the Osaka stations are one stage removed from main network programming, they are much freer to experiment and try out new ideas on their local audience; if a show succeeds, then they can push it for the network. 'The Tokyo stations are always cautious and conservative,' a TV critic told me, 'but two Osaka stations, ABC and MBS, are giving their producers a much freer hand.

All the new talent is coming from there. MBS has one "Laugh-In" type show built around all the young talent in the city and encouraging audience participation that is the most original entertainment in years.'

The commercial networks, naturally, are geared to entertainment. Although they may schedule English conversation at 6 a.m., there is no pretence of culture at 6 p.m. In the evenings they pump out a steady diet of variety shows with pop singers belting out their latest hits, samurai dramas, home dramas (local for soap operas) and a Japanese phenomenon known as 'hard-training' dramas. 'The Japanese people like series about characters training hard to achieve some special goal, either in their job or in sport,' a TBS programme director explained. 'They love the theme of dedication to the almost impossible.' TBS themselves set the pace with a hard-training series *V for Victory* about a girls' high school volley-ball team toiling to win a local championship. Once victory was indeed obtained the series fizzled out—'training' slackens off and so does the audience. TBS replaced it promptly with *Attention Please*, a fictionalised account of the trials, tribulations and loves of seven Japan Airline hostesses learning how to cater to the 340 individual whims of passengers on a Boeing 747 Jumbo Jet.

The home dramas, of course, are very like soap operas everywhere. The most popular one in 1971 was *Wife at Eighteen*, a tale set in a Tokyo high school in which a student of eighteen and her history teacher are trying to keep their marriage secret. Another epic, produced by MBS in Osaka for NET's network, chronicles a lady dentist's love affair with a paediatrician.

The most popular home dramas, however, cannot quench the Japanese love of action, whether it is provided by a sixteenth-century samurai saga or a twentieth-century crime series. Hour after hour private eyes, both ancient and modern, snap necks with karate chops, send thugs hurtling into oblivion with the flick of a well judo-trained wrist or, in fine kick-boxing style, administer a flying scissors kick on some villain's jaw.

'hese traditional Japanese sporting skills are heaven-sent to ıe TV producer. And while the samurai cut swathes through ıe armies of evil with their swords, the modern private eyes all ırow a deadly knife. Guns are out of fashion, but gore is in.

No one seems unduly worried by all the violence. The ommercial stations took considerable comfort from a survey y a sociologist at Kyoto University of 448 juvenile delinuents in Osaka who had been charged with murder or manlaughter. This enquiry, apparently, indicated that only 2·4 per ent of the boys and 3·5 per cent of the girls had been inuenced in their crime by television; most of them claimed to ave drawn their inspiration from films and magazines.

The commercial broadcasters are more worried about the ree rein of sex on the screen. The ethics committee of the Iational Association of Commercial Broadcasters stopped a ariation of strip poker on NTV in which the clothes of losing ontestants in a quiz show were gradually snipped away with a air of scissors. They also ruled out women's professional restling on the Japan Science Foundation's Channel 12, 'hich they felt was stretching the interpretation of science ducation just a little too far.

Controls, however, are few; the industry is left to police self. The Ministry of Posts and Telecommunications has verall responsibility for licensing the stations, but is conerned primarily with administration rather than programme ontent. The Minister accepts without apparent qualms, for xample, National Educational Television's far-reaching deinition of 'educational' programmes. There is no equivalent of he U.S. Federal Communications Commission, Britain's Inlependent Television Authority or the Australian Broadcasting Control Board to call the commercial broadcasters to account.

The maintenance of programme standards, however, in face f the rising costs of television, is beginning to tax even the nost prosperous commercial stations. All four 'key' stations in Tokyo make profits, but the competition is intense. According o Nobuo Shiga, a leading Japanese television critic, there is really only enough advertising in Tokyo to sustain two and half commercial stations if they are to keep up good standarc and develop their technical facilities; the fact that there a five, including the Science Foundation's channel, means th profits—and the plots—are thin.

For many years the TBS network, with twenty-five affiliate stations, has been the most profitable; frequently TBS had te or twelve of the shows in the top-twenty ratings. TBS' un doubted lead is now being challenged strongly by Fuji, whic has cornered most of the new UHF stations; the Fuji networ now comprises twenty-seven stations, including ninetee UHF, and is the biggest in Japan.

The success of networks is often seasonal. NTV, which i strongly orientated towards sports, does well during the sum mer months for the simple reason that they own one of Japan' favourite baseball teams, the Yomiuri Giants. They are guaran teed exclusive coverage of all the Giants' games and, as th team plays five nights a week from 8 p.m. till 9.30 from Apr to September, NTV is assured of fine ratings for those si months. Actually, the Giants owe their existence to Matsutar Shoriki, the founder and for many years president of NTV who was also known as the 'father of baseball' in Japan. Whil securing for NTV the first commercial TV licence he was als organising baseball teams.

NTV's preoccupation with sports persists throughout th year; they promote most of the major kick-boxing events an are now trying to encourage the Japanese to play soccer. Thei most popular winter programmes are two cartoon series abou a boy baseball player and professional wrestling. They are th only Japanese network not to have succumbed to the samura craze. Instead, they have developed a documentary depart ment, under Junichi Ushiyama, which has won an interna tional reputation reporting everything from the gorgeous gi pearl fishers of Ainu, to the Stone Age peoples of New Guine and a journey by wood-fired train across South America. The are now linked with Yorkshire Television, the Canadia

Broadcasting Corporation, Swedish and Russian television in a ong running co-production series, *Under One Sky*. One proect was for each contributing country to make a ten-minute lm on a child 'genius'; the film from each nation was then blended into a world-wide view of exceptional children. NTV hope that this co-operation can be expanded into building up n international film encyclopaedia for the dawning cassette ge.

Despite their preoccupation with entertainment, the commercial stations all devote a considerable proportion of their budgets and programme time to news. TBS, which has always had a strong reputation for news reporting, devotes fourteen per cent of its budget to news, has a news staff of three hundred and five foreign bureaus. NTV has three hours of news bulletins and news magazines every day. The rivalry to be first with a news story is fierce; all have radio cars, helicopters and outside broadcast vans ready to leave instantly on any major tory. The six senior news editors at TBS all carry electronic 'bleepers' to alert them in a crisis if they are within a twentymile radius of their office. Stations delight in broadcasting that hey are first with the news. Once, when a Boeing 727 crashed n Tokyo Bay, TBS just beat all its rivals to the nearest pier with an OB van, commandeered the only boat and were first to ocate the wreckage; the other networks were fuming back on he quay. The rivalry ceases only for satellite transmissions, which are normally shared through a pool because of the high costs.

The real people to beat on news, however, are NHK. They ake their role as Japan's public-service broadcasting organisaion exceptionally seriously. NHK was modelled originally on he BBC in the days when the image of Lord Reith was exremely strong. Lord Reith, whose ideals of high thinking and plain living earned the BBC the affectionate nickname 'Auntie', has persisted longer as an influence at NHK than at the BBC. Their mission, NHK like to remind visitors, is 'to contribute to the elevation of the cultural level of the nation'.

For almost ten years the president of NHK (i.e. director general) has been a remarkable man named Yoshinori Maeda who was perhaps the single most influential man in television in Japan, or indeed in Asia, during the 1960s. Maeda began his career as a foreign correspondent with the Asahi newspaper group, then worked his way up through NHK's news service to the presidency of the corporation. He is still, at heart, a journalist, a great believer in the potential role of television in disseminating news and information to the Japanese people not only about their own nation but the world at large. 'Maeda,' says one of his colleagues, 'has always insisted that NHK is not just a Japanese broadcasting organisation, but a world-broadcasting organisation, dedicated to international co-operation with other broadcasters.'

His great preoccupation is with NHK's news coverage in trying to preserve its independence from any kind of government or other pressures. 'We must be quite free from pressure from any quarter,' he insists. His own position at NHK depends on the approval of a board of twelve governors, who select him initially and can renew his term every three years. The governors, like those of the BBC on which NHK's constitution is largely based, are chosen from a cross-section of leading Japanese citizens; during 1970 the board was composed of five industrialists, two diplomats, a lawyer, a scientist, a college president, and representatives of the fisheries and farming industries. The Prime Minister appoints the all-male board, but he must have the approval of both houses of the Diet. Left-wingers in Japan often charge NHK with following the government line and, like many other public-service broadcasting corporations, it has an inevitable reputation of giving the 'official' view. However, the government must be exceptionally careful of trying to control the broadcasters' views. As in Germany, there are many bitter memories of government manipulation of radio before and during World War II, which have established especially strong resentments at any attempts to meddle in radio or television today.

Maeda's concern with news occasionally makes it seem as if NHK's general service is putting out nothing else; almost six hours a day—one-third of total broadcast time—is given over to news and news analysis. The general news bulletins are amplified by three special reports from overseas correspondents, together with a five-minute bulletin for children. The news division obtains its foreign reporting chiefly from the largest corps of foreign correspondents maintained by any broadcasting organisation in the world. The network was originally established by Maeda himself as director of NHK news in the 1950s, and comprises twenty-four foreign bureaus (the BBC has fourteen and CBS has nine). The news division can pre-empt all other programme time for major stories. During my own stay in Tokyo four hours every afternoon on three consecutive days were given over to live coverage of a crucial debate in the lower house of the Diet on pollution. This extended coverage is accepted at NHK as a natural part of their responsibility to the Japanese public.

Besides this heavy allotment of news, NHK describe a further nine hours of their programmes each day as 'cultural' or 'educational', leaving a mere five hours or less for entertainment. Even in its entertainment programmes NHK tries to carry through that feeling of cultural uplift. 'Our aim,' explained an NHK executive, 'is fair and healthy entertainment. We have our duty to raise the level of understanding of the Japanese public.' Their most successful evening programme, for example, is a regular Sunday-night samurai drama, *Ten to Chi to* (Heaven and Earth), which is about the only occasion in the week when they can beat their commercial rivals in the ratings during golden time. While swordplay abounds, the producer explains, 'we try to make our samurai play on a higher level than the commercial stations; we include much more about the ancient customs of our people.'

This Reithian concern for achievement and moral virtue pervades everything that NHK produces. One of their very best documentary series of fifteen programmes in colour looked at the accomplishments of the early Meiji pioneers who introduced Western civilisation into Japan and began the modernisation of the nation. NHK campaign constantly, both in news and documentary programmes, on everything from pollution to stopping traffic accidents. One major undertaking, which they hope will run right through the present decade, is a monthly ninety-minute colour documentary *Our World in the Seventies*, which is based on coverage by NHK teams around the globe of important trends—the problems of youth in France or America, the increasing infiltration of computers into almost every sector of life.

NHK's education channel, of course, is even more serious-minded and it is watched by a small, but remarkably constant audience. From the moment it comes on the air at 6 a.m. until midnight it rarely has less than a hundred thousand viewers or more than four hundred thousand. Over three-quarters of its programmes are strictly educational; the remainder are billed as cultural, which may mean a symphony concert, ballet or Kenneth Clark's successful BBC series *Civilisation*. Six hours each day are devoted to schools programmes, which are viewed extensively at all levels of the Japanese educational system; the science programmes for primary schools, for example, are watched by eighty-two per cent of all primary students. Outside school hours, half an hour every day is given over to special programmes for handicapped or mentally retarded children. There are lessons in English, French, German, Spanish and Chinese; university courses in sociology, jurisprudence, mathematics, history and economics, together with lectures for women on running the home, on shop management and, for teenagers, on playing the guitar.

Both NHK's television channels, together with three radio networks, are financed out of licence fees of £4·50 a year for a black-and-white set and £6·50 for colour. Unlike all other public-service broadcasting organisations whose fees are collected by a third party, NHK itself signs a contract with every household that has a TV set and its own staff go door to door ollecting the fees. Licence evasion, so NHK claim, is almost on-existent. 'Everyone,' they say, 'is very honest.' This nethod of licence collecting gives NHK a unique relationship vith its viewers; on the doorstep you are bound to get the full ent of any public dissatisfaction.

Whether NHK pays enough attention to complaints is de-atable. Television critics often suggest that the corporation is o busy giving the masses its version of enlightenment, that it as no time to heed their views. Rather curiously for an rganisation that has a large public-opinion research depart-nent, NHK does no daily audience research; they rely on atings provided by an outside commercial company and on two r three major surveys of their own each year. Maeda and his rogramme executives clearly watch the ratings as closely as nyone else in television. Nevertheless, they go to some lengths o explain that they are not slaves to the ratings game. 'Clearly ve like a good audience,' says Tadashi Yoshida, deputy direc-or of the general network, 'but we don't follow commercial ormulas.' NHK are, in fact, on that endless high-wire act that aces all public-service broadcasters in nations which also allow commercial television: they try to maintain a balance between easonable standards and a large enough slice of the viewing udience to justify the compulsory licence fee.

Actually, NHK is consistently top of the ratings by day and, lmost as consistently, bottom in the evenings. Between 6 a.m. nd 6 p.m. NHK normally holds the top seven positions in the atings, and a total of fifteen out of the top twenty; in 'golden ime' it is lucky to get two places low down in the top twenty (for the samurai drama on Sundays and a Folk Song Festival n Thursdays). Rarely does NHK's evening audience equal hat peak of thirty-one million it achieves with its news at 7 very morning. No other major television organisation that I now gains its maximum audience at dawn.

Moreover, only a handful of programmes on the commercial networks, even in golden time, ever win as large an audience as NHK does with the breakfast news; a twenty-million audience for an evening programme is excellent.

While NHK's earnestness makes for admirable and highly professional television, one does wish for a few more touches of frivolity. The phrase 'our responsibility to the public' came up almost too frequently. A little irreverence might be fun from time to time and amplify NHK's unquestioned daytime leadership into night-time superiority also.

'The trouble with NHK,' says the TV critic Nobuo Shiga, 'is that they are so sober that new creative talent simply cannot express itself in their programmes.' Shiga's recent book *Naked NHK* (which made him *persona non grata* at NHK) suggested that all the creative genius in the corporation was being channelled into technical wizardry rather than programmes. Certainly NHK's automated Broadcast Control Centre in Tokyo is regarded as the ultimate technical showplace by broadcasters everywhere. 'When you get to Tokyo,' everyone urges, 'you *must* see that centre.'

Well, they are right. If you sit for the afternoon in the Technical Operations Centre there, which handles the transmission of two thousand programmes a week on NHK's two TV and three radio networks, you begin to wonder after a while why the four young men on duty did not just stay out for a long lunch. Two IBM 360 computers are doing all the work. Occasionally, just to reassure themselves that the computers are on the job, these technicians glance at a formidable galaxy of television monitors and computer display screens. On five display screens an IBM 360 has spelt out just what it is doing with each network. On the GTV monitor the computer has printed out in red letters that it is supervising a Keep Fit programme for housewives, which will end at 4.15; the educational TV display alongside reports a science lecture is being transmitted. The computer has also printed out in green letters on each screen details of the next scheduled programme. The GTV will have a children's puppet show from NHK's Osaka studios. The computer knows that the videotape of this show is already loaded on the videotape recorder in Osaka. Naturally, it has

lready thoughtfully double-checked a coding on the puppet-
ıow tape against a similar coding in its programme-schedule
emory-bank to confirm that no foolish human in Osaka has
ıadvertently put on the wrong tape. (If they had, the com-
uter sounds the alarm, so that the correct tape can be installed
ell before broadcast time.) Then, precisely at 4.15, the com-
uter switches out the Keep Fit lesson and switches on the
uppet show; in the same moment it also remembers to change
rom a science to a Chinese lesson on the educational channel.
adio programmes are changed with equal adroitness. An
utomatic apology can even be interjected in the event of a
emporary fault.

Since the majority of NHK's programmes are pre-recorded
n videotape, the essential role of all this automation is simply
witching tapes on and off at the right split-second. The com-
uters are equally adept, however, at coping with a live news
rogramme. NHK's News Centre is hooked into the computer
omplex and the entire sequence of each newscast is mapped
ut on plastic cards which are slotted into a gadget known as
esources Random Selector. All the producer has to do is push
single button which commands the selector to 'read' the next
ard and, following that instruction, automatically switch in a
tudio camera on the news reader, a news film projector, a
ideotape recorder or even a live satellite transmission from
alfway around the world. The system is so flexible that, if a
ate story comes in while the news is on, the whole running
rder can be altered just by rearranging the sequence of plastic
ards. Sudden newsbreaks outside regular news time can also
e accommodated by ordering the computers to bypass the
egular programme schedule and cut immediately to the news
tudio; the computers need just two minutes to reorganise their
houghts and comply.

The transmission of programmes is merely the final chore in
complex computer operation, which NHK has christened
Total On-Line Program and Information Control (TOPICS).
Earlier, TOPICS has presided over every moment of a pro-

gramme's progress, from the first vague plan to the finished taping. Two hundred offices at NHK are hooked into TOPICS through their own computer terminal and display screens. This enables a programme's birth to be charted so closely that critics occasionally suggest that computers have replaced people completely at the corporation. TOPICS, in fact, co-ordinates all requests for actors, musicians, designers, lighting experts, announcers and outside broadcast units, and juggles the bookings for all NHK's thirty-six videotape recorders and twenty-one studios. A producer working out his schedule can call up the computer and find in an instant when a particular studio is available and tap out a reservation on his keyboard. At any moment the computer will obligingly print up on any one of the two hundred display screens a complete briefing on the status of the project, outlining whether the script is complete, who are the actors and technicians assigned, when and where all rehearsals and the final taping will take place, together with a provisional airing date. Alternatively, the computer can conjure up the entire network schedule weeks ahead for instantaneous review or alteration.

'TOPICS can handle eighty different types of production facilities,' says Yoshinori Maeda proudly, 'previously our staff were writing out five thousand requests a day for studios or announcers or OB vans; it often took hours for these to be delivered and for them to get an answer—now it's instantaneous.'

NHK's latest notion is to ask its computers to memorise their entire film library. At the moment, if a producer wants to get a shot of Mount Fuji from the north at dawn he may have to look through fifty rolls of film to locate the precise view he has in mind. Once the computers have added the library to their repertoire, they will advise the producer in a few seconds on precisely which roll of film he can find the view of Fuji. Hours of frustrating viewing will be eliminated.

While squeezing every last advantage from their computers NHK displays equal efficiency in planning such mundane hings as floor coverings. The endless miles of studio corridors re laid with three different colours in floor tiles; green tiles ndicate a special visitors' route through the building, so that he seven thousand daily sightseers can find their own way hrough the building without a guide—they are just told 'stay n green floor', orange tiles guide artists and performers direct o the dressing and make-up rooms; grey tiled corridors are for taff only—they are supposed to know their way through the naze.

Those seven thousand sightseers trudging down the green tourist' corridors of NHK every day reflect the Japanese ascination, almost obsession, with television. They have the nost voracious appetite for TV anywhere outside the United States; eighty per cent of the population spend at least two iours every day watching TV, thirty per cent spend four hours r more. The average Japanese man views for $2\frac{3}{4}$ hours on veekdays and $3\frac{1}{2}$ hours on Sundays; his wife is even keener—he looks in for $3\frac{1}{4}$ hours during the week and 3 hours 40 Minutes on Sundays. This represents a major slice of their eisure time; indeed, according to Naomichi Nakanishi of NHK's Public Opinion Research Institute, the Japanese spend lmost twice as much of their leisure time watching television s do the Americans. The housewife in Japan spends fifty-six er cent of all her leisure before the box—compared with wenty-four per cent for the American housewife.

The moment she has seen her husband off to work and the hildren are on their way to school, she tunes in to a cosy little ifteen-minute home drama, *Rainbow*, on NHK's general hannel. *Rainbow* chronicles the life of a Mrs Tanaka, who is narried to an archaeologist. They have several children one of vhom, appropriately, works for NHK. After 8.30 she has the hoice of several *Today* type shows, all aimed at women; there s *Hello Madam* on NHK, the *Kazu Nara Morning Show* on NET, the *Hiroshi Ogawa Morning Show* on Fuji or the *Jiro Kimbara Show* on NTV. The remainder of the day is whiled away with cooking lessons, Keep Fit classes, several traditional

Japanese tea ceremonies and a good choice of short, home dramas normally about the conflict between parents and children in some modern Japanese family.

Traditionally the Japanese wife has always been obedient and even subservient to her husband: her role has been one of complying with his every whim, having a piping hot bath ready for him when he comes home, scrubbing his weary back, then serving him a delicate dinner. Moreover, as Nakanishi points out, 'the majority of Japanese housewives have never had any opportunities to train themselves on how to spend their leisure hours.' Television, consequently, has become 'indispensable', a new window to a wider world in which men are not always such superior beings. Can that arduous back-scrubbing ever be quite so dutiful again? The Japanese housewife is not yet in open rebellion, but the new perspectives she observes through television are slowly changing the rigid family structures. NHK, probing the influence of TV on its viewers, found that in 1970 one-fifth of them reported 'TV programmes have promoted the democratisation of human relationships within the family.'

The same enquiry also revealed that television viewing time is still increasing, especially in the thirty per cent of Japanese homes that now have two or more television sets, as family conflicts over which programme to watch are reduced.

The prospect for the future is that the Japanese will have an even greater choice of programmes, although most of them are likely to be embellishments of the educational pattern already established. The government have one channel reserved on the UHF waveband for an Open University of the Air, relying heavily on television for its teaching. The issue is whether the government runs this itself or pays NHK to do it for them. NHK, always anxious to preserve their independent status, are extremely reluctant to undertake the production of government programmes. Moreover, they have their own ideas for expanding their educational projects.

But everyone in Japan, of course, is really brimming with

lans for the era of cassettes. All the commercial networks have et up special subsidiary companies linked with electronics irms to exploit the cassette potential. The electronics indus-ry's exceptional expertise at miniaturisation and its competi-ive costs may well mean that the Japanese will be the first to roduce a cassette-player that is cheap enough for the ordinary ome. The initial players that went on the market in Tokyo in 971 cost about £130 each, with the programme cassette cost-ng £42 for a half-hour's tape. 'Although these first cassette layers are beyond the budget of the ordinary Japanese fam-ly,' said an executive of the National Association of Com-ercial Broadcasters, 'I am quite sure we can develop cheap ideo packages for home use by the late 1970s.' If the Japanese ppetite for television is anything to judge by, the country ould become the first mass market for the cassette.

Japan's leadership in television in Asia is so great that it is mpossible to envisage any other countries there ever beginning o challenge her. Already the Japanese sphere of influence is preading swiftly. Three Japanese directors are on the board of he Pakistan Television Corporation, where all the equipment s Japanese. More than five hundred engineers and broad-asters from other Asian nations have already been trained by NHK's Central Training Institute in Tokyo and scores more fly in every year.

En route from New Delhi to Bangkok I travelled next to a young Indian girl on her way to Tokyo to join her husband, who was learning how to make television sets; once he had the skill he was to return to India to start manufacturing sets there. 'No one in India really knows how to make television sets,' she said to me, 'the Japanese are so far ahead of us.'

AUSTRALIA

19

Linking up Down Under

'OR two hundred years after Captain James Cook made his rst landfall at Botany Bay in 1770, Australia always seemed at he ends of the earth; an enormous, almost empty continent of ed, brown and orange deserts and sheep farms with, perched round its rim, a handful of cities reached only after weeks board ship or some thirty tedious hours in a jet. That isolation nded, in one sense anyway, in November 1966 when the first 'acific INTELSAT satellite relayed television pictures of a mall group of English immigrants, specially gathered at a ortable earth station at Carnarvon in Western Australia, to heir relatives assembled at a BBC television studio in London. It was not a fantastic piece of television programming,' Walter Hamilton, assistant general manager of the Australian Broad-asting Commission (ABC), conceded later, 'but the world was hrinking for us at last.'

The satellite bridge to Australia really proved itself, how-ver, in July 1969 when Neil Armstrong first stepped from Apollo 11 on to the surface of the moon. A special NASA racking station at Honeysuckle Creek near Canberra and Aus-ralia's own giant radio telescope at Parkes were first to home n on the scene and relay it via the Pacific satellite to Houston nd the watching world. 'Just for one big occasion Australia ad the picture first, at least three hundred milliseconds before nyone else,' ABC's Hamilton added proudly. 'Just for once ve were not at the end of the line, our accustomed place "down under".' (EBU Review, November, 1969.) Regularly now, thanks to INTELSAT, Australians can watch their tennis stars winning at Wimbledon and Forest Hills or their cricketers trouncing England in pursuit of the Ashes.

Australia may have been at the end of the line before satellites, but she was by no means bottom of the viewing league. Although the Outback can be cut off five hundred miles from the nearest TV station, in the big cities of Sydney, Melbourne, Brisbane and Adelaide there is a choice of the ABC's public-service and three commercial channels. Over half of Australia's twelve million population is gathered together in these cities, where they can enjoy a choice of more television channels than anyone in Europe (always excepting those addicts with high roof aerials in Brussels, who pick up programmes from four surrounding countries). They can also watch for longer hours because the commercial stations are on the air at least seventeen hours a day. Indeed, only in the United States and Japan is the quantity of television offered greater; total TV programming in Sydney is an extraordinary 445 hours each week—in Britain and West Germany, by comparison, it is just under 200 hours. While this may sound an achievement, television 'down under' is, in fact, an object lesson in what happens with too much programming and too little money. The results can be as barren as Australia's deserts.

The splendid submissions of prospective programmes made by some commercial operators in applying for their licences have fallen forgotten by the wayside. One applicant in Melbourne grandly announced that his station's output 'would reflect an Australian environment, encourage an awareness of the achievements of Australia and advance the arts and culture of the nation.' Yet in 1970, the amount of programme time devoted to 'the arts' on Australian commercial television was so small that it could not be rated in official programme content analysis; a footnote merely remarked 'less than 0·05 per cent'. The general manager of one commercial station told me

ankly, 'Our promises in applying for the licence bear no
semblance to what we are doing now.'

The Australian Broadcasting Control Board, from the best
motives, simply adds to the trouble. In granting the licences
id regulating the commercial stations the board insists that
alf their programmes must be locally produced. They also
becify that six hours of Australian drama must be transmitted
y each commercial station weekly. While this policy has the
lmirable aim of limiting the flood of imported package pro-
ammes and stimulating home production, in effect it places
o great a strain on local resources. Australia has little theatri-
l or film-making tradition on which television can draw.
elevision has had to pull together its own group of talents
om scratch to satisfy a colossal demand; in Sydney or Melourne more local programming is required each week than is
roduced either by the BBC or commercial television in
ritain, or indeed, by any European television organisation.
Iot surprisingly, standards suffer. One Australian television
coon, explaining why he objected strongly to any increase in
ie proportion of Australian programmes, stated flatly that he
as not going to be responsible for foisting 'muck' onto the
ustralian people.

With two hundred broadcasting hours still left to fill each
eek, after the local quota has been aired, Australian television
as long been a lure for international programme salesmen.
he BBC sold almost eight hundred productions there in
969, earning a third of the total income of BBC Television
nterprises. The British viewer visiting Australia consequently
els entirely at home: he can watch *Softly, Softly*, *Dr Finlay's
asebook*, *The Troubleshooters* and *The Power Game*. Sir
ew Grade at Associated Television also has a long running
ontract with Channel 7 in Sydney, supplying everything from
he Saint to *Tom Jones*. There is a special fondness for Brit-
h programmes among the commercial stations that has
othing to do with sentiment: commercial stations are allowed

to count a half of each programme as 'local production' in ful filling their domestic quota.

Yet the Americans sell just as well. Australia is one of th few countries with a well-developed television system wher American programmes still gallop into the Top Ten. For som years, to prevent costly bidding and to keep prices down, th commercial stations and the ABC formed a pool for thei American buying. Each station listed the programmes i wanted and a ballot was then held to determine who should b the lucky one to show *Lucy* or *Ironside*. At one point, th Americans countered by refusing to sell to the pool for almost year. It only came to an end, however, when Channel 7 i Sydney broke loose and went on a grand American buyin spree.

Amazingly, the avalanche of programmes is transmitte without a true commercial network. The ownership of com mercial stations is tightly regulated; control of more than tw television stations by any person or company is forbidden Only loose programme-producing groups have been formed; Melbourne station embarking on a new series will seek assur ances from outlets in Sydney, Brisbane and Adelaide that the will take the show, but essentially the stations in the citie operate independently. Anyone from Sydney travelling to Mel bourne or Adelaide may find their favourite programme goe out on a different night of the week. Only the ABC has a tru network carrying programmes simultaneously nationwide.

Outside the major cities of Sydney, Melbourne, Brisban and Adelaide, each with three commercial stations, and Pert with two, there are thirty 'country' stations, generally owne by small newspapers or local businessmen. These countr stations have no direct link with the metropolitan stations They originate few programmes, apart from local news, bu simply shop around the big city stations to fill the few hour that they are on the air each evening. This unsystematic pur chasing hampers the metropolitan stations, since it never guar antees countrywide sales for any programme. With three mai roups of commercial producers, the programme market is vercrowded and countless shows are never aired outside the najor cities.

Although commercial networks are prohibited, formidable oncentrations of power have arisen in Australian television hrough major newspaper groups. With no more than the two ations that the government permits to any one owner, newsaper owners still find it possible to wield great influence in elevision's development throughout the country. Newspaper nagnates' dominance of television in Australia is perhaps more otent than anywhere else in the world.

Leading the field is Sir Frank Packer, renowned both as ewspaper owner and yachtsman, whose Australian Consoliated Press publishes the Sydney *Daily Telegraph* and several nagazines. He owns TCN Channel 9 in Sydney (the very first ommercial station in Australia) and GTV Channel 9 in Melourne. The John Fairfax group, owners of the *Sydney Morng Herald* control ATN Channel 7 in that city and are major hareholders in BTQ in Brisbane. Down in Melbourne, Sir ohn Williams' *Herald* newspaper owns HSV Channel 7. Rupert Murdoch, who is now extending his empire into Britain with his purchases of the *Sun, The News of the World* nd a slice of London Weekend Television, has a large stake in ADS Channel 7 in Adelaide through his company, Advertiser Newspapers. *The News* in Adelaide are also owners of NWS Channel 9.

The lone non-newspaper tycoon in Australian commercial elevision is the airline millionaire, Sir Reginald Ansett, who wns stations in Melbourne and Brisbane. Ansett arrived in elevision rather late, when the third commercial stations were icensed in the main cities. He has had a hard time breaking nto the market. As his losses and those of the two other nonnewspaper owned stations in Adelaide and Sydney mount, heir executives often criticise the newspaper alliances of their ivals or lament that they have no such link themselves. 'The newspapers that own television stations promote them quite

shamelessly,' complained one bitter executive. And Talb
Duckmanton, the quiet, pipe-smoking general manager of th
Australian Broadcasting Commission explained, 'You will fir
hardly any newspaper outlets that are not linked to televisio
It's very hard for us at ABC to get write-ups of our pro
grammes.'

A check of these complaints reveals that they are often justi
fied. The *Sydney Morning Herald* for instance, publishes
weekly four-page pull-out TV guide, including a full page
articles previewing programmes. Not only are the programm
for its own Channel 7 listed first, although the natur
sequence is to print Channel 2 (ABC) first and then Channel
9 and 10, but *all* articles in guides I have seen preview on
programmes on their own channel.

Newspaper partiality for its own channel is understandabl
but the exclusion of editorial comment on the others is a diffe
ent matter. Blatant pressure on TV critics is also unmaske
from time to time. One television critic was fired by a wel
known newspaper baron for criticising programmes on h
paper's station. When the critic protested he was trying to b
impartial, the magnate snapped, 'What about being imparti
our way?'

The stations with newspaper tie-ups hotly deny any on
sidedness. 'The newspaper interest is not all that importan
protested Clyde Packer, Sir Frank's son, who runs TCN
Sydney. 'Look, we're top station in Brisbane and Melbourn
where we don't even own newspapers.'

With and without newspapers, the metropolitan and countr
commercial stations comfortably beat the public-service AB
ratings. The concept of the Australian Broadcasting Commi
sion is close to that of the BBC in Britain and of NHK
Japan. The ruling body consists of nine government-appointe
commissioners selected from prominent Australians in bus
ness, education and the professions; the commissioners mu
include one woman. They, in turn, appoint the general ma
ager (director-general) of the ABC, who presides over day-to

day running and policies. But one crucial difference in organisation distinguishes the ABC from the BBC and NHK—the ABC's revenue does not come from licence fees. Although there is a licence costing £6 a year for owning a TV set in Australia, the money from the 2,300,000 licences goes into the Government's general revenue kitty. Each year, the general manager of the ABC has to go, cap in hand, to the government and ask for money, which is then paid out of government funds. This means the ABC does not have a guaranteed income based on the number of television sets in the country. Normally the ABC's grant is close to licence fee revenue (about £23 million a year) in the early 1970s, but its isolation from that fee can be crucial. Equally inhibiting is the fact that the appointment of all ABC's staff paid over £3,450 has to be approved by the government's Public Service Board. If the ABC wants to offer a high salary to a good director from a commercial station, they have to seek approval from the board to pay him above the standard rate for directors. 'Unfortunately, our reputation for independence is not as strong as the BBC's,' an ABC executive admitted, 'but we are now trying to build it up.'

The ABC successfully rebuffed the Postmaster-General, Alan Hulme, in 1969 when he threatened a curb of their current-affairs budget because he objected to the tone of the programmes. The commission pointed out that the Broadcasting and Television Act clearly gave them control over programme policy and, eventually, the Minister backed down. 'The government here is very afraid of television,' said the same ABC executive 'and we need a strong chairman of the commission to stop them interfering.'

The ABC's brief is also much vaguer than for most other public-service broadcasting organisations; they are required simply to provide 'adequate and comprehensive programmes'. Understandably, just what that means is open to many interpretations. For several years the ABC left entertainment mostly to the commercial channels and concentrated instead on a rather solid diet of programmes with a nice moral tone. 'We assumed there was an ABC viewer who came home at 7 and sat down to watch "worthy" television,' one ABC man told me. 'We offered a little bit of everything that was good for him.' This policy gained the ABC a microscopic proportion of the audience.

Since Talbot Duckmanton became general manager in 1965, the ABC have suddenly become more conscious of how to please large audiences with popular entertainment. 'We must compete for audiences,' said Duckmanton. 'If we don't, our audience will diminish beyond the level at which we can claim we are a national broadcasting authority. Some people would like to see us maintained merely for the satisfaction of minority audiences, while they themselves were free to attend to the majority audiences. But we could then no longer be regarded as a national body. If public-service broadcasting is to be effective, it must be comprehensive.'

The ABC's most conspicuous audience winner has been a gossipy little fifteen-minute soap opera *Bellbird*, about life and loves in a small Australian town. *Bellbird* is shown each weekday evening just before the main news at 7 p.m. and occasionally slips into the Top Twenty programmes. But even then it attracts barely a quarter of the audience in the cities. A more enterprising ABC series *Dynasty*, a saga of a newspaper–television tycoon and his family, took a swipe at newspaper control of commercial television. The script was carefully tailored to avoid libel suits by identifying too closely with any single Australian newspaper-owning family, but there were no prizes for guessing the autocrat on whom the series was modelled.

The real achievement of the Australian Broadcasting Commission, however, has been to reach a high level of current affairs and documentary programmes, a field almost completely ignored by the commercial stations (they gave a mere 1·1 per cent of their time to current affairs in peak evening periods during 1969–70). Every evening, from 7 until 8, the ABC boldly present a full hour of news and current affairs, which wins them consistently their best audiences of the day (apart from *Bellbird*). The audience for this evening hour is actually double that for almost any other time; on the graph of their ratings it stands out like Mount Everest.

The dilemma facing producers, both at the ABC and the commercial stations, is that their audiences have long been accustomed to the professional standards of imported programmes, which they find very difficult to match. 'It's a tragedy that we didn't have much stricter quotas to begin with,' an ABC drama producer said. 'By the time we started making more of our own shows the audience was already accustomed to overseas standards. Now they can reject our efforts.' But the problem is not necessarily one of quotas; the Australians simply have too many television stations on the air for too long each day. The money and the talent available cannot make the programmes worth while.

Of the home-grown dramas the most successful have been two police series, *Division Four* and *Homicide*, but several others have been dropped at considerable cost after poor audiences for the opening episodes. Nowadays all the commercial stations and ABC are hunting overseas for partners for co-productions to be made in Australia. Channel 7 in Sydney has been making pilot programmes for CBS, and Channel 9 worked with Paramount on a series *Flea Force*, about a team of Australian commandos in the Pacific in World War II. ABC have joined up with the BBC for a 13-part 'Down-Under Western' on Ben Hall, an Australian bushranger of the Ned Kelly brand.

Any attempt at liveliness on the part of local producers has often been curbed, however, by one of the strictest rule-books of television standards anywhere. Australia's stand as the last bastion against the permissive society is clearly reflected in her television. There is no television on Sunday mornings and all stations must put out at least thirty minutes of religious services each week. Sex education on television is explicitly ruled out. 'References to sex relations should be treated with discretion,' says the rule-book, 'reference to illicit sex relations should be avoided where possible and should on no account be presented as commendable.' The rules also specify 'Respect for the state of marriage and the importance of the home and family should be maintained.'

Attitudes have eased slightly, however, in the last few years. 'I remember a script a few years ago in which an unmarried couple met in a bar,' recalled an ABC drama producer. 'This had to be changed so that they met over a ham sandwich in a sandwich bar.' The relaxation is due not so much to Australian boldness as to imported BBC shows. 'The BBC has been an ice-breaker in pushing forward the frontiers of permissiveness all round the world,' said the ABC producer. 'It's helped us enormously—we just argue that if the BBC does it, then we can too.'

Nevertheless, all imported films destined for television are still subject to the approval of the Commonwealth Film Censorship Board. The board grades them either G, indicating they may be shown on television at any time; A, meaning they are not recommended for children and must not be shown before 7.30 in the evenings; or AO, adults only, which may be shown only after 8.30 p.m. The censorship rules also spell out that before 7.30 p.m. 'parents should be able to feel secure in allowing children to watch television without supervision.' This responsibility is taken seriously by the television companies and after 7.30 it is quite usual to see the caption over the opening titles 'This programme is not suitable for children'.

While Australia's television producers are working to nourish local writing and acting talent, the technical challenge of the seventies is to extend television into the Outback. Although ninety-six per cent of Australia's population already live within television range, the remaining four per cent are thinly scattered over thousands of square miles. The cost of bringing television to them, as demanded by the ABC's public-service concept, will be enormous. Thirty-eight new low-power ABC television stations are being built in the Outback in 1972–3, ut these will bring only a further 110,000 people before the ox. Communities like Darwin and Alice Springs, which are vell over a thousand miles from the nearest city cannot be ooked neatly into a microwave network. Indeed, the answer or them, as for so many other small settlements in Australia is satellite to feed community receivers. Just as the Pacific IN-TELSAT satellite finally ended Australia's visual isolation rom Europe and America, so eventually an Australian or sian satellite tuned to bounce signals into every corner of the esert could end the loneliness of the Outback.

AFRICA

20

A Symbol of Independence

AFRICA is proving as hard for television to penetrate as it was for Livingstone and Stanley. Steamy tropical climates wreak havoc with sensitive electrical equipment, colossal distances defy the establishment of networks, electricity often does not extend more than a few miles outside main towns, while television sets are quite beyond the means of the average family. In Sierra Leone there were still less than one thousand sets eight years after the beginning of television—and no one was sure how many of those were working. Only two television sets out of one hundred installed for an educational television project in Ghana survived the first two years without succumbing to heat and humidity. Upper Volta, on the southern fringes of the Sahara Desert, started television with a flourish, but gave up daily programming after a few months through lack of money. They now have television only two nights a week. 'Television is still in its infancy in Africa,' said Levinson Nguru, the director of the Kenya Institute for Mass Communications, 'ownership of a set here is still a matter of prestige—a set costs £150. None of my friends can afford that.'

As late as 1971 there were just 250,000 television sets in the whole of Africa south of the Sahara; or one television set for every thousand people. Nations as diverse as Tanzania, Malawi, Angola, Mozambique and South Africa had no television at all. South Africa, the last developed country anywhere without television, is finally proposing to take the plunge in

1975 when it will introduce first an all-colour channel in English and Afrikaans for the European population and later a separate colour channel for the Africans. Despite this late start South Africa will have the only colour TV in Africa and conceivably more sets in use almost from the beginning than the rest of Africa combined: the commission which recommended the establishment of television estimated 700,000 sets would be sold in the republic in five years.

This is entirely feasible since in Rhodesia, which has had television since 1960, there are fifty thousand sets, ten times more per head of the population than in Africa as a whole. Rhodesian television however, is very much the odd man out; it is aimed at the white population. Moreover, since UDI in 1965, it has not been able to buy programmes openly from Britain or America, although this has not prevented it from getting prints of the latest shows by various roundabout methods.

Television's slow start in Africa has surprised many people who felt a decade ago that it would be a mass medium there within a matter of years. Not only the British, American and French equipment manufacturers who competed for contracts have been disappointed; even educationalists, who believe that television can be an invaluable tool in both adult and school education, have felt thwarted. They often wonder if, for the time being, they should put more emphasis on radio. The cheap transistor radio is firmly implanted in most homes even in the remotest villages and seems much less sensitive to the hazards of climate. Politicians are aware of this. 'Most African nations are being created out of what was previously just a collection of tribes,' a Kenyan broadcaster pointed out. 'If you want to mobilise these people you must use radio.'

This has not discouraged most African leaders from enthusiastically approving the opening of every television station. Indeed, television has widely become a symbol of newly won independence, along with a flag and an airline. Everywhere it is under the close supervision of the Ministry of Information nd, for all its present limitations, is regarded as a formative nfluence in welding together disparate tribes into one nation. Much of the local programming tends to be given over to nation-building propaganda, with news cameras dutifully following presidents and ministers as they open hospitals, schools nd roads. When I was in Kenya enormous efforts were being made on television to persuade everyone in the country to plant one tree: the Minister for the Environment gave a ten-minute special broadcast exhorting everyone to plant a tree next day.

Limited treasuries have forced almost every African country to accept advertising on television as one source of income, supplemented by licence fees or direct grants. Advice on the kind of station that a country can afford has poured in from all sides. Together with the major American, European and Japanese equipment manufacturers, organisations such as Thomson Television International (TTI), Television International Enterprises (TIE) in Britain, L'Office de Co-opération Radiophonique (OCRA) in Paris (now merged with ORTF) and Radio Television International (RTV) and NBC International from New York have been bustling all over the continent. They offer package television stations to suit all pockets, management expertise, programme and advertising representation and training programmes for local staff. In former British colonies both radio and television has often been modelled on the BBC. Indeed, not only in Africa but throughout the old British Empire, broadcasting was almost invariably moulded originally to the BBC's traditions and BBC men were seconded to found the services. The kind of free-for-all scramble for television licences that has happened in Latin America or the Philippines never occurred. This liaison with Britain has been maintained even after former colonies have gained their independence through the Commonwealth Broadcast Conference. The Conference meets every other year and maintains a permanent secretariat at the BBC in London. Some thirty-seven Commonwealth nations from Africa, Asia and the West Indies

as well as Canada, Australia and New Zealand belong to th
Conference. This mutual assistance enables the smalle
countries to call in expert advice on the development of thei
broadcasting. Sierra Leone, for instance, sought help in 196
from a team of British, Canadian and Ghanaian broadcasters t
prepare a report on the expansion of their radio and televisio
services. All Conference members must be public-servic
organisations (the commercial networks are excluded) and i
opposes what it calls 'international operators' out to make a
quick profit by selling package television stations to developing
countries.

While Britain has been active in her former colonies
France's ORTF is influential in old French colonies and in the
territory of Afars and Issas (former French Somaliland) and
the island of Réunion out in the Indian Ocean. The French
have been particularly tenacious in maintaining a hold on television in several countries. The Ivory Coast at one time considered signing up with Thomson Television International in London for a package station, until the French reminded the government of the Ivory Coast that their economy relied heavily on exporting coffee to France. The French won the contract. They also outmanoeuvred the Americans from RTV in Congo (Brazzaville) by simply offering to train television personnel free which RTV, as a commercial organisation, could not afford to do. The competition for contracts has now become even keener with the arrival of the Japanese in force. Their first major coup was to win the re-equipping of Uganda's television network.

Package television stations come in all shapes and sizes and can be tailored to the requirements of the country. The cheapest cost £60,000 for equipment and installation and can be run for about £80,000 a year (about the same as it costs to make one episode of *Bonanza* for American television). 'We created "bespoke" television stations,' explained Desmond O'Donovan, the managing director of Thomson Television International, who helped set up TV in Kenya, Sierra Leone and

Ethiopia. Actually, stations are sometimes 'off the peg' rather than 'bespoke', for governments have a notorious tendency to dither for years about whether or not to have TV and then demand overnight that it be ready for some celebration next month.

The record for swift installation is held, by general consent, by TTI, who had a television station operating in Addis Ababa just *nineteen* days after Emperor Haile Selassie suddenly ordered that it must be open for coverage of the anniversary celebrations of his coronation—then less than three weeks away. All the equipment had to be airfreighted from London, and set up in makeshift studios on half a floor of the Addis Ababa municipal office building. Matters were not helped because the head of customs in Ethiopia was personally against the introduction of television and, despite the fact that it was the Emperor's express command that it be installed, insisted that all the normal formalities be carried out in clearing the equipment at the airport. However, right on time, the station went on the air with the Emperor in the studio to watch the transmission. Moreover, the Ethiopians themselves, who had never even seen a television set, let alone sophisticated cameras, control console or a transmitter until a couple of weeks before, handled everything. The British advisers, who had installed the equipment and given them instant training, stood to one side with fingers crossed. All went off perfectly and the Emperor was delighted.

From that auspicious beginning in 1964 the Ethiopians have continued to run their station, putting out about three hours of programmes a night, nearly half of them locally produced. Several of the senior staff have been to Britain for short training courses at the Thomson Foundation's television school near Glasgow, and TTI still supplies a chief engineer, but otherwise there is no outside advice. Admittedly, it is hardly a grand set-up. All the props are stored in the passage outside the director-general's office; there is a small news studio about the size of a modest bedroom and the main studio is little larger than a family living-room. Yet the Ethiopian Television Ser vice's half-dozen producers have shown an instinctive flair fo the medium and conjure up all kinds of programmes; they have even produced a Chekhov play translated into Amharic

I spent an afternoon watching one young producer tape a half-hour variety show. The studio, which is ventilated simply by opening the windows, was like a sweat box. Somehow, a nine-man band and a squad of singers and dancers were working away in there before two cameras. Every now and then the producer would leap up from the control panel, nip into the studio and move around one or two arches that formed the scenery. With a little bit of manipulation of the arches and the cameras he could make the studio floor look like half an acre. The whole show was taped on the station's one videotape recorder—a rather ancient piece of apparatus acquired second hand (the station originally managed without a VTR at all and did all local programmes live). Considering the heat and the cramped conditions, everyone was remarkably good-natured. The producer sustained himself with long pulls at an enormous bottle of fizzy mineral water between his forays into the studio to change the scenery. 'You should have been here when we did these variety programmes live,' he said; 'that really wore us out!'

Although their television is partly financed by commercials, the Ethiopians take a serious view of their role as educators and builders of national unity. 'People don't move around very much in this country,' said Kassaye Damena, the director of programmes, 'so it is our job to make people in villages aware of what the rest of their country looks like, to create a national consciousness. Just now we are making a series of documentaries about the historic towns of Ethiopia and their role in our development.'

Inevitably, the Ethiopians have to rely on buying many of their entertainment programmes from abroad; quite apart from their limited studio facilities they simply cannot afford too much local output. Their income is £80,000 a year. Since it

›sts them £350 to make a half-hour show of their own, but
ıey can buy *Bonanza* for £20, they end up purchasing about
alf their programmes. They also get a few free; the French
:mbassy in Addis Ababa provides them with *Panorama* in
'rench once a fortnight. But most evenings, you can hope to
atch *Startrek*, *UFO* or *Land of the Giants*. All are presented
n English without subtitling or dubbing, which is too expen-
ive. 'Most of those American stories are so simple that you can
ınderstand them even without speaking English,' said Kassaye
Damena. 'My father loves *Bonanza* although he doesn't know
the language.' One of the few programmes the Ethiopians
steered clear of was *The Avengers*. 'We didn't take to THAT
LADY,' said Damena, referring to Steed's judo-adept partner.
'Ethiopian woman don't throw people around like that.'

The real challenge for Ethiopian television is to extend its network; at the moment pictures can be received only within a few miles of Addis Ababa, and there are a mere fifteen thousand television sets. The aim is to extend the service as rapidly as possible to the northern city of Asmara and thence to the other main population centres.

While Ethiopia has the distinction of possessing the fastest-installed television station in Africa, Nigeria had the first. This was a commercial station, WNTV, set up with the help of the British company, Overseas Rediffusion, in 1959 at Ibadan in Western Nigeria. WNTV is run by the provincial government and is conceived purely as a commercial operation, relying heavily on imported American programmes. A relay station boosts its signal into the capital of Lagos, where it has a sharp rivalry with the federal Nigerian Broadcasting Corporation's television service. The corporation, which is a public-service organisation loosely modelled on the BBC, got into television much later. When television first started in Africa, the corporation was still run by BBC men, who had been seconded to Lagos to establish a nationwide radio network in Nigeria. The director-general, an Englishman, argued that the corporation were still too preoccupied establishing radio to become in-

volved in television and the federal government should wai
The government, however, enjoying the first heady momen
of independence from Britain, were eager to have televisior
especially as the provincial government of Western Nigeri
already had WNTV. So they simply shopped elsewhere. The
signed a five-year contract with NBC International of Nev
York to instal and manage a television station. This new federa
television service opened in 1962 and was operated by NBC
International until 1967. By that time the Nigerian Broadcasting Corporation was run by the Nigerians themselves and they
felt ready to cope with television as well as radio. The American contract was not renewed and the Nigerian Broadcasting
Corporation took television under its umbrella.

Under the corporation's wing the television service has become one of the most ambitious in Africa. Despite the fact that it had only two studios and its signal is received by a mere fifty thousand sets in the Lagos area, it produces forty-five per cent of its own programmes. The director of television, Michael Olumide, believes strongly that his programmes must reflect the local culture and way of life. 'If I were to put out imported programmes all the time that just showed the American or the British heritage I wouldn't be beginning to broadcast,' he told me. 'In Nigeria we are very fortunate in having more writing, acting and musical talent to draw on than most other African countries.' The real problem is money. The NBC exists on a government grant and commercials, but the total budget for television is no more than £400,000 a year. 'The government just does not realise the importance of television,' said Olumide; 'we have the most potent medium in the country, but we are starved of money so that many of our artists are really working for us from charity. Nigeria has creative talent, but we cannot really pay enough to nourish it. We have a weekly drama series called *Village Headmaster*—about a schoolmaster in a little village but we can pay the leading actor only £10 for a half-hour play.' The NBC's most popular programme, an hour's live variety show, *The Bar Beach Show* on Saturday nights, gets by on a budget of under £100. 'The real danger of all this is that you settle for mediocrity,' said Olumide, 'that you accept sub-standard work just so you can keep going. But I would rather cut our time on the air than do that.'

The real difficulty, of course, is that television in Nigeria, as elsewhere in Africa, is still available only to the upper classes living in the capital city. Until the network extends throughout the country and sets are counted in hundreds of thousands, no government is going to give television priority for funds. Meanwhile they stagger along as best they can. 'I was showing some visiting American television people our studios recently,' said Olumide, 'and explained that we made half-hour dramas using two cameras and, as we have no videotape editing equipment, we simply shoot the whole thing non-stop from beginning to end. They did not believe me.'

The West African nation that began television with the highest hopes was Ghana. While Kwame Nkrumah was President he determined to build a nationwide network to produce most of its own material, including many educational programmes. 'Originally Ghana's plans were the most pragmatic conceived anywhere in Africa,' said Frank Goodship, a Canadian broadcaster, who helped establish Ghanaian television. 'They planned a nationwide network, good production facilities and trained plenty of people before they went on the air. They aimed at five hours of local material every day, including schools television every morning.' Initially the Ghanaians did not buy much packaged entertainment or westerns from overseas. Africans who are new to television will sit glued to the set for hours watching instructional films about farming or fisheries —until you show the first western. That opens the floodgates and they then want nothing else. 'If you really want to use television to teach people about the world, then you must not import cowboy shows,' said Frank Goodship. The Ghanaians under Nkrumah, ambitiously determined not to develop the appetite for cowboy pictures. They began producing more than eighty per cent of their own programmes. The only trouble was the money simply was not there to sustain them. With less than fifteen thousand sets in the country, the annual licence fee of £5 could not provide enough revenue. After a while, Ghanaian television began to accept advertising and, as a corollary, the advertisers demanded popular shows. So the floodgates to the western opened after all and today Ghana's television service produces only forty per cent of its output.

Yet even advertising cannot really raise enough money to sustain television in Ghana or other African countries. With a mere fifteen to twenty thousand sets in most countries no advertiser is prepared to spend more than a few pounds per minute for spots. The scarcity of sets means that even the combined income from licences and advertising does not add up to a worthwhile television budget. Only commercial radio is a profitable operation anywhere in Africa.

Zambia and Kenya, for instance, each with about twenty thousand sets, face exactly the same problem of minuscule budgets. 'My total programmes budget is about £60,000 a year,' said Morris Mwendar, controller of television at Voice of Kenya (VOK) in Nairobi. 'We manage to do about forty per cent of our own programmes, but our facilities weren't really designed for extensive local production—and there is very limited local talent.' The Kenyans and Zambians concentrate on news (introduced naturally with a beating of message drums) and nightly news magazines. The Kenya magazine *Mambo Leo* from 6.30 to 7.15 each evening follows very closely the old BBC *Tonight* or NBC's *Today* show format of interviews and filmed reports. The one difference is that it is conducted in two languages: English and Swahili. The two anchormen switch happily back and forth from one language to the other according to the linguistic ability of their guests. The local politicians love it, and are for ever ringing up seeking to get on to expound their views—African politicians, apparently, have become just as addicted to appearing before the cameras as politicians everywhere.

For more general entertainment the Kenyans fall back

heavily on imported programmes. The exception is a delightful weekly, local comedy show, *Mzee Pimbi* about an amiable old rogue called Pimbi and his wife Mana Tefi who live in a small village outside Nairobi. Pimbi is a game little fellow who feels he must get involved in everything that's going on. During the East African Safari motor rally he naturally turns up to participate in a beaten-up jalopy and, if there is a local boxing championship, he's in the ring mixing it with all-comers. The show is sponsored by a local dairy, so he is also seen drinking gallons of milk. The show is popular with everyone in Nairobi except European expatriates (who tend to be the people who can afford television anyway), because all their servants are falling about with laughter before the set instead of serving dinner. The best place to watch the show is in one of the local police stations around Nairobi: they are all equipped with television and become a social viewing centre for the neighbourhood. Often a hundred people may be gathered before one police set.

Whatever they may be viewing, you can be sure of one thing—there is no violence on television. Kenya has quite the strictest rules I have encountered anywhere regarding violence on TV—no killing, no shooting, no fighting, no poisoning, no stealing may be shown. That, of course, rules out many imported shows. The Kenyans have to restrict themselves to a fairly light diet of *Tom Jones, Rolf Harris,* the *Andy Stewart Show, The Planemakers* and *Not in Front of the Children* from Britain, plus carefully selected episodes of *Peyton Place* and *Disneyland.*

The reason for the violence ban, according to Morris Mwendar, is that 'people here believe what they see. Out in the villages many of them have seen films on mobile cinemas—these are usually educational—showing them how to grow coffee or tea. So they see a film as speaking the truth. If they see somebody shot on television they believe he is dead, and you can't tell them that he isn't: they've seen the gun fired and the blood coming out.'

The restriction on violence is, of course, an extension of the strict political censorship that is part of the way of life of television in every African country. No one makes any secret of the fact that censorship exists. The usual justification for it is exactly the same as that given for not allowing violence, namely that the people are totally unsophisticated: they believe everything they see on the box, so it is much the best that they see a nice government line and nothing else. Not that everyone is taken in. I met a well-known BBC news reader in one African country where he was spending a month, teaching the local television announcers how to present the news. That afternoon one of them had enquired politely at the end of his lecture: 'When you are giving the television news on BBC and you know that what you have to read is lies, how do you present it?'

Television stations are true seats of power and some that I visited were as difficult to get into as a gold vault, for they are the natural first place to capture in the event of a *coup d'état*. Occasionally, the precautions have quite embarrassing results. In Zambia, when President Kaunda was away at the Commonwealth Prime Ministers' Conference in Singapore early in 1971, the military decided to run through their anti-coup drill to make sure all was secure in the President's absence. A squad of troops came rolling up to the television station in late afternoon and surrounded it: no one was permitted to enter or leave. Inside, the broadcasters were busy putting the finishing touches to the *Tonight* show. But the troops outside would not allow any of their guests in. When the time finally came for the programme, the anchormen went on the air alone and said, 'I'm sorry, we don't have a programme for you this evening. Our station is surrounded by troops who will not let the guests through to the studio. If any senior army officer is watching perhaps he would come down here and change the orders.' An embarrassed officer arrived post-haste and the programme went ahead, rather late.

One of the real dilemmas facing television in Africa has been hortage of trained staff. Most African nations, quite naturally, vant their stations run by their own people, but sometimes the echnical standards are so bad as to make the whole effort neaningless. I saw a long interview with General Gowon of Nigeria over VOK in Nairobi, when the general was on a state visit there, in which the sound quality was so bad that the general's remarks were totally unintelligible.

Happily, the Kenyans are now making a serious effort to raise their whole training standard. They have established in Nairobi at the Kenya Institute for Mass Communications the only television training school in Africa. To begin with, it is a modest affair training ten students at a time in one small studio with three cameras. They are not only thoroughly briefed on all the equipment, but also make their own television programmes. One or two that I saw were already as good as anything being put out on Voice of Kenya. The potential importance of the institute is not just the training—but that the Kenyans are receiving it in their own environment. If the Kenya Institute develops, it could become the major fountain for television talent that not only Kenya but all Africa requires.

The great debate is how much educational television can really advance in Africa over the next few years. Ethiopia, Ghana, Nigeria, Zambia and Uganda already have educational programmes shown on the general television service during the day, but their effect has been often blunted through lack of co-operation from schools, the limited coverage of transmitters or simply through inadequate knowledge of how to operate the sets and maintain them. A teacher-training college in Ghana received its first set in 1965, but it never worked; the following year a new set was put in—that did not work either. In all it was three and a half years between the time the college first had a set and received decent pictures.

In Ethiopia, which has a very good educational television service, putting out nearly two hours of programmes five days a week since 1965, sheer lack of transport makes regular maintenance of sets impossible. When I visited Addis Ababa, the

Mass Media Centre of the Ministry of Education, which run the service with help from the British Council, was sitting o 130 television sets which it could not deliver to schools i outlying villages because no transport was available. Despit the excellent intentions of everyone working there, the educa tional television service, which transmits its programme in th daytime over the Ethiopian Television Service transmitters lives a hand to mouth existence, never knowing when the nex money will come in. Once they got down to seven pence in the kitty. Even so the programmes on geography, mathematics, social studies and English are seen by some sixty thousand Ethiopian children every week. And their response shows how significant television could be in raising education and living standards everywhere in Africa if it can be more extensively used. 'You go to these schools in the villages,' one of the British Council's advisers told me, 'and there are children in rags with no shoes sitting on the floor—there are no chairs or desks—bellowing back answers to questions on television. Often there is no teacher there to supervise them, but they are quite entranced.'

'The pity is that many countries still do not fully realise the advantages of educational television,' said Tom Singleton, the director of the Centre for Educational Television Overseas (CETO) in London (now merged with the Centre for Educational Development Overseas). But he believes that this picture may change radically in the seventies. 'Ministers of Education in developing countries are now being brought face to face with the financial realities of education. They want five years of primary education for everyone—but the cost makes it a dream many years away. This is where television should come in, not only in educating classes but in helping to upgrade the whole standard of teaching.'

The real test case for Africa is in the former French West African colony of the Ivory Coast. Faced with a soaring bill for education and a desperate shortage of qualified teachers, so that less than half the children had any chance even of primary-school education, the Ivory Coast, with the advice and help of UNESCO, has staked £200 million over the next twelve years on a nationwide educational television project. They hope that by 1975 more than half a million children will be watching the daily television lessons, and that by the mid-1980s television's shouldering of much of the burden of education will enable all children to be enrolled in primary schools. The educational programmes will all be made in the Ivory Coast at a fine new production centre in Bouake, a city in the interior, 150 miles north of the capital of Abidjan. The World Bank, in its first major investment in educational television, has contributed £4·5 million to the building of the centre and the French goverment has chipped in with a further £400,000.

The TV lessons will cover the whole range of primary school education and should, for the first time, provide a high quality of instruction throughout the country. The problem in the past has been that the capital, Abidjan, and one or two large towns had good schools with quite high enrolment, but elsewhere schools have been almost non-existent—less than ten per cent of the children receive any education in the rural areas of the north. Besides nearly three hours of TV lessons daily, there will be an hour's live briefing for teachers over the network at 7 each morning. This will outline the day's programming, advise the teachers on how to prepare the class and deal with any queries arising out of earlier lessons. The programmes will be transmitted over the existing commercial television network, which already covers more than two thirds of the country. Since many of the rural areas have no electricity, hundreds of battery-operated television sets are being supplied to schools and schemes worked out for maintenance because of the ravages of the humid tropical climate.

The Ivory Coast experiment will be watched closely, not only in Africa but throughout the Third World. If it is successful, many other countries will certainly turn much more rapidly to harnessing television to education. While educational schemes expand, the other real requirement is for closer liaison between African broadcasters on all aspects of television. The nucleus for co-operation already exists in the Union of National Radio and Television Organisations of Africa (URTNA), but its membership is limited primarily to West African countries and it has not yet been a potent co-ordinating force. 'We haven't really started to explore the possibilities of co-operation yet,' said Morris Mwendar in Nairobi. 'I am sure that television in Africa will not play its full role unless and until we use it to show what is going on elsewhere on this continent. Most of us have no idea what other television services are doing; we ought to be working with them on co-productions, trying to create television that is truly African in character.' That ideal, however, may be difficult to achieve before television has really found its feet within the individual countries. At the moment, most governments see it as one means of welding together a complex conglomeration of tribes into a nation; while that fragile task proceeds they are likely to keep television very much within their own control.

But at the heart of the matter really is Africa's need for a cheap, durable television set and more electrification. Until these requirements are fulfilled, television can do little to penetrate the continent. Television sets are being assembled locally in Nigeria, Ghana and Kenya. They are cheaper than imported models, but they are still beyond the means of, say, a Masai tribesman—even assuming he wanted to buy one. And an enterprising firm in Nairobi has also developed a small, petrol-driven generator especially to power a television set. But again, the combined cost of generator and set is too high for the individual family and can only really be used for community viewing in villages without electricity. 'The real trouble, you know,' an African broadcaster admitted, 'is that we all rushed into television for prestige reasons long before we were ready for it. Often we were oversold on the idea by manufacturers of equipment. They all said "it'll turn you on". So one country got it and then it became a matter of keeping up with them to maintain face.'

CONCLUSION

21

Towards 1984

TELEVISION channels these days resemble an amoeba—constantly dividing and multiplying. Ten years hence, if we look back, the choice of two, three or even half a dozen channels, that most of us in Western Europe, America, Japan or Australia now enjoy, may seem tremendously restrictive. The advance in technology since World War II, which has already made television so dominant in our lives will propel its expansion even faster in future. The latest series of Intelsat IV communications satellites positioned above the Equator during 1971 can handle no less than twelve colour-television channels simultaneously (plus nine thousand two-way telephone conversations). In San Jose, California, a cable system capable of disseminating forty-two different channels is already hooked into many homes.

What is in store for television, in fact, is so exciting that it makes fiction pall. Electronics engineers talk quite seriously of the prospect of multi-channel television sets on which the viewer can dial up, not only a wide selection of conventional programmes or films, but his bank for a screening of his statement or the supermarket for a display of the day's top bargains. Against this potential, today's broadcasting becomes, as the chairman of the American National Cable Television Association put it, 'rather like a narrow cart-track to a forty-lane super highway'.

Effectively television is moving forward on three fronts:

satellites, cable and cassettes. The satellites will shortly becom
so high-powered and sophisticated that they will be able t
relay pictures direct to home receivers by the 1980s. A Unite
Nations study of the likely timetable has revealed that withi
five years direct broadcasting from satellites into specially 'aug
mented' home television sets will be feasible; the ordinar
family set, the report indicated, could be 'augmented' for be
tween £20 and £110. Relays from nuclear-powered satellite
direct to 'unaugmented' home receivers are predicted for the
mid-1980s.

Such a breakthrough could be of immense advantage in the developing countries, where television has still hardly established a foothold. A single regional satellite could reach every village in Africa or India or the pattern of islands that makes up Indonesia. The expensive infra-structure of microwave networks to span the vast distances need never be contemplated. Regional satellites could lift television out of the cities of the Third World into the backwoods. A village of five hundred people in some remote valley that would inevitably be bypassed by microwave links can be enfolded overnight.

The delicate question, of course, is going to be who makes the programmes? The Arab States Broadcasting Union, for example, are very keen to have a regional satellite for educational television throughout the Arab world—but who actually prepares the television lessons? The Egyptians? Will the Libyans or the Sudanese accept their version of history? South America faces the same dilemma: does right-wing Argentina make the programmes that will also be beamed to schools in left-wing Chile? The political hurdles of the age of satellites are likely to be much more difficult to overcome than the technical ones.

For this reason I am sure that, although satellites will prove invaluable eventually for education in developing nations, their prime use will remain for sports and news events of universal importance. The current form certainly suggests this. Of the 996 hours of television relayed on the Intelsat system in 1970, the majority were of sport. During the World Cup football in Mexico City, for instance, three different matches were being relayed simultaneously to Europe by satellite. The additional channels now available on Intelsat IV mean that for the next World Cup half a dozen or more matches could be covered at once, ensuring that every country can see its own team play.

One afternoon in Washington D.C., in the offices of COMSAT, which manages the Intelsat system on behalf of the seventy-seven participating nations, I looked over the individual pattern of transmissions, country by country, for 1970. Japan, for example, transmitted 56 hours of television to the Pacific and Indian Ocean satellites and received 32 hours of pictures relayed by them; Britain sent 62 and received 114. But the little island of Puerto Rico took 135 hours of satellite transmission and Venezuela 99 hours. The explanation of this enormous—and expensive—satellite usage by such small countries was simple, they take the baseball games every weekend from the United States.

While broadcasters speak quite rightly of our being in the age of global television, most of us are really interested in our own backyard—unless the home team is playing away. Although technology may make it possible for us to tune in in the 1980s to a Chinese satellite relaying Peking's version of *Bonanza*, the mass audience may look at it out of curiosity but after that will probably switch back promptly to their own home channels.

Moreover, those channels may well become more absorbing if cable television and cassettes live up to their advance publicity. So far, apart from the special case of Hong Kong, cable television has made most impact in Canada, where a quarter of the homes are plugged in to twelve Canadian and American channels. The United States is catching up fast, particularly now that the FCC has finally decided to permit rapid expansion of cable systems. The lead was given by President Johnson's Task Force on Communications Policy, which recommended late in 1968: 'We conclude that one of the most promising avenues to diversity (of programming) is the distribution of television to the home by cable.' The FCC's new chairman, Dean Burch, told the National Cable Television Association's annual convention in 1970: 'The time is ripe for a breakthrough in your industry.' Already the number of homes linked to cable systems has doubled between 1963 and 1971; by the end of this decade at least a third of all American homes are expected to be connected.

Europe has moved towards cable much more slowly, primarily because the public-service television networks there have always covered the whole of their countries with a conventional signal, eliminating the need to bring in distant signals by cable to remote towns or villages. However, most new apartment blocks in the Netherlands and Belgium now have cable, bringing them television from West Germany and France. And one Munich suburb has its own closed-circuit television service. In Britain, apart from an abortive Pay TV experiment in London, its use has been limited mainly to closed-circuit educational systems in London and Glasgow. But the prospect of the 'wired nation'—of cable television in every home—is foreshadowed in the new town of Washington in County Durham, which is laid out with ducts for cable TV's lifeline—the coaxial cable. The real advantage of cable over conventional television is that while airwaves become jammed with relatively few channels, a coaxial cable can easily pipe twenty, forty or even eighty channels into every home. Many systems now being installed in American towns have the option of twenty channels and, as noted earlier, San Jose in California has forty-two.

But how much genuine diversity will cable really offer? Although American systems with over 3,500 subscribers now have to originate their own programmes, in addition to relaying normal television stations, the choice is hardly scintillating. They rely heavily on local news and sports events. 'Cable TV is best at local programming,' Wallace Briscoe of the National Cable Television Association told me; 'we can identify with a ommunity just like a local newspaper covering politics or high-chool events.' A technological revolution to relay the local chool plays seems pointless.

At the moment the cable scene in America and Canada is ragmented; there is no nationwide network. But once systems do begin to link up first into regional associations, then possibly into a national system, the opportunities for good programming are greater. So are the potential profits. The Clay–Frazier fight in 1971, although not carried by cable systems, started everyone counting up how much the purse might have been if it had been piped into ten million American homes at a special price of £4. Although most cable systems charge a fixed monthly fee, it is possible to scramble signals so that certain channels are received only after extra payments.

What every viewer really cares about is what he finally sees. His best hope is the cassette. This newcomer, quickly nicknamed 'Son of TV', is the visual cousin of a tape-recorder. The equipment consists of a video-player, which can be plugged into the aerial socket of any normal television set, and cartridges or cassettes of programmes. The cassette is simply inserted in the player—rather like putting a tape on a tape-recorder—and the programme is seen on a spare channel on the TV set.

What is widely called 'the cassette revolution' was originally pioneered by Dr Peter Goldmark of CBS, the man who also invented the long-playing record back in 1948. Dr Goldmark's system, known as EVR (for Electronic Video Recording) uses miniaturised photographic film. CBS, together with ICI in Britain and the Swiss chemical firm CIBA, have invested nearly £20 million in launching EVR in the United States, Japan and Europe during 1971 and 1972. But EVR's lead is being challenged by a cluster of rivals. Philips and Sony have devised a player using magnetic tape rather than film. Decca and Telefunken prefer plastic discs (not unlike refined long-playing records), while RCA's Selectavision uses a laser beam to imprint images on vinyl tape. The only trouble is that none

of the rival systems are compatible: an EVR cartridge will no
function on a Sony or a Decca player.

Each manufacturer, however, is eagerly lining up all kinds o
programmes for his own version. CBS bought 1,500 ol
movies from 20th Century Fox and are busy putting them o
EVR film. They have also tapped the BBC's archives in Britai
for a series of travel films and have signed up the great Italia
publishing corporation, Mondadori, to make educational film
for them. Everyone else is rushing round trying to corner a slice
of the cassette market—and to decide which of all the different
systems is really going to prevail in the long run. Time-Life
have Robert Redford signed up to make a series of skiing lessons for cassettes and Leonard Bernstein contracted to lecture
on music. David Frost has joined the board of a New York
company, Optronics, which has scooped up the rights to over
six thousand films, documentaries and cartoons. Out in Japan
all the major commercial television networks have formed
cassette subsidiaries, while the mighty NHK is trying to decide
how to get the maximum advantage from converting the great
treasure house of video tapes, produced for its eighteen hours a
day educational channel, into cassettes. In Britain Sir Lew
Grade, together with the ABC network in the United States,
has concluded a five-year contract with the National Theatre to
film all their productions for cassettes. Thames Television in
London have made a series of thirteen half-hour programmes
on the British Museum. They will be shown first on television,
but Thames regards them as perfect cassette material.

Initially, the first players that trickled on to the market in
1971 were too expensive for the family buyer: they all cost
from £130 for the player itself, with at least another £20–£30
for each half-hour cassette. They appealed much more, therefore, to schools and universities. A school, for instance, will
soon be able to buy a complete set of cassettes of Shakespeare's
plays and use them again and again. The great advantage for
educational use is that the film or tape can be stopped at any
point for a single frame to be studied. It can also be reversed so

ɿat a short sequence can be repeated immediately—most useɿl for studying a complex dramatic scene in *Hamlet* or even ɿhe arm action for serving in a tennis lesson.

Obviously the costs will come down eventually until the ɿrdinary family can afford the cassette. And cassette libraries ɿvill enable viewers to hire their favourite old Cary Grant or ɿGary Cooper movies (or a golf lesson) for a weekend at less ɿhan the cost of going to the cinema.

But cassettes are unlikely to be for regular home use in the 1970s; most broadcasters foresee their full impact being felt during the eighties. They point to the relatively slow growth of colour television as an indication that although the technology may exist, the private purse cannot necessarily afford it. Even in 1971 rather less than 40 million of the 250 million television sets in the world were in colour (and of those about 30 million were in the United States, and 5 million in Japan). For most television executives the seventies will be the decade for colour to break through. The BBC in Britain is looking for most of its increased income to the higher licence fee from colour; Italy and Spain are still waiting to take the final plunge in selecting PAL instead of SECAM. The seventies, therefore, will come to terms with colour; the eighties with cassettes and cable.

As for the Third World, television there still has to become a mass medium. It can only do so when the cost of a set comes within the means of the ordinary man. At the moment his budget stretches at best to a transistor radio—a stage that was reached in Europe or America more than forty years ago. In Copenhagen, Laurits Bindslov, the director of Danish television, pointed out the findings of a survey in Denmark: they revealed that a skilled worker there put in the same number of hours' work in 1929 to earn the price of a radio, as in 1953 to earn a black-and-white TV, and in 1968 to earn a colour set. Africa and India, by the same token, are really at the 1929 level today. Although their development will undoubtedly be telescoped, it does suggest that television will only really get into its stride there in the 1980s.

The prospect, therefore, for the first man to step out of his space craft on to the surface of Mars some time during the 1980s is that perhaps three billion people—or rather more than three quarters of the world's population—will be watching him. That makes the audience of 723 million who watched Neil Armstrong step on to the moon in 1969 seem like a turn-out for a matinée. So far we have really had only a preview of what television can do. As a leading European broadcaster, reviewing the difficulties of keeping up with the latest technological breakthrough, remarked: 'We already have such fantastic tools at our disposal that I find it impossible to understand what broadcasting will be like by A.D. 2000. I often feel like a village boy suddenly placed at the wheel of a Rolls-Royce already in motion.'

BIBLIOGRAPHY

This bibliography is a general guide to other books on the world television scene today or to useful books giving more detailed background on the development of television in individual countries.

Erik Barnouw — *A History of Broadcasting in the United States*, 3 vols (*A Tower in Babel, The Golden Web, The Image Empire*) Oxford University Press, 1966–1970.

J. G. Blumler and Dennis McQuail — *Television and Politics*, Faber & Faber, London, 1968.

Asa Briggs — *The History of Broadcasting in the United Kingdom*, Oxford University Press, 1965 (3 vols published to date).

Communications in the Space Age; The use of satellites by the mass media, UNESCO, 1968.

Wilson P. Dizard — *Television: A World View*, Syracuse University Press, Syracuse, NY, 1966.

Walter B. Emery — *National and International Systems of Broadcasting; Their History, Operation and Control*, Michigan State University Press, East Lansing, Michigan, 1969.

Fred Friendly *Due to Circumstances Beyond Ou Control*, Random House, New Yor 1967.

Hugh Greene *The Third Floor Front; A View o Broadcasting in the Sixties*, The Bodle Head, London, 1969.

History of Broadcasting in Japan, NHK, Tokyo, 1967.

Stuart Hood *A Survey of Television*, Heinemann London, 1967.

Alexander Kendrick *Prime Time; The Life of Edward R. Murrow*, Little, Brown & Co., Boston, 1969.

Robert MacNeil *The People Machine*, Harper & Row, New York, 1968.

Joe McGinniss *The Selling of the President 1968*, Trident Press, New York, 1969.

James W. Markham *Voices of the Red Giants, Communications in Russia and China*, Iowa State University Press, Ames, Iowa, 1967.

Burton Paulu *Radio and Television Broadcasting on the European Continent*, University of Minnesota Press, Minneapolis, 1967.

Public Television, A Programme for Action; The Report of the Carnegie Commission on Educational Television, Bantam Books, New York, 1967.

Anthony Sampson *Anatomy of Britain Today*, 1965, *The New Anatomy of Britain*, 1971, Hodder and Stoughton, London.

The New Europeans, Hodder and Stoughton, London, 1968.

E. G. Wedell — *Broadcasting and Public Policy*, Michael Joseph, London, 1968.

John Whale — *The Half Shut Eye*, Television and Politics in Britain and America, Macmillan, London, 1969.

Magazines and Reviews:

Educational Television International, Journal of the Centre for Education Television Overseas, London.

EBU Review, European Broadcasting Union, Geneva.

Radio, Television; Review of the International Radio and Television Organisation, Prague.

The following broadcasting organisations also publish valuable yearbooks:

ARD and ZDF, West Germany; BBC and ITA, Britain; JRT, Yugoslavia; NHK, Japan; ORF, Austria.

Index

INDEX

INDEX